Thinking of the Laity
in Late Tudor England

Thinking of the Laity
in Late Tudor England

PETER IVER KAUFMAN

UNIVERSITY OF NOTRE DAME PRESS

Notre Dame, Indiana

Manufactured in the United States of America

Library of Congress Cataloging-in-Publication Data
Kaufman, Peter Iver.
Thinking of the laity in late Tudor England / Peter Iver Kaufman.
p. cm.
Includes bibliographical references and index.
ISBN 0-268-03304-8 (cloth : alk. paper)
ISBN 0-268-03305-6 (pbk. : alk. paper)
1. Puritans—England.   2. Laity—Church of England—
History—16th century.   3. Church of England—
Government—History of doctrines—16th century.
4. England—Church history—16th century.   I. Title.
BX9334.3.K38   2004
262'.15'094209031—dc22

2004011328

∞ *This book is printed on acid-free paper.*

Contents

Acknowledgments   vii

Abbreviations   ix

Introduction   1

1   Coming to Terms: "Puritans" and "The People"   7
     Convictions
     Puritans
     The People

2   "We are all priests": Early Reformers Thinking of the Laity   31
     "Laymen as wise as the officers"
     Complaints, Commoners, and "Strangers" in the Reign of King Edward VI
     Protestant Opposition and Exiles at the Time of Queen Mary

3   Into the 1560s: Elizabeth I's "Alteracion"   63
     "The Unsettled Settlement"
     Lay Leadership in Reformed Parishes
     "Hot Troublesome Dissensions": John Jewel's "Simple People"

4   Populist Initiatives and Government Reaction: Into the 1570s   103
     "That Old and True Election . . . by the Congregation"
     Prophesying and the People

5   Patronage to the People?   139
     Rudesbies
     Browne and Fenner
     Too Great a Perfection

     Afterword   167
     Index   171

Acknowledgments

John Craig, Lori Anne Ferrell, John Headley, Norm Jones, Carolyn Wood, and an anonymous reader for the press commented on earlier drafts of the entire book. *Thinking* and my thinking, I think, got better as a result. I am also grateful to Karen Bruhn, Todd Butler, Patrick Collinson, George Demacopoulos, Hans Hillerbrand, Christopher Marsh, Scott McGinniss, Julie Mell, Michael Pasquarello, Neandra Perry, and Albert Rabil for repairs ordered and remarks offered in the margins of chapters, with coffee, over dinner, during seminars, or while walking. David Ganz, Barbara Harris, Peter Lake, and Linda Levy Peck entertained inquiries, proposed answers, and, at critical moments, pointed. What wonderful colleagues all!

Mention of my debts to other generous colleagues at archives and libraries hardly repays them. They made my sifting things so much easier, and they deserve so much more than mere acknowledgment, yet unless the sales of this volume surprise me, that is all they will get. Profound thanks, then, to the staffs of Davis Library at the University of North Carolina, Chapel Hill—notably, John Rutledge—and of the Divinity School Library at neighboring Duke University. And *Thinking* could not have reached this stage without thoughtful, tremendously helpful colleagues at the Bodleian and at Queens College, Oxford; at the UL, the Parker Library at Corpus Christi College, the Pepys Library at Magdalen College, and the library of Emmanuel College, Cambridge; at record offices in Chester and Bristol; and, in London, at the Guildhall Library, the Library of the Inner Temple, the Institute for Historical Research, Dr. Williams's Library, the British Library, and the Public Record Offices at Chancery Lane and Kew.

Barbara Hanrahan at the Press is inspirational; her colleague, Rebecca DeBoer, kind and wise in the ways of production; Jack Kirshbaum, insightful and helpful between the lines.

For over twenty years, for friendship and counsel, I've counted on John Wilson, Professor in the Department of Religious Studies and then Dean at Princeton University before his retirement last year. Conversations with John always get me closer to where I ought to be going. This book is for him.

Abbreviations

AM	*The Acts and Monuments of John Foxe*, 4th ed. 8 vols., ed. Josiah Pratt (London: Religion Tract Society, 1887).
AM (1563)	*John Foxe, The Acts and Monuments of the Christian Church* (London, 1563).
APC	*Acts of the Privy Council of England*, ed. John Roche Dasent (London: H. M. Stationary Office, 1890–).
ARG	*Archiv für Reformationsgeschichte.*
BIHR	*Bulletin of the Institute for Historical Research*, London.
BL	British Library, London.
Bodl.	Bodleian Library, Oxford.
BRO	Bristol Records Office.
Browne	*The Writings of Robert Harrison and Robert Browne*, ed. Albert Peele and Leland H. Carlson (London: Allen and Unwin, 1953).
CCCC	Parker Library, Corpus Christi College, Cambridge.
ChW	Churchwarden accounts.
Concilia	*Concilia Magnae Britanniae et Hiberniae*, vol. 1, ed. David Wilkins (London, 1737).
CMP	*Correspondence of Matthew Parker*, ed. John Bruce and Thomas Thomason Perowne (Cambridge: Cambridge University Press, 1853).
CR	*Corpus Reformatorum.*
CRO	Chester Records Office.
CRO, EDA	Ecclesiastical, diocesan records.

CRO, EDC	Ecclesiastical, diocesan consistory court.
CSP	Calendar of State Papers.
CUL	Cambridge University Library.
DWL	Dr Williams's Library, London.
EEA	*Elizabethan Episcopal Administration*, 3 vols., ed. William P. M. Kennedy (London: Mowbray, 1924).
EHR	*English Historical Review.*
HJ	*Historical Journal.*
Institutes	Jean Calvin, *The Institutes of the Christian Religion*, 2 vols., ed. John T. McNeill (Philadelphia: Westminster Press, 1960).
JEH	*Journal of Ecclesiastical History.*
Jewel	*The Works of John Jewel*, ed. John Ayre (Cambridge: Cambridge University Press, 1845–50).
JPQE	*The Journals of all the Parliaments during the reign of Queen Elizabeth*, ed. Simond d'Ewes (London, 1682).
Laws	Richard Hooker, *Of the Laws of Ecclesiastical Polity*, ed. John Keble (Oxford: Oxford University Press, 1836).
LPL	Lambeth Palace Library, London.
Miscellanea	*Records*, vol. 1, ed. J. H. Poller (London, Catholic Record Society, 1905).
OL	*Original Letters relative to the English Reformation*, 2 vols., ed. Hastings Robinson (Cambridge: Cambridge University Press, 1846–47).
Peel	*The Second Part of A Register*, Albert Peel (Cambridge: Cambridge University Press, 1915).
Perkins	*The Works of that Famous and Worthie Minister of Christ . . . W. Perkins*, 3 vols. (London, 1616–17).
Perkins (1631)	*The Works of that Famous and Worthie Minister of Christ . . . W. Perkins*, (London, 1631).
PRO	Public Records Office, London.
Proceedings	*Proceedings in the Parliaments of Elizabeth I*, vol. 1, ed. T. E. Hartley (Leicester: University of Leicester Press, 1981).
Register	*A Part of a Register* (Middleburg, 1593).
Remains	*The Remains of Edmund Grindal*, ed. William Nicholson (Cambridge: Cambridge University Press, 1853).
Strype(1)	*John Strype, Ecclesiastical Memorials relating chiefly to Religion and the Reformation of it*, 3 vols. (Oxford: Oxford University Press, 1822).

Strype(2)   *John Strype, Annals of the Reformation and Establishment of Religion,* 4 vols. (Oxford: Oxford University Press, 1824).

Synodalia   *Synodalia: A Collection of Articles of Religion, Canons, and Proceedings of Convocations in the Province of Canterbury,* vol. 1, ed. Edward Cardwell (Oxford: Oxford University Press, 1842).

TRHS   *Transactions of the Royal Historical Society.*

Troubles   *A Brieff discours off the troubles begonne at Franckford in the year 1554* (London, 1575).

TRP   *Tudor Royal Proclamations,* 3 vols., ed. Paul L. Hughes and James F. Larkin (New Haven: Yale University Press, 1964).

WA   *D. Martin Luthers Werke, kritische Gesammtausgabe,* vol. 11 (Weimar, 1900).

Whitgift   *The Works of John Whitgift,* 3 vols., ed. John Ayre (Cambridge: Cambridge University Press, 1851–53).

ZL   *The Zurich Letters, comprising the correspondence of several English bishops and others with some Helvetian reformers,* 2 vols., ed. Hastings Robinson (Cambridge: Cambridge University Press, 1842–1845).

ZL(ET)   Epistolae Tigurinae, *ZL,* vol. 2, separately paginated.

Thinking of the Laity
in Late Tudor England

Introduction

How thoroughly reformed was the English laity during the second half of the sixteenth century? Did laymen enthusiastically accept, acquiesce, or resist? Historians have variously answered those questions for years. They sift churchwardens' accounts, visitation records, complaints filed with church courts, wills, ballads, and broadsheets, searching for Protestant commitment, religious indifference, and residual Catholicism. In what follows, we will have occasion to revisit some of their sources and draw on what has already been learned from them. But other, related, though far less frequently asked questions preoccupy us here: What were reformers thinking of the laity? How and why did their thinking change?

To most English Protestants in the 1560s, 1570s, and 1580s, Roman Catholicism was a religion "expound[ing] *ecclesia* to be a state opposite unto, and severed from the laietie."[1] To be sure, this complaint exaggerated Catholic clericalism and conveniently forgot about subparochial structures that encouraged lay initiative and lay leadership. *Thinking of the Laity* will do little to offset the exaggerations and forgetfulness with spirited discussions of late medieval laicism and clericalism, for this volume is a study of

---

1. DWL, Morrice MSS. B.2, 235v, and C, 452. The critic (T.N.) was almost certainly Thomas Norton, the son-in-law of Henrician reformer and archbishop Thomas Cranmer. Norton offered his definition of *ecclesia* in 1583, twenty years after he translated John Calvin's *Institutes* into English. Thomas More, the recusant descendant of his famous namesake, all but substantiated Norton's charge, for when More was arrested in 1582, a confession of faith found among his papers claimed that *ecclesia* referred only to persons in holy orders. More's confession insisted that scripture only "semeth to call the whole churche" together for important decisions. Cambridge, Emmanuel College MS. 76, 9v–10r.

sixteenth-century perception and prejudice. It concentrates on reformers who saw or imagined a "sever[ing] from the laietie" and sought to remedy it. The more impatient among them are known now as puritans, the most "forward" of whom favored an extraordinarily controversial remedy: broadly participatory parish regimes. They commended lay involvement in parish elections and suggested greater lay say in disciplining delinquents. Their critics perceived participatory solutions or initiatives as problems and opposed experiments with laicization, democratization, and local control. And by 1590, the critics prevailed. John Whitgift, Richard Cosin, John Aylmer, Matthew Sutcliffe, and Richard Bancroft made sure that few contemporaries thought of the laity as favorably as had the likes of Robert Browne, William Fulke, John Field, Thomas Lever, Dudley Fenner, and John Udall. Their story is one of false starts and foolhardy sentiments, and it sprawls across our last two chapters. At the end, though, we find that the advocates themselves had second thoughts and had grown skeptical and suspicious of lay and local control.

That advocates were dissuaded (as were other reformers who were more ambivalent from the start, notably, John Jewel, Edwin Sandys, Thomas Cartwright, and Walter Mildmay) accounts, in part, for the general neglect of the tale we tell. For historians are usually more intrigued by what was than by what might have been. "What was," in this instance, is an Elizabethan puritanism that has been expertly repossessed and redeposited in the mainstream of English Protestantism by Patrick Collinson, Nicholas Tyacke, and others. "What might have been" would likely have resembled later congregationalism. This work features fresh evidence that Elizabethan partisans of broadly participatory parish regimes publicly confronted their critics, and it collects shards of expectations and regrets that survive in a few petitions, in manuscript records of university controversy, in recollections volunteered by advocates of lay and local control, and in the exaggerated fears of their adversaries. To assemble these fragments is to find forgotten moments in the Elizabethan polity debates and to recover thinking about the laity that gave "revolutionary force" to late Tudor puritanism, a force that, Tyacke admits, has gone missing. And, as we discover why, by whom, and to what end, plans were made to pass along power to the people, we are reminded that roads not taken are as yet important parts of the historical landscape.[2]

---

2. Nicholas Tyacke, "The Rise of Puritanism," in *From Persecution to Toleration: The Glorious Revolution and Religion in England*, ed. Ole Peter Grell, Jonathan I. Israel, et al.

But who were "the people" puritan partisans of lay and local control expected to participate influentially in parish deliberations, debate doctrine, and elect pastors? And precisely who were the puritans who assumed some degree of democratization was consistent with and instrumental to religious reform? Chapter 1, "Coming to Terms," arrives at answers while proposing definitions.

That chapter begins toward the end of the sixteenth century, when the popular preacher William Perkins created Eusebius, an uncommonly articulate commoner who dramatizes how the reformers' convictions countenanced lay assertiveness. Let Eusebius be a lesson, Perkins seems to say, a demonstration that ordinary people can internalize the reformation's good news about the gratuity of God's grace, can discipline themselves— although they tend to misbehave—and can usefully preach grace and discipline to others. Yet the story concludes ambiguously. Eusebius is both independent and deferential. Might Perkins somehow have been commending both social control and religious individualism? He was a particular favorite among puritans, many of whom reportedly partnered with eminent parishioners to keep the commoners down and out. Other puritans, connoisseurs of spiritual conflict, did not gravitate to the aristocracy's side in social conflicts. They, too, would have admired Perkins' Eusebius, an emblematic commoner or Protestant Everyman, avidly involved in the "perennial struggle of the godly for assurance of their elect status." Involvement in that struggle, puritan populists suggested, prepared the laity to participate as well and as responsibly in deliberations prevenient to critical congregational decisions.[3]

Partisans of participatory parish regimes allowed that lay participants could be drawn from a vast cast of characters beneath the gentry and above the chronically indigent. For centuries, people of that "caste" were known

---

(Oxford: Clarendon, 1991), 17–18. Patrick Collinson, *The Religion of Protestants: The Church in English Society, 1559–1625* (Oxford: Clarendon, 1982), 275–76, comments on the "containment" of radical elements, as he does in his "English Conventicle," in *Voluntary Religion,* ed. W. J. Sheils and Diane Wood (Oxford: Blackwell, 1986), 249–51.

   3. Peter Lake, "Defining Puritanism Again," in *Puritanism: Transatlantic Perspectives on a Seventeenth-Century Faith,* ed. Francis Bremer (Boston: Northeastern University Press, 1993), 3–29, identifies puritanism as "a style of piety" responsible for various degrees of opposition to reformed religious settlements depending on the strength of the puritans' "impulse toward incorporation." For the place of "perennial inner struggle" in that "style of piety," see Alexandra Walsham, *Providence in Early Modern England* (Oxford: Oxford University Press, 1999), 19–20.

as *"mediocres";* during the sixteenth, they were called "the middling sort." We refer to the puritans proposing to give them a greater part in parish government as "populists," but with a crucial proviso or stipulation, because puritans did not claim to express the will of the people as did the populists of later periods. Quite the contrary, puritan pastors generally mistrusted their parishioners and urged them to repent much of what they willed. Yet "forward" puritans also exhibited a populist's faith in the virtues and common sense of the godly commoner. Hence, "Coming to Terms," settles for an anachronism to underscore "the revolutionary force" of proposals that died in infancy when suspicions about the commoners' competence could neither be allayed nor answered convincingly.

Elizabethan puritans were not the first sixteenth-century English reformers to suggest that parishioners pick their pastors. The second chapter surveys a stretch from later lollardy through Marian Protestantism, pausing first for William Tyndale, who argued that select laymen were "as wise as officers" of the church.[4] He predicted that when the wisest of laymen, his king, Henry VIII, reformed the realm's religion, commoners would ensure that churches not return to that sad state to which "the practice of prelates" had consigned them, namely, to the corrupt patronage practices of Catholics.

Thomas Cranmer, the king's archbishop of Canterbury, was more restrained while Henry lived, though he openly opposed the clericalism of conservative Henricians. Later, he welcomed many reformed refugees from the continent, permitting them their experiments with participatory parish practices. They apparently took his permission as an enthusiastic endorsement and inferred that the polity and discipline of all the realm's churches would soon resemble theirs. Yet Cranmer was cautious, even after 1547, with the inconstant Henry in his grave. Ardent and more constant reformers were influentially positioned in the new king's court, but Cranmer imagined that laymen long loyal to Catholicism were still under its spell despite the decade and more of reform. The laity, therefore, was unprepared to accept and usefully exercise authority. And it would likely remain so, he suspected, until he and the likes of Hugh Latimer had more time to train clergy and commoners alike.

But there was too little time. Young King Edward VI died in the summer of 1553, before Cranmer's reformed preachers and theologians, imported from abroad, could make over the middling sort and before he could

---

4. William Tyndale, *Doctrinal Treatises and Introductions to Different Parts of the Holy Scriptures,* ed. Henry Walter (Cambridge: Cambridge University Press, 1848), 236–41.

implement modest changes in polity and procedure that might have promoted greater lay participation in parish administration. On Edward's death, his half-sister and successor, Mary I, overcame opposition to rule and recatholicized her realm. Inadvertently, though, her measures to suppress Protestantism encouraged lay leadership. In England commoners stepped forward to preach and protest when their reformed pastors were arrested. And nothing showed lay initiative to advantage better than the conditions of exile.

The exiles returned on receiving news of Mary's death in 1558. They expected their new queen, Elizabeth I, to favor reform but found she favored, above all, "obedyent subjects" and assumed hierarchy was "necessarie for [the] preservation of obedience and order among the clergy." Probably neither queen nor council gave much thought to lay participation in the parishes. Instead, the regime was more concerned with the strictly political choices that their "giddy" commoners might make.[5]

Churchwardens, other commoners, and local priests, however, did give considerable thought to lay participation in decisions affecting parish policy and personnel. Into the 1560s commoners continued to serve as aldermen and on juries; they collected revenue for their churches and supervised expenditures. On occasion, they joined with fellow parishioners to choose their ministers. Partisans of such practices had precedents aplenty. Returning refugee and foremost apologist for the new religious settlement, John Jewel stressed the laity's competence and seemed to contemplate a degree of democratization, even after he became one of the queen's new bishops. But reservations about the realm's "rude and rash people" kept him from proposing or endorsing what more radical reformers found to be the polity implications of increased lay literacy and of the priesthood of all believers.[6]

In the early 1570s the radicals lobbied parliament for participatory parish regimes and took their case to the public. They argued that "thrusting" pastors on parishes without counsel or consent of the parishioners "cause[d] many mischeefes." Could churches be instruments of saving grace when prevailing patronage practices corrupted the ministry or emptied pulpits of preachers? Proponents of lay authority and local control said that "examples of all the apostles in all the churches and in all purer times" proved their

---

5. I. B. Cauthen, ed. *Gorboduc, or Ferrex and Porrex* (Lincoln: University of Nebraska Press, 1970), 61: "so giddy are the common people's minds" (1562). For "obedyent subjects," see LPL MS. 2002, 61r (1559).

6. *Jewel*, 2:687–88.

point. Critics countered that it was irresponsible to subject pastors or policy to parishioners' whim. Laymen were to be led, not looked to for leadership.[7]

Just then, diocesan and government authorities limited lay assertiveness elsewhere. They commanded that "the people shulde be excludett" from prophecies, discussions of reformed doctrine and discipline that ordinarily followed a series of market-day sermons. The public face or phase of such "exercises" was suppressed from 1576, in large part, because, as one onlooker reported, prophesying tempted "every artificer" to become a "reformer and teacher."[8]

Dudley Fenner, curate in Kent, mourned the passing of prophesying and urged superiors to grant the laity greater say, albeit not "sway," in parish affairs. But by the 1580s diocesan officials were disinclined to give ground. They were on guard against "the multitude" or mob and even suspicious of requests to restrict pluralism in the parishes, requests which struck them as the thin edge of a menacing wedge, specifically, as a puritan "introduction to bringe patronage to the people."[9]

But puritans, too, grew skeptical that the proles could be preached to piety and trusted with power. Enthusiasm for lay and local control waned. Fenner retained more confidence in lay discretion than most—and Robert Browne, more still—yet the critics of participatory parish regimes were relentless. They vilified dissidents who dared favor them until only a very rare renegade suggested in print that a sound ministry might well depend on an enlightened and empowered laity. During the 1580s the puritans increasingly looked to personal piety rather than to a presbyterian or more broadly participatory polity for assurance that the realm's reform was genuine and lasting. *Thinking of the Laity* goes no further because it seemed more important to nearly all our protagonists late in that decade to be moved to repentance by one's pastor than to possess the power to remove him. William Fulke as much as conceded that populist puritanism had gotten nowhere, that the victories worth celebrating were not institutional but personal, with God "confirming and lightning oure minde inwardly."[10]

---

7. Bodl., Selden Supra MS. 44, 32r; *Whitgift*, 3:296–300; and BL, Cotton Titus VI, 21v.

8. DWL, Morrice MSS. B.2.8, C.218, for "every artificer"; BL, Lansdowne MS. 23, 7r, 20r, for "excludett."

9. BL, Lansdowne MS. 30B, 203v–4r; Bodl., Ashmole MS. 383, 70r and 81v; and Dudley Fenner, *Counter-poysen* (London, 1584), 149.

10. William Fulke, *The Text of the New Testament* (London, 1598), C6v and 132v–33r.

Coming to Terms

"Puritans"
and "The People"

William Perkins was probably the most widely read English theologian at the start of the seventeenth century. By then he had been teaching and preaching at Cambridge for more than a decade. He trained a generation of Calvinist pastors and encouraged them to expect the reformed laity to display an assurance of election as well as a faith in divine sovereignty and in the gratuity of grace. Perkins' protagonist in his dialogue on "the state of a Christian," Eusebius, shows just how those convictions might be developed in an intense, lively struggle with doubt, guilt, and despair. Perkins' script turned the reformed layman into a theologian and an evangelist of sorts. Eusebius preaches his struggle and convictions to stir and structure others' desires for faith and assurance of election. The objective was to shape the very subjectivity that became characteristic of the godly, known at the time, and to this day, as puritans.

Late Tudor puritanism is ordinarily distinguished as a conspicuously "forward," implacable opposition to the Elizabethan religious settlement. It is permissible—and perhaps preferable—however, to define it as an acute awareness and approval of personal, spiritual conflict, that is, as "a style of piety" or subjectivity. To whom did puritans pitch their convictions? Whom did they hope to involve in broadly participatory parish regimes? Historians who suspect they were only interested in edifying and empowering elites may be startled to learn that several outspoken reformers were ambitious for the "plaine countrie man," for the commoner, that is, who was lodged in the society's capacious middle, between the indigent and truly privileged. Queen and regime might think of that mass (or of the masses) as a mob, as "a multitude" easily carried away by unwelcome "novelties." Yet puritans with a populist streak envisaged great good coming from the commoners conferring on the direction and pace of religious reform and on the nature of religious leadership.[1]

Convictions

What did reformed Christians believe? And when did they believe it? Preachers told them they were still wicked; doctrine assured them Christ had died for the wickedness of this world. Could they presume that the amnesty extended to them? Or were they too broken to mend?

When they read the Bible or had it read to them, laymen learned that the apostle Paul had enjoined them to "walk in the spirit," "to walk after the spirit," "to crucify the flesh with its lusts and appetites." Injunctions of that sort seem to have signaled there was something sinners could or should do to put their lives in order. Indeed, a case for self-management likely would have been made more often from pulpits had leading reformers not been obsessed with sin. But they harped on its pervasiveness. "There remain relickes of syn" in the most righteous Christians, William Fulke said in 1574, "a lust unto syn contrarye to the spirit of God, which also breaketh out some tymes into actual syn." The good that one came across in this life was "inchoacted," imperfect, and "made perfect [only] in the lyfe to come." Here

---

1. BL, Lansdowne MS. 25, 92r–93r, for Elizabeth's mistrust of the mob or multitude. Puritan populism is ordinarily associated with the opposition to select vestries that surfaced during the 1620s and 1630s, for which, Peter Lake, *The Boxmaker's Revenge: "Orthodoxy," "Heterodoxy" and the Politics of the Parish in Early Stuart London* (Stanford, Calif.: Stanford University Press, 2001), 391–92.

and now, reformed Christians were simultaneously sinners by experience and saved by faith.[2]

Correctly, but often too exclusively, this simultaneity is identified with the reformed religion of the sixteenth century. Sensing the "relickes of syn" within and experiencing how they corrupted conduct, reformed Christians were desperate for assurances that they were among the elect. "Relickes of sin" or "lust unto syn" made everyone's "walk" appear crooked and contrary to what the apostle required. Was the crookedness a cause of divine displeasure or a symptom of it? Were the faithful off to a false start? If doubts swarmed, would their faith hold? Could they hold on to the conviction that they were righteous by imputation, that Jesus Christ's atonement covered a multitude of sins, among which theirs were surely numbered?

Assurances of election inspired strenuous effort to repay God's immense mercy with an abundance of goodwill and good work. At least that was what the reformed preachers seemed to think or hope. Perhaps they hoped as well that assurances of election and eternal rest would take some bite out of hardships here and now. In any event, repeated assurances were always in season, as were sermons on the "relickes of syn" likely to capsize confidence. Preachers were constantly convicting or assuring. The prolific William Perkins confided that he could only conceive of lasting assurances of election after abandoning the idea that faith was tantamount to equanimity, to a state or stasis beyond "wavering, doubting, [and] distrusting." It seemed to him that assurances were "ever assailed with desperation." When faithful Christians realized how badly they behaved, guilt reduced their faith to "almost no faith at all." Perkins wanted to help them (and to help them help themselves), so he lectured, preached, and composed consoling commentary on biblical passages and on their "wavering, doubting, [and] distrusting." In Cambridge, from the 1580s to his death in 1602, he redefined assurance and rearmed faith against the inevitable onslaughts of self-doubt.[3]

He often wrote about religious rearmament. He said faith and doubt were locked in interminable combat, which now looks like an inescapable, intrapsychic consequence of the simultaneity of sin and salvation at the heart of reformed doctrine. Perkins posed two related questions in one of his

---

2. William Fulke, *Comfortable sermon of fayth* (London, 1578), C6v–C7r.

3. William Perkins, "A dialogue of the state of a Christian man," in *Perkins*, 1:385–90, for "wavering" and for what follows here on Eusebius and Timotheus.

didactic fictions, both of which will become increasingly important as we proceed here: how disastrously did doubt disable the faithful, and how fully would faith emancipate or empower them?

Perkins created protagonist Eusebius to persuade conversation partner Timotheus to accept that every reformed Christian was "both sinner and no sinner." Timotheus could not imagine how "no sinner" could withstand temptation? "Flesh is like a mightie, gyant, strong, lusty, stirring, enemie to God, confederate with the divell." When the "relickes of sin" press from within and temptations beset from all sides, Timotheus inquired, "in what case are you then?"

Eusebius answered from experience. "Times were hard," he recalled; "I and my family were put to great pinches," surviving on slender rations, not an animal left in the pen. But a wealthy neighbor had managed to look after his large flock of sheep—all the more remarkable an achievement because cruel circumstance in that ruinous season and region had turned many honest husbandmen into thieves. "There was such great stealing," Eusebius figured that the risk of detection would be low; so he stole a lamb and explained to his family that the meat had been a gift. He seemed safely away though sorely troubled. "I did eate with thanksgiving (as my maner is) but surely very coldly, and me thought my prayer was abhominable in God's sight." Still, two days passed without incident. But during the third night, remorse struck. Eusebius awoke from a bad dream to discover it was part of a ghoulish plot.

The devil was throttling him with his own guilt, suggesting his trespass was symptomatic of a crippling character disorder. Eusebius became convinced that his one slip showed he could not and would not be saved. The devil did it all "to persuade me that God had cast me away." Later Eusebius understood that his nightmarish ordeal was one of God's redeeming strategies or methods—later, that is, when he had learned that only the regenerate possess a capacity for self-scourging remorse. But at that instant—that third night—he was, he recalled, "turmoiled" and "stung with the conscience of sin." He would not concede he was a castaway. He must have been an idiot to take the devil's word for it. Instead, Eusebius retired to a quiet corner, and, "there upon my face groveling, I confessed my sinne and praied":

> on this manner praying, I continued many hours, and God, which is neere to all them that call upon him, heard me, eased my paine, and assured me of the remission of my sinne. After presently, for the more easing of my conscience, I went to my neighbor, and betweene him and

me upon my knees, confessed my fault with teares, desiring him to forgive me, and I would (as God's law requireth) restore that which I stole fourefold. He (and I thank him) was contented and took pitie on me and ever since hath beene by God's mercy my good friend.

This reconciliation may well suggest how Perkins regarded the social role of reformed religion. It bears comment, and we will return to it shortly, but Eusebius wanted to press on and to impress on Timotheus that "the grounde-worke of salvation is laid in God's eternal election, and a thousand sinnes cannot overthrow God's election." If consciousness of sin meant that election were forfeit, where would King David or the apostle Peter or the fleet of other biblical (un)worthies have landed? Yet proofs impersonal did not satisfy Timotheus who apparently found Eusebius' previous confidences quite compelling. "What meanes do *you* finde most effectuall to strengthen your faith and to raise you up againe when you are fallen?"

"I have very great comfort by the sacrament of the Lord's Supper," Eusebius replied, although he might have been expected to neglect sacrament for sermon. For Perkins, his creator, was tremendously popular among Calvinists nowadays known as puritans, and Elizabethan puritans believed "gaping at the mass" was Roman and retrograde. Nonetheless, Eusebius was encouraged that

God of all his mercy and of his infinite pitie and bottomlesse compassion set up his sacrament as a signe upon a hill where it may be seene on every side farre and neere, to call againe them that be runne away. And with the sacrament hee, as it were, clocketh to them as a hen for her chickens to gather them under the wings of his mercy and hath commaunded his sacrament to be had in continual mercy laid up for us in Christ's blood.

Churches in London scheduled monthly communions, but the turnout disappointed officials. Enforcement of the law requiring Christians to attend no fewer than three communion services each year was uneven.[4] Perkins

---

4. Arnold Hunt, "The Lord's Supper in Early Modern England," *Past and Present* 161 (1998): 45–47, 56–57; J. P. Boulton, "The Limits of Formal Religion: The Administration of Holy Communion in Late Elizabethan and Early Stuart London," *London Journal* 10 (1984): 139–40.

must have known of the disinterest and disappointment when he recommended more frequent communion, calling it "a source of spiritual and emotional sustenance." His Eusebius urged daily repetition, "continuall use," for the sacrament was proof of God's "bottomlesse compassion." Perkins understood its public drama as a complement to the private play of self-incrimination, the play he scripted for the "cloase corner" of Eusebius' home. To struggle with one's guilt was to discover the "relickes of syn" within and to confront that unpardonable part of the reformed Christian that any just judge would condemn. But to see, smell, taste "the bread broken" and "the wine powred out" was to remember God's mercy. The sacrament assured sinners that celestial compassion tempered justice. "I have very great comfort," Eusebius acknowledged. But should sinners find no comfort in communion, they might yet seek assurance of election in self-accusation when "humbl[ing themselves] before the Lord more heartily."[5]

It would be hard to imagine Eusebius "more heartily" humble. Yet leading reformers assumed that, left to themselves, sinners only "partlye knowe" the nature and extent of their sins. They needed help to build to the crescendo of self-contempt and the pitch of remorse required of the repentant. And help came with the sermons and prayers recited to prompt "sighing and sorrowing." "I come into publicke assembly [to] heare the minister preach the word which doth laye open and displaye my sin and misery," George Gifford let on, explaining that "the like may be said when the congregation doth pray with [its] pastor" and when preachers "apply the holy and wholesome Word of God to the heart and conscience of the[ir] people."[6]

Gifford occasionally traveled from his parish in Essex to Cambridge to consult with Perkins. They agreed on the value of prescribed, public prayers. Perkins was convinced that reformed Christians' sincerity should not be doubted simply because they borrowed others' syllables to express their sorrow. "[A]s a man that hath a weake back or a lame leg may leane on a crutch," so might a Christian "leane" on another's lament. But Perkins also allowed that "sighes of the heart" seldom waited on set prayers. "Secret and sudden," sighs and sorrows "lifted up the heart to God" wherever and whenever the heart's host penitently sifted sins—with or without liturgical prompts. After

---

5. *Perkins*, 1:374.
6. George Gifford, *A short treatise against the Donatists of England* (London, 1590), 22–25, 42–43.

all, Eusebius learned that "sorrow for sinne usually commeth on a suddane as lightening into a house."[7]

Historians today cannot make house calls in the sixteenth century to sift for sources, but we do know what Perkins and puritan preachers he educated and inspired expected from parishioners' homework. Parishioners were to inventory their offenses and to experience remorse and repentance, from which they would develop what Richard Greenham called a "craving" for God's compassion.[8] Greenham preached about longing and craving for more than twenty years in the small village of Dry Drayton, an hour from Cambridge by slow horse. He hoped, as did Perkins, Fulke, and Gifford, to shepherd parishioners to and from worries quite like those illustrated at the start of this chapter. Yet we do well to keep in mind that the worriers we meet in the sermons were preachers' creatures, whose passages from guilt and grief, through grace, to assurance of election were scripted for them. Did any or many laymen actually develop the convictions and cravings imagined for them? We can never be sure; as Margaret Spufford concedes, evidence for the religious beliefs of ordinary people "is, and always will be, thoroughly unsatisfactory." At present, Eusebius is all we have—an ideal type sighing, sorrowing, and seeking assurance.[9]

Eusebius is also something of an enigma. Perkins made him a humble husbandman or, lower on the social scale, a hired hand as well as an authority on remorse, a lay moral theologian with an appreciable talent for teaching. Eusebius was one of that caste of commoners whom the likes of John Foxe and George Gifford had transformed into celebrities. They have become emblems of lay intelligence and independence. Foxe had millhards and cowherds outsmarting Catholic clerics in stories of English martyrs, first published in 1563; Gifford's book on "country divinity" has Zelot lecturing Atheos, much as Eusebius instructed Timotheus. Was Perkins suggesting lay competence and sanctioning lay initiative or would he have been happier if we drew a different lesson from his fiction? His Eusebius was in awe of the sacrament and deferential to the wealthy neighbor he had wronged. Perhaps Perkins told his tale of remorse and recompense, crafted

---

7. *Perkins*, 1:365; and *Perkins* (1631), 2:67–68.

8. "Exposition of the 119th Psalm," in *The Workes of the reverend and faithful servant of Jesus Christ, M. Richard Greenham*, ed. Henry Holland (London, 1612), 483–84.

9. Margaret Spufford, *Contrasting Communities: English Villagers in the Sixteenth and Seventeenth Centuries* (Cambridge: Cambridge University Press, 1974), 352.

Eusebius' convictions, and dramatized lay deference to shore up late Tudor aristocracies—lay as well as clerical.

The second lesson seems likely when one recalls what happened during the 1540s and early 1550s when gospelers got wind of "great pinches" similar to those that squeezed Eusebius. Sermons of that time brimmed with indignation and with sympathy for the "thousands in England" impoverished by sudden economic downturns or by the greed and opportunism of their more fortunate neighbors, with sympathy and appeals, that is, for the "thousands who begge nowe from dore to dore." Bernard Gilpin pressed for remedies from the pulpit, recalling that the earth was the Lord's and not the landed gentry's. Hugh Latimer showered blame on the affluent for hoarding large herds while their fellow Christians were driven by "the dearth" to larceny, as Eusebius was. But in the 1560s the descendants of Gilpin and Latimer were relatively silent about social injustices. In the 1580s Perkins' peasant was sorry, and also, perhaps, a sorry result of what historian Andrew McRae calls a "widely consistent shift of focus in preaching, from social justice to social order."[10]

Did Perkins protest the shift? Or was he contemptuous of the laity in the lower strata of society? Had he and nearly all other religious radicals become social conservatives? It is said that many did—and influentially so—and that clerical and lay elites, assured of their election, conspired to discipline inferiors. But the now familiar argument that Elizabethan puritans polarized the people, dividing the privileged few with a divine right and duty to rule from the unruly multitude, is by no means conclusive, as we shall see. First, though, we ought to come to terms with what "puritan" and "the people" signify in this application.

Puritans

For centuries, historians assumed they could distinguish Tudor puritans from other Protestants by their plumage, call, and habitat. Puritans were

---

10. Andrew McRae, *God Speed the Plough: The Representation of Agrarian England, 1500–1660* (Cambridge: Cambridge University Press, 1996), 61–72. Also consider the contrasts between Philip Sidney's "cold-blooded comments" and expressions of sympathy for the dispossessed composed at midcentury, in Penry Williams, *The Late Tudors: England, 1547–1603* (Oxford: Oxford University Press, 1995), 440–43. For "thousands" of beggars, Bernard Gilpin, *A Godly sermon preached at court* (London, 1581), 49–52; and, for the gospelers' social radicalism, Susan Brigden, "Popular Disturbance and the Fall of Thomas Cromwell and the Reformers, 1539–1540," *HJ* 24 (1981): 272–78.

plainly attired in their pulpits, claiming that elaborate clerical vestments were Roman and retrograde. They called for simplicity in worship, for emphasis on sermons rather than sacraments, for a saintliness that looked to much of their world like an obsessive austerity, for voluntary forms of religious association, and, increasingly, for alternatives to episcopacy. And historians looked for puritans particularly in London, Essex, Kent, and around Cambridge. But that description of puritanism no longer holds. It was too tidy to survive the accumulation of detail that came to complicate historians' search for the essence of puritan reform and for puritans' enduring affections and disaffection. To be sure, parts of the old view survive in the two definitions of puritanism that have developed over the last thirty years. The first features puritans' commitments to a thoroughgoing institutional reform; the second, their dedication to personal regeneration. Both are based on an ostensibly sturdy scholarly consensus about crucial changes in England and in puritanism from Elizabeth's accession to the century's end, a consensus worth reviewing.

Protestant exiles who returned to England were prepared to be patient. They cheered the few reforms that the new government was inclined to try in 1559, yet they were hoping for more. John Jewel explained to friends whom he left behind on the continent that the new queen, Elizabeth I, "notwithstanding she desires a thorough change as early as possible," would likely proceed slowly "lest the matter should seem to [be] accomplished . . . in compliance with the impulse of a furious multitude." It was regrettable, he admitted, that the religious reforms were neither more radical nor more swift. For the regime's "dilatoriness grievously damped the spirits of our brethren." Nonetheless, Jewel predicted, regret would quickly change to rejoicing when queen and regime brought before the parliament a more resolutely reformed religious settlement.[11]

He was no prophet. The government proceeded cautiously from the 1560s to the century's end. When reformers lobbied in convocation, parliament, or print for more sweeping changes, conformists conjured up the specter of mob rule and the "furious multitude." Moderates soon agreed with conformists who suspected for some time that radicals' talk of further reform camouflaged contempt for compromise and disrespect for degree. And all that talk disposed clerical and lay elites to greater vigilance and stricter social control.

---

11. *ZL*, 1:17–18.

Keith Wrightson and David Levine find that respectable, godly citizens in Essex "invest[ed] apparently petty sources of social friction with massive moral significance," prevailing on constables and church officials to keep a tight rein on members of the underclass. Rich, influential villagers, along with the Calvinists who preached to them, "withdrew" from the multitude, dissociating themselves from the stew of impulse, impatience, fury, and burlesque that is often equated nowadays with early modern popular culture. Marjorie McIntosh calculates the cost: "withdrawal" and "aggressive regulation," she observes, "were disruptive of precisely those values that had previously lain at the core of the social thinking of the local communities: order, harmony, and some accommodation to the needs of the poor."[12]

In such tales of "withdrawal," the poor are the dreaded, "furious multitude"; their sins—drinking, cursing, flirting, dancing—are said to have preoccupied puritan disciplinarians. "Reformatory campaigns" in towns like Rye, Chester, and Ipswich were cranked up as early as the 1570s; in rural parishes, later. Nearly everywhere, delinquency concerned citizens far more than did destitution. During the 1590s puritans reportedly pushed off from the poor and exaggerated the "social distance" between "the better sort" and the ungodly.[13]

A second take on this development does not dwell on the socially divisive consequences of withdrawal as much as on the puritan accommodation to and integration with the social concerns of local elites. On this reading, puritans came to cooperate with moderate reformers on the episcopal bench. Puritanism disappeared for a time as a protest and acquired what historian Patrick Collinson now calls "a neo-clerical ideology."[14] But whether one stresses withdrawal and polarization or integration and accommodation, the chronology associated with the puritans' commitments to completing the reform of the English church is roughly the same. It compasses their impatience during the 1560s, their experiments with alternative polities into the early 1570s (especially with presbyterianism), and their growing conser-

---

12. Marjorie McIntosh, *Controlling Misbehavior in England, 1370–1600* (Cambridge: Cambridge University Press, 1998), 206–7; Keith Wrightson and David Levine, *Poverty and Piety in an English Village: Terling, 1525–1700*, 2nd ed. (Oxford: Oxford University Press, 1995), 179–81; and Peter Burke, *Popular Culture and Early Modern Europe* (New York: New York University Press, 1978), for general comments on "withdrawal."

13. Wrightson and Levine, *Terling*, 212–13.

14. Collinson, *Religion of Protestants*, 111, 178–88.

vatism thereafter. A complete account of the impatience, opposition, experi-
mentation, and accommodation would show that they were circumstantial,
not substantial and defining characteristics. Puritans, therefore, might be
more usefully defined by their distinctive approaches to personal regeneration rather than by any single position (or by any set or sequence of positions) toward institutions and authority. From this second perspective, the
puritans distinguished themselves from other Elizabethan Calvinists as avid
connoisseurs of inner, spiritual conflict.[15]

Eusebius' conflict is emblematic. His theft signaled that he had lost his
first struggle with "the relickes of syn" within. Panic followed his felony;
remorse followed the panic. Remorse and repentance expressed his yearning for divine mercy, which assured him of his election. Such was Eusebius'
and most puritans' preferred route to redemption. Perkins said it was to be
traveled repeatedly. Intrapsychic conflict was "continuall," according to
William Fulke. It was an ongoing dialectic between perceived estrangement
and real reconciliation, a conversation of sorts between doubts and assurance of election, between faith and despair. Thomas Wilcox, coauthor with
John Field of the puritans' first *Admonition* to parliament in the early 1570s,
compared the results with the seasonal flowering of what appeared, in win-
ter, to be dead wood, a barren bush. For assurances flowered in the faithful, even though, and arguably because, they figured for a time that one or
another or all of their offenses had put them beyond the pale.[16]

Puritans wanted reformed worship purged of "popish" costumes and
customs. They wanted a reformation of manners to proceed from their
reformulation of doctrine. But what set puritans apart from contemporaries

---

15. On Wrightson's watch, connoisseurs of spiritual struggle became impresarios of
social struggle, organizing withdrawal from the underclasses and thus polarizing their
parishes. But see, in this connection, Patrick Collinson's suspicions about the "false di-
chotomies," which, he says, inform Wrightson's view: Patrick Collinson, *Puritan Character:
Polemics and Polarities in Early Seventeenth-century English Culture* (Los Angeles: William
Andrews Clark Memorial Library, 1989), 23–24. Also note Margaret Spufford's criticisms
of Wrightson in "Puritanism and Social Control," in *Order and Disorder in Early Modern
England,* ed. John Stevenson and Anthony Fletcher (Cambridge: Cambridge University
Press, 1985), 43–46. Wrightson replied to critics in a postscript composed for the second
edition of *Terling.*

16. "Treatise tending unto a declaration whether a man may be in the estate of damna-
tion or in the estate of Grace," in *Perkins,* 1:377–78; "Dialogue concerning the conflicts
between Sathan and the Christian," in *Perkins,* 1:406; Fulke, *Text,* 444r; and Thomas
Wilcox, *Large letters for the instruction and comfort of such as are distressed in conscience* (London, 1589), 57–59.

was "the strenuous message of puritan pietism" and "a style of subjectivity" that, as Peter Lake says, survived "the puritan impulse toward incorporation within the various establishments of late Tudor and early Stuart England."[17] Puritans, in other words, desired to structure desire. Thomas Wilcox admitted the importance of their objective, maintaining the "desire of mercy [was] the obtaining of mercy."[18] Edward Dering, preaching at Cambridge and at court in the 1560s and early 1570s, anticipated Perkins and claimed that the experience of acquiring assurance was "full of wavering and doubting." When despair or doubt seemed likely to defeat faith and hope and when the faithful felt irredeemable, it was useful to remember that "the nearer we feel we are to hell the further we are from it."[19]

John Calvin frowned on frequent bouts with despair. He had seen how they demoralized reformed Christians. Richard Greenham, however, held that a lively faith was never livelier than when the faithful "travell[ed] to see" their sinfulness. "The most righteous are their own greatest accusers," Greenham explained, presuming that self-accusation and shame inflamed their desires for righteousness and pardon—the very desires that made them righteous.[20] Thus, despite Calvin's demurrer, his admirers in England melded righteousness and despair, and their puritanism, Patrick Collinson now confirms, was "equivalent to [the] full internalization" of protestantism. But "internalization" here should not suggest they were ready to dispense with sacraments and sermons. Perkins' Eusebius extolled the eucharist. Puritans' sermons summoned sinners to repentance, inspired contrition, and turned the faithful into prodigals. That puritans expected so much from pulpits when there were so few capable preachers to fill them was quixotic, perhaps, yet they trusted God to move their queen and her council to supply the political ways and means.[21]

---

17. Lake, "Defining Puritanism," 9–19. For puritans' "very strong experiential bias," also see Lake's *Moderate Puritans and the Elizabethan Church* (Cambridge: Cambridge University Press, 1982), 166–68.

18. Thomas Wilcox, *A discourse touching the doctrine of doubting* (Cambridge, 1598), 273.

19. Edward Dering, *Certaine godlie and verie comfortable letters full of consolation* (Middelburg, n.d.), B3r; Dering, *Godlye private prayers for householders* (London, 1574), A3r.

20. Compare Calvin's *Institutes*, 3.2.24, with several of Greenham's sermons, notably, "Sweet comfort for an afflicted conscience," in *Works* (London, 1612), 102–3; "Quench not thy spirit," in *Works* (London, 1605), 243–44; and "Sermon on Proverbs 28:15," in *Works* (1605), 797–801.

21. John Phillip, *A sommon to repentance* (London, 1584), D1v–D4r. Also consult Collinson, "Popular Religious Culture," in *The Culture of English Puritanism, 1560–1700,*

Their challenge was to stir and structure personal desire, although they knew that no human initiative could change God's eternal decree: the elect were chosen before all time. Sorrow for sin was not the cause of their salvation. Their sorrow and saving were God's doing: "if he doe not effectually batter men's stonie and hard hearts, they cannot return to him."[22] God revealed his will in his Word and saw to it that the Word was conveyed and applied in sermons. And God's gift of faith guaranteed that the revelation and its applications were received—and animated all that followed, from self-accusation to assurance of election. Here, too, puritans kept faith, so to speak, with the nascent Protestant tradition; they stressed sermon, solafideism, and scripture, insisting that the last be accessible in English.[23] To critics who held that it confused the people, that the Bible was "high and hard," William Fulke responded that scripture was intelligible to every soul God intended to move by it. And to critics who argued that censorious sermons antagonized laymen, the puritans answered that it was far better to be called to account and racked by guilt than to be "rockt aslepe in the cradle of security."[24]

Puritans noticed that parishioners were often "rockt aslepe" at worship and that bishops increasingly deprived parishes of the sermons that might awaken their drowsiest members. For outspoken preachers who called the laity to account effectively were being denied licenses to preach simply because they objected to reforming religion at their bishops' slow pace. And while preachers were silenced, from the 1560s, and occasionally thereafter, nonpreaching pastors, spurning passionate pulpit oratory, read homilies that were written by others. Puritans thought such reading was no better than silence, that curates who read rather than preached were "dumbe" dunces in robes, and that patrons, clerical and lay, who appointed them were terribly irresponsible. Dudley Fenner had just the remedy in the 1580s: parishioners ought to have the right to consent to patrons' nominees. He trusted the local

---

ed. Christopher Durston and Jacqueline Eales (New York: St. Martin's, 1996), 47–50, for the importance of puritans' sermons; and, for "internalization," Collinson, *The Birthpangs of Protestant England: Religious and Cultural Change in the Sixteenth and Seventeenth Centuries* (London: Macmillan, 1988), 95.

22. Wilcox, *Doubting*, 116.

23. Fulke, *Text*, 311r.

24. Fulke, *Text*, 63r–64r, and Peter Iver Kaufman, *Prayer, Despair and Drama: Elizabethan Introspection* (Urbana: University of Illinois Press, 1996), 54–56, 68–69, citing Greenham, Perkins, Arthur Dent, and others to that effect.

laity would know what kind of leadership and preaching it required. Others before Fenner said the same and were branded as "the hottest kinde of protestants." Critics accused them of thinking their zeal, intelligence, and rectitude made them superior to or "hotter" than everyone around them. Not so, Fenner said: the puritans had faith in the people; they favored parish government of and for the people.[25]

The People

Who were "the people?" Yeomen, say Keith Wrightson and David Levine, allowing a few substantial tradesmen and fewer husbandmen to join the company. Tudor puritanism was "socially selective," they go on; "firmly committed puritans" were of and for the yeomanry.[26]

Wrightson and Levine would have gotten no argument from William Harrison, conformist canon of St. George's Chapel at Windsor from 1586 but puritan preacher in Essex from 1559 and chronicler of the intervening years. For Harrison was careful to distinguish yeomen from the queen's base or inferior subjects, as did Thomas Smith, his Essex neighbor. Borrowing passages from the *Description of England* that Harrison was composing and revising, Smith parked yeomanry alongside the landed gentry, described yeomen in glowing terms, and set them as pillars of their parishes. Yeomen were enterprising, clever, responsible men who studded English shires with impressive, though not garish homes. And they were honorably opportunistic, investing prudently to enlarge their holdings when creditors dismembered the estates of "unthriftie gentlemen" and put the pieces on the block. But, from the 1560s, yeomen also appear to have taken advantage of the "surge of farming prosperity." They were known to drive copyholders from arable land and to enclose common land to make room for their own huge herds. Smith and Harrison expressly regretted the evictions, enclosures, and, above all, the loss of work: "where forty persons had their livings," a single shepherd ambled among the dozens of plows "laid down" and left behind. But neither Smith nor Harrison accused the yeomen, whom they

---

25. Dudley Fenner, *An answere unto the confutation of John Nichols* (London, 1583), 87v, and *Defense of the godly ministers against the slanders of Dr. Bridges* (London, 1587), 66–68, 132–33.

26. Wrightson and Levine, *Terling*, 173–75.

all but idealized. Admittedly, yeomen were not gentlemen, but they were "goodmen," "among the best in the realm," and "exempt from the vulgar and common sorts."[27]

But it is hard to get a fix on social hierarchy in early modern England. For instance, estimates range from 5 to 25 percent when cliometricians try to calculate what portion of the population was trapped in poverty. Statistics abound, though conclusions drawn from them tend to vary with the settings (rural or urban), seasons (crisis or normal), and specifications of what poverty was. Historians cannot even agree on general trends. Some scholars suppose hygiene and improved health, crop failures, inflation, and enclosures swelled the sixteenth-century labor supply, reduced the real value of wages, and drove to destitution the people whose grandparents had been beneficiaries of a higher mortality, labor shortages, common land, and climatic and economic stability. Rival scholars think the tale of Tudor hard times is less credible. They paint a much brighter picture and cite the flourishing foreign trade, domestic consumerism, the "industrial character" of the realm's newest cities, and the impressive yields of some late Tudor experiments with fertilizers and other agrarian technologies. But downturn or upswing, poverty remained a problem. On one account, puritanism provided a way to cope with and to control the people beneath the uppermost tier of peasant society at which yeomen and lesser gentry were found. Puritan preachers reportedly countenanced "withdrawal" and "social distance" from the common sort, licensing elites' moral and political authority over inferiors.[28]

---

27. *Harrison's Description of England in Shakespeare's Youth*, ed. Frederick J. Furnivall (London, 1877), 306–7, and William Harrison, *The Description of England*, ed. George Edelen (Ithaca, N.Y.: Cornell University Press, 1968), 120–21, 193. Also see Thomas Smith, *De republica Anglorum*, ed. Mary Dewar (Cambridge: Cambridge University Press, 1982), 74–75. Mildred Campbell conceded subsequently that yeoman opportunism was sometimes less than honorable, but she was quite reluctant to soil the celebrity Harrison and Smith had acquired for their yeomen. Her study, though, is still valuable and the most comprehensive available on *The English Yeoman under Elizabeth and the Early Stuarts*, reprint ed. (New York: A. M. Kelly, 1968), especially 91–94, 105–7, 220. For farming and prosperity, consult D. M. Palliser's *The Age of Elizabeth: England under the Later Tudors, 1547–1603*, 2nd ed. (London: Longman, 1992), 178–79; and, for yeo-mania, see Edmund S. Morgan, *Inventing the People: The Rise of Popular Sovereignty in England and America* (New York: Norton, 1988), 153–59.

28. Palliser, *Age of Elizabeth*, 228–34, 305–8, 451–52; C. G. A. Clay, *Economic Expansion and Social Change: England, 1500–1700*, vol. 1 (Cambridge: Cambridge University

That account or interpretation is clearly, comprehensively expressed in charges leveled by Christopher Hill and elaborated by David Zaret. Hill and Zaret allege that puritanism not only assured that inferior sorts would be controlled but content and conscientious as well. Yeomen and craftsmen were getting ahead and just "beginning to give employment to a wider circle than their own famil[ies] and an apprentice or two." These emerging elites, as employers, needed a dependable labor force, men and women who "no longer waited at the rich man's gate for charity, but went out to offer their services." Tudor puritanism filled the bill; puritans preached the poor from alms to wages, on Hill's watch. In effect, they justified England's transition from welfare to its Elizabethan version of "work-fare." Without puritanism, the new elites' desires to acquire were likely to have been thought "a deplorable, if natural frailty," and those desires would never have become a "mainspring of emerging capitalist society."[29]

Zaret's investigation of late Tudor social prejudice and economic exploitation adds a word about puritans' motivation. He imagines that the puritans nested with affluent, influential patrons to protect themselves. They feared that the "radically democratic implications" of reformed religion, if ever realized, would likely dismantle all elites, clerical as well as lay. The puritans, therefore, put distance between their godly patrons and the multitude, defending the former's (their retainers') respectability by identifying material success with sanctity. Their sermons were spurs and bridles, Zaret says—spurs to urge acquisition and bridles to restrain and train the poor. And, as the "servitors" of social climbers, Zaret's puritans preached to the likes of Perkins' Eusebius, trying to transform resentments of those left behind into deference to, and reverence for, those getting ahead.[30]

Bridles? One gets a decidedly different impression from Richard Bancroft's complaints about reformers who "endevoreth with the multitude,"

Press, 1984), 223–24. Also consult the more controversial studies of late Tudor economic development and hardship, particularly Eric Kerridge, *The Agricultural Revolution* (New York: A. M. Kelly, 1968); A. L. Beier, *The Problem of the Poor in Tudor and Early Stuart England* (London: Methuen, 1983); and Paul Slack, *Poverty and Policy in Tudor and Stuart England* (London: Longman, 1988).

29. Of Hill's many papers on reformed religion and economics, see "William Perkins and the Poor," reprinted in *Puritanism and Revolution: Studies in the Interpretation of the English Revolution of the Seventeenth Century* (London: Secker and Warburg, 1958), 219–38.

30. David Zaret, *The Heavenly Contract: Ideology and Organization in Pre-Revolutionary Puritanism* (Chicago: University of Chicago Press, 1985), 64–67, 192–95.

"rebelling and rayling" and inciting the very people Hill and Zaret claim were bridled, tamed, trained, and restrained.[31] Bancroft almost certainly exaggerated the "rayling" and rebellion to win the propertied for the puritans' conformist critics. He exaggerated the danger, that is, to make those who had the most to lose suspicious of religious enthusiasm, but unless he wholly invented the puritans' pitch to the people, to "the multitude," Zaret's case for bridles is in bits, and an argument could be made that puritans tried to draw in, and not withdraw from, the common sort. "A man may have a king's hart in his breast and yet a begger's coate on his backe," explained Zelot, George Gifford's protagonist in the *Country Divinity* (1581).[32] Beggars and their slightly better-off brethren were important to Gifford and his fellow reformers. For if commoners were left unattended, they might return to the unreformed religion they or their parents practiced twenty years earlier. But "let the people be taught to know wholsome doctrine, and they will never abide the rotten drugges of . . . Roman apothecaries."[33]

Puritans thought themselves educators of, and advocates for, the common sort of Christians, although the word "commoner" may have caused some consternation after Thomas Elyot published his *Boke named the Governour* in 1531. At its start, Elyot agonized over the word "commonwealth," deciding finally to reject it; proposals he attributed to "communers" seemed to him to undermine the community. "Communers" were a "vulgar people" who would have the "slouthful or idell participate with hym that is industrious and taketh payne whereby the frute of his labours shulde be diminished."[34] But Elyot's fears were unfounded. And later, puritans were no socialists. The plight of the Elizabethan "communers" or "commonaltie" moved them to teach doctrine, not to preach insurrection. Their challenge, from the 1560s, as they saw it, was to explain reformed religion *ad plebem*, as their forebears in the first centuries after Christ explained "among the common people" what was worthy of reverence.[35] From the 1580s, after

---

31. Richard Bancroft, *Dangerous positions and proceedings published and practised within this island of Brytain under pretence of reformation* (London, 1595), 44–46, 61–62.

32. Gifford, *Briefe discourse of certaine points of the religion which is among the common sort of Christians and which may be termed the countrie divinitie* (London, 1598), 96.

33. See the anonymous *Dialogue concerning strife in our church* (London, 1584), 5v–8r.

34. Thomas Elyot, *The Boke named the Governour*, vol. 1, ed. Henry Herbert and Stephen Croft (New York: E. P. Dutton, 1967), 6–8.

35. See, for example, the conversation in King's Lynn on eucharistic language and "the unlerned," CCCC, MS. 102, 247–49.

failed attempts to legislate commoners' participation in parish patronage and administration, puritan partisans of lay and local control did not take to the streets. So when George Gifford tried to stir "communers," their social superiors had no cause for alarm. Gifford's "common sort" was not Elyot's; indeed, they were "plaine countrie men," unexceptional and unassuming but, truth be told, uncooperative as well.

For Gifford's "plaine men" stubbornly persisted in equating righteousness and redemption with every minimally good intention. "I do what I can," his Atheos says in *Country Divinity*, expecting heavenly reward, for "God hath made me able to do no better." But "let [such] people be taught," Gifford trumpeted, acknowledging, though, that most commoners, like Atheos, were mulish and needed kicking as well as educating. They "armed themselves against true repentance" and would have pastors "for nothing but friendship." But every pastor's best course was to be belligerent. Angry words jolted the complacent as well as the combative commoners, keeping "plaine countrie men" from Roman Catholicism—and in the reformed churches. Wrightson, Levine, Hill, and Zaret depict the puritans' belligerence as a distancing device, but their "harsh utterances" now seem to have been intended as something of a wake-up call, a tactic that seemed to Gifford and his kind more inclusive than isolationist.[36]

Some puritans were heard to grumble that the laity wanted only good news from personable and consoling pastors, as Gifford implied; other puritans trusted that their parishioners expected severe reprimands from the pulpit, welcomed them, and were at a loss without them. "Poore people of the countrie," for whom the *Lamentable complaint of the commonaltie* was filed, were said to be desperate for "an holie preaching ministerie," specifically for sermons that "take an edge by exhortation" and shame sinners to repent. Bishops told nonpreaching curates to procure at least four sermons a year, but the *Complaint*'s "poore people" looked for more and suggested that the sharpest rebukes, if delivered only quarterly, were unlikely to have much effect. "The mighty oak of sin cannot be felled by four strokes of an axe."[37]

To be sure, the "commonaltie" attached to that sentiment in *Lamentable Complaint* was dreamed up—as were Perkins' Eusebius and Gifford's Zelot.

---

36. See Gifford, *Countrie Divinitie*, A2v–A3r, 49–53, and, to put those "harsh utterances . . . in the context of [puritan] mission," Eamon Duffy, "The Godly and the Multitude in Stuart England," *Seventeenth Century* 1 (1986): 31–55.

37. *Register*, 206–7, 221–23, 269.

Unprepossessing laymen outnumbered "plaine" yet proficient lay protagonists, who debated learned priests in John Foxe's *Acts and Monuments* and elsewhere, in John Bridges' sermon of 1571 and Gifford's *Country Divinity* ten years later, travestied explanations of condign and congruent merit and ridiculed "rustic Pelagianism."[38] Most "plaine" people were conspicuously plain, in other words, both in narratives as well as in parishes, yet the fictions that survive tell us what some puritans thought a commoner's common sense, when awakened and informed, was capable of doing.[39]

From the 1560s, they imagined "plaine countrie men" were the realm's most formidable defense against Catholic reconquest. They looked to involve their "plaine" protagonists in the selection of pastors. Critics of broadly participatory schemes and regimes—reformers of all stripes—worried that the commoners were less capable and more Catholic than generally perceived. The critics, that is, thought proponents of lay participation and local control were naive; we may think of them as populists, though only if an obvious anachronism is allowed—if we suspend the requirement that populists reflect the opinions of those whose participation they promote. For the Elizabethan puritan partisans of broad participation advocated the involvement of laymen whose repentance, perseverance, and longing for God's love they mistrusted, even while they lay all three as cornerstones of a reformed church and commonwealth. They hoped first to enlighten and then empower the common sort.[40]

Their "populism," therefore, blended with paternalism. Nicholas Bownde's instructions to householders are an example of how that worked. Bownde challenged heads of households to impart the rudiments of reformed faith to their extended families every sabbath. "Wee have a greate help by our inferiours in many things, so the Lord would have us helpe them in the chiefe

---

38. John Bridges, *Sermon preached at Paules Crosse* (London, 1571), 73, 80–82; for John Foxe, *infra*, 54–57, 145–47, and Richard Helgerson, *Forms of Nationhood: The Elizabethan Writing of England* (Chicago: University of Chicago Press, 1992), 264–66.

39. Patrick Collinson, *Tudor England Revisited* (London: Queen Mary and Westfield College, 1995), 5. Collinson cautions against overstating the puritans' admiration for commoners' common sense. Christopher Haigh, "The Taming of the Reformation: Preachers, Pastors, and Parishioners in Elizabethan and Early Stuart England," *History* 85 (2000): 576–78, suggests that many puritans preferred accommodation to confrontation.

40. See Debora Shuger's remarks on the term "populist" in "Subversive Fathers and Suffering Subjects: Shakespeare and Christianity," in *Religion, Literature, and Politics in Post-Reformation England, 1540–1688*, ed. Donna Hamilton and Richard Strier (Cambridge: Cambridge University Press, 1996), 60–61.

and principal." Church attendance was not enough. Householders must see to it that servants, apprentices, and family members "spend the rest of the [sabbath] in holy exercise." "Caus[e] them to conferre" about the sermon or about passages from scripture, Bownde directed, one authoritarian to others.[41]

But Bownde's populist streak was conspicuous when he prowled around the apostle Paul's correspondence to document the earliest Christians' dedication to such conferences. He lined up several passages behind the apostle's encouragement to "let the word of Christ dwell in you plenteously in all wisdome, teaching and admonishing your selves." The greatest shame of the reformed regime, Bownde grieved, was that people were still "so ignorant as to imagine that to conferre of the scripture is proper to the ministers and not belonging to the common people which once to dreame of [was] a thing more meete for the darke night of poperie wherein it was defended than of the midday of the Gospel which doth so manifestlie gainsay it."[42]

Bownde tirelessly filed old saws. "Though every one give but a little yet the summe amounteth to a great deal." "Though every man hath some grace of God's spirit in himselfe, yet it is greatly increased by conference." "[T]he knife that is blunt, being rubbed upon the whetstone (though it be more blunt than itself) receive thereby a sharpness which it had not before." "Even as though there be no fire in the flint stones, yet one of them striking upon another do bring forth betweene which commeth not from any one of them but from both and both of them striken together." Striking and rubbing suggest disagreement or friction, yet Bownde did not explicitly commend dispute. "That which every man severallie cannot doe, al of them together . . . joyning their strengths, shalle be able to bring to passe." And "the knowledge of many being put together shall increase that which was in every man before." Sabbath sociability, conversation, and collaboration document the populist impulse in Bownde's patently patriarchal narrative, making "every man" a beneficiary, insofar as "conferring about things [the commoners] shall come to that knowledge . . . which not onely none of them had before, but not any one of them could have by himself alone attained unto."

41. Nicholas Bownde, *The doctrine of the sabbath plainely layde forth* (London, 1595), 260, 270–73.

42. Bownde, *Sabbath*, 214–17, citing Colossians 3:12.

Bownde figured that the apostle Paul knew the limits of what anyone may "attain unto" alone, that he was being truthful rather than just courteous when he told Christians in Rome he was coming not only to bestow spiritual gifts on them but to be counseled and comforted by their faith (Romans 1:11–12). Bownde wrote to make the implication of Paul's admission clear to the heads of households: they were just as likely to learn from, as to teach their apprentices, children, and servants. Granted, it is risky for historians to infer practices from purposes, but the broadly participatory character of household conferences in this suggestive example of prescriptive literature seems important. And what we know of the exchange of small gifts—paper gloves and garters with edifying messages and lists of pious resolutions—also suggests congenial and somewhat "classless" classes at home.[43]

Bownde's sabbath conferences, compassing the "upstairs" and "downstairs" of a late Tudor household seem continuous with, and perhaps a culmination of, the puritans' proposals to empower the people. But we should learn to expect considerable imprecision when we listen for the voices of— and catch only the advocates for and critics of—"the people." Even yeomen, with whom leading Elizabethan reformers are said to have made common cause, are hard to locate. It would help tremendously had the sixteenth-century yeomen subscribed to an ideology of class conflict or, for that matter, to any single idea, yet students of yeomanry only come up with catalogues of virtues (thrift, intelligence, neighborliness, and the like) and the most perceptive students are far from arguing that any virtue settled exclusively at one socioeconomic stratum. Moreover, there appears to have been no agreement at the time—and there is none now—about the amount of property, number of household servants, or size of a surplus that husbandmen had to acquire to establish their standing as yeomen. Regional variations further complicate the sketch. Cumbrians, for example, styled themselves yeomen more casually than farmers in Cambridgeshire, where, as a result, yeoman literacy was much higher than in the north.[44]

---

43. Bownde, *Sabbath*, 218–22. For small gifts, see Tessa Watt, *Cheap Print and Popular Piety, 1550–1640* (Cambridge: Cambridge University Press, 1991), 248–51.

44. David Cressy, "Describing the Social Order of Elizabethan England," *Literature and History* 3 (1976): 29–44 and *Literacy and the Social Order: Reading and Writing in Tudor and Stuart England* (Cambridge: Cambridge University Press, 1980), 150–61. Also see Theodore Leinwand, "Shakespeare and the Middling Sort," *Shakespearean Quarterly* 44

One generalization seems to stand a chance at survival, namely, the statement that yeomen were attached to the land. A landless yeoman, after all, seems something of a contradiction. Yet there were many ways to hold acreage. Pastures in Norfolk were deeded to some citizens of Norwich who rarely left the city and had country neighbors cultivate their investment. Did owners become yeomen on purchase? The farms and fields they acquired certainly gave them status that tenements in town did not.[45] But while the countryside and prospects for gentrification beguiled affluent townsmen, the cities beckoned the landed and lesser gentry. They came to compete with wealthy merchants, perhaps also with tradesmen, whom Marjorie McIntosh now calls "urban yeomen."[46] William Harrison watched the traffic at the time, referring to it as "a mutual conversion." People in the cities "changed estate" with country cousins.[47] There seems to have been so much change and movement that one may be justified in suspending efforts to distinguish yeomen from husbandmen, upwardly mobile cottagers, merchants, tradesmen, and urban professionals in Elizabethan England's "broad middle layer."[48]

Late Tudor puritans mostly had that "middle" in mind when they were thinking of the laity and advocating broadly participatory parish regimes. Sixteenth-century literature refers to the "middling sort" or "middle sort." Yet the lesson that we learned about imprecision while looking for yeomen applies here as well: discriminations at the margins will always be arbitrary and imprecise. Historians may try or pretend to say exactly what level of resourcefulness was needed for cottagers and members of undercapitalized trades to rise to the middle or above, but we must not expect to discover the specific amount of investment and industry necessary to lift someone from poverty into the middle or higher still. The solution, I submit, is to admit the

---

(1993): 284–303, and, for "massive variations within the non-elite social stratum," J. A. Sharpe, *Early Modern England: A Social History* (London: Arnold, 1987), 199.

45. See S. J. Payling, "Social Mobility, Demographic Change, and Landed Society in Late Medieval England," *Economic History Review* 45 (1992): 51, 66–67; and Robert Tittler, *The Reformation and the Towns in England: Politics and Political Culture, 1540–1640* (Oxford: Clarendon, 1998), 248.

46. Marjorie McIntosh, *A Community Transformed: The Manor and Liberty of Havering, 1500–1620* (Cambridge: Cambridge University Press, 1991), 193.

47. Harrison, *Description*, 115.

48. For that "broad layer," see Tim Harris, "Problematizing Popular Culture," *Popular Culture in England*, ed. Tim Harris (New York: St. Martin's, 1995), 1–22.

imprecision yet provisionally to define the vast caste of characters in the middle as people (1) aspiring to the wealth and cultural values of the elite, (2) ever more strenuously trying to distance themselves from the poor, and (3) welcoming chances to participate in the administration of their livery companies, municipalities, and parishes.[49]

To calibrate discrepancies in soil, surplus, or swagger, within this middle and to develop subsets or "classes" from those differences seemed unpromising exercises to me. Without subsets, though, it may not be the best use of our time here to approve or disprove the contention that puritanism was an "ideological accomplice of certain processes of social differentiation."[50] Besides, the preachers who polarized could be no more interesting than those Elizabethan puritans who, thinking about the laity, advocated broad lay participation and local control of their churches.

49. My provisional definition fuses J. A. Sharp's comments with Ian Archer's analysis of citizen participation. See Sharpe, "Social Strain and Social Dislocation, 1585–1603," in *The Reign of Elizabeth I: Court and Culture in the Last Decade,* ed. John Guy (Cambridge: Cambridge University Press, 1995), 208–29; and Ian Archer, *Pursuit of Stability: Social Relations in Elizabethan London* (Cambridge: Cambridge University Press, 1991), 14–17. For the characteristic preoccupations of those in "the broad middle," see Keith Lindley, "The Maintenance of Stability in Early Modern London," *HJ* 34 (1991): 986–88; Keith Wrightson, "Sorts of People in Tudor and Stuart England," in *The Middling Sort of People: Culture, Society, and Politics in England,* ed. Jonathan Barry and Christopher Brooks (New York: St. Martin's Press, 1994), 41–48; and H. R. French, "The Search for the Middle Sort of People in England, 1600–1800," *HJ* 43 (2000): 284–93.

50. Compare Tittler, *Reformation,* 338, with Lake, "Defining Puritanism," 12–13.

TWO

"We are all priests"

Early Reformers Thinking of the Laity

Lollards in England are generally thought to have been forerunners of the Protestant reformations of the sixteenth century. They were confident "the secret motions in private men" more adequately conveyed God's will than what they were learning from their priests. When those "private men" went public—reading scripture, teaching, and preaching, though they were laymen—the English church might be truly reformed and refashioned, perhaps without prelates.

William Tyndale, known for assailing "the practice of prelates" in a treatise with that title is also known for trying to get English Bibles into the hands of commoners whom he trusted to transform the church. Tyndale's critics presumed that literate laymen were nonetheless unprepared to comprehend what they read and altogether incompetent to assess or alter King Henry VIII's church. Thomas Cranmer, archbishop of Canterbury from 1532, shared that skepticism into the next decade and in the next reign. He did not believe the laity was ready to participate meaningfully in parish government, though he welcomed to King Edward VI's England several refugee reformers from the continent who did. Congregations of "strangers" put lay authority in play, but caution was the order of Cranmer's day.

At the heart of a program approved from 1553 by Queen Mary I and her principal adviser, Cardinal Legate Reginald Pole, was the effort to restore the laity's "habits of obedience" to Rome. Disobedient pastors were arrested. Resourceful, reformed, antiestablishment commoners occasionally took their places. Marian bishops had a gathering sense that such expressions of local autonomy and lay assertiveness would probably undermine their counter to previous English reforms. They must not have been happy to hear the likes of miller Edmund Allin, thinking of the laity, say that "we are all priests." The hundreds who chose emigration to reformed cities on the continent over England under Mary were thinking of the laity as well. The exigencies of exile in Emden, Frankfurt, and elsewhere drew laymen into positions of power. Congregations assembled for elections and interrogations, signaling a confidence in commoners' discretion, and makeshift arrangements, notably their few experiments with participatory parish regimes, amounted to an intriguing preface to what was to follow.

"Laymen as wise as the officers"

Historians tend to associate literacy with learning and wisdom. They discover that the sixteenth century was a good age for brains and books. Statistics suggest an increasing number of Englishmen could read as decades passed, and, from more readers, we should probably infer there were more questions about what they were reading. As the commoners consulted their vernacular Bibles, they likely questioned their clergy. And as the most avid readers ranged over the pamphlet literature complaining about the church's economic and interpretive powers, their questions seemed to become combative.

John Champneys called himself "an unlearned lay manne" and "a poor lay man of small literature," but he was familiar enough with his Bible to comb it and compose from its parts his *Harvest is at hand* in 1548. Combing and composing, he came to the uncontroversial conclusion that "the onely trewe and perfect remedy" for bondage to sin was "for all reasonable people to seeke of God in prayer the regeneration promysed in Christ." *Harvest* is contemptuous of the other remedies on offer at the realm's churches—

sacraments, penances, and priests presiding over both. Champneys thought all that was quackery, worse than worthless. They were distractions. "Every lively member" of the reformed churches, he claimed, possessed the "spirit of Christ" or was possessed by it; either way, possession put the "intelligence of the word of God" into one's head, even into the heads of the thickest-headed commoners. "Unnedefulle ministers," self-proclaimed curators of divine mysteries, made Christianity too mysterious for Champneys, who maintained that "every lively member" could do very well without the curatorial staff. As for the members yet unpossessed and unlively, they were better off listening to laymen of little, though profound learning.[1]

Champney's approach was not new. In the fifteenth century, comparable criticisms drew fire from Reginald Peacock and Thomas Netter, who said they derived from the scant learning of the laity. Netter insisted that commoners' intuition was no substitute for the trained intelligence of priests.[2] Peacock argued that laymen who memorized passages from scripture and preached commentaries on what they remembered ("kunnen suche textis bi herte an bi mouth") spread heresy and harm. Amateur exegetes, he went on, increased the need for that supposedly "unnedefulle" ministry. For without priests, the flotilla of errors that accompanied expressions of lay "learning" would certainly go uncorrected.[3]

Peacock wrote against commoners who repeated John Wyclif's criticisms of the clergy. They styled themselves "trewe, faithful lyvers"; their enemies called them lollards. When cornered, they were known to have declared that all clerical distinctions—from priest to pope—were unscriptural and unwarranted. They were not surprised, they said, to find priests prescribing a steady diet of sacraments, penances, pilgrimages, and the like—passing off the pomp and ceremony as something remotely biblical. After all, priests "lyven all oute of Goddis lawe" so "noo . . . person of the clergie cometh into the trewe and dew undirstondinge of Holi Scripture."[4]

---

1. John Champneys, *The harvest is at hand* (London, 1548), B3v–B4r, D8r, E5v–E6v, G2r.

2. Thomas Netter, *Doctrinale fidei Catholicae*, 3 vols., ed. Bonaventure Blanciotti (Venice, 1757), 2:719 ("Quid docere poterit cum ipse non didicit"). Also see 3:379 for the lay usurpation of sacerdotal prerogatives.

3. Reginald Peacock, *Repressor of over much blaming of the clergy*, vol. 1, ed. Churchill Babington (London: Longman, Green, Longman, and Roberts, 1860), 88–90.

4. Peacock, *Repressor*, 102–4.

Later lollards were as disrespectful of the clergy. Early in the sixteenth century, they suggested something of a non-sequitur to express and justify their dissent. From the premise that there were no priests "in Christ's time" they concluded that priests of any subsequent age could not but play false with the good news of that time. Priests were not to be trusted. Lollards preferred to read the Bible or have it read to them by other laymen.[5] Their reading in homes and fields attracted small crowds, and crowds attracted the attention of diocesan authorities eager to learn what more was said when the Bible was read. Were local priests rebuked? Were all clerics savaged? Was reading a prelude to rebellion? Who organized and who joined such "societ[ies] convented for heresy"?[6]

Authorities trawled for heretics in nearly every diocese. They caught a few renegade priests who, like John Drury near Worcester, spoke caustically about pilgrimages and ridiculed parishioners for offering candles to images. Drury was charged as well with having taught his servant to read the Bible. Occasional cleric William Sweeting was a cattlekeeper when apprehended and executed in 1511 for speaking "against oblations and images."[7] On the whole, though, later lollardy was a lay movement, if we may refer to it as a movement at all. Neighbors passed the word. Intrepid lay itinerants kept lollards in one village informed of the piety and protests of like-minded persons in the next. There was little chance that clerics' efforts against anticlericalism would end the criticism. Surveillance and repressive measures, however, limited the number, range, and effectiveness of itinerant critics. Later lollards spoke of their "sects" and "congregations," echoing John Wyclif's inflated accounts of his influence a century before, but they consistently proved better at colonizing individual consciences than at organizing their "convented" societies into "a system of gathered churches."[8]

---

5. *AM*, 4:230, for remarks to that effect attributed to dissidents Richard Vulford and Thomas Geffrey. When I use Foxe and his sources to document or comment on later lollardy and the Marian martyrs, I refer to Josiah Pratt's edition (*AM*), but I am aware that it obscures the development of the text during Foxe's career. Later in this chapter and in the next, I shall include references to the first edition, *AM*(1563), to signal what early Elizabethan readers learned from Foxe.

6. *AM*, 4:219–20.

7. *AM*, 4:237, for Drury; 4:214–16, for Sweeting.

8. Derek Plumb, "A Gathered Church? Lollards and Their Society," in *The World of Rural Dissenters, 1520–1775*, ed. Margaret Spufford (Cambridge: Cambridge University Press, 1995), 132–63, goes looking for that "system" among fifteenth- and early sixteenth-

Unless one thinks of reading as a ritual, lollards shared no liturgy. There was no sacrament unique to them, as, for example, the *consolamentum* was unique to the Cathar. What distinguished the lollards from other restless, yet generally restrained, late medieval Christians was a landmark lay assertiveness that made their otherwise unexceptional complaints about clerical corruption insufferably offensive at the time. Isabel Morwin confided to her sister early in the sixteenth century that purgatory and pilgrimage were scams perpetuated solely for the priests' profit. Asked if she had picked up that idea from her curate, Morwin answered that knowledge of such swindles, quite like the "intelligence of the word of God," could be drawn from observation, without benefit of clergy.[9] Historian Anne Hudson suggests that observations of that sort derived from a doctrine of predestination that provided lollardy with "a coherent program for reformation" as well as with a proto-Protestant conception of the priesthood of all believers.[10] Perhaps so, although one can imagine that indignation was passed along without any "coherent program." Whatever the case and conveyance, the source of subversive sentiment need not be located with precision to propose that lollard leveling moved commoners like Isabel Morwin to profess contempt and inclined layman Richard Sawyer to declare war on the clergy.[11]

A century after Sawyer, Richard Bancroft heard and repeated rumors of just such a war. Sawyer and other long-buried lollards were no threat at that time, but Elizabethan puritans were. They boasted biblical precedents for their "zeale *extra ordinem*" and justified their belligerence with examples of

> Phineas who in zeale killed the adulterers; of Ahad who in zeale killed Sifara. . . . To those that know these principles, how can it be eyther obscure or difficult what they are both to thinke and judge when they shall heare of extraordinary callings and secret motions in private men,

---

century lollards and finds nothing that might pass for it. Yet Richard Davies, "Lollardy and Locality," *TRHS* 6 (1991): 191–212, claims to have discovered lollard "micro-networks."

9. *AM*, 4:221.

10. Anne Hudson, *The Premature Reformation: Wycliffite Texts and Lollard History* (Oxford: Clarendon, 1988), 168–73, 508.

11. See John A. F. Thomson, *The Later Lollards, 1414–1520* (Oxford: Oxford University Press, 1965), 77–79, for Sawyer's deposition. For a different take on coherence and leadership among the lollards, see Shannon McSheffrey, *Gender and Heresy: Women and Men in Lollard Communities, 1420–1530* (Philadelphia: University of Pennsylvania Press, 1995), notably, 7–10, 47–48.

whereby they shall take upon them (through the assistance of giddy and seductive malcontentes) to correct and amend, to set up and throwe down, to deliver and to restraine, to punish and execute how, what, where, when, and whom . . . according to their owne pleasures, and all under the pretence of such directions as they shall affirm the Holy Ghost doth minister unto them.[12]

Bancroft might have allowed his characterization of puritan zeal and dissent to stand also for lollard protest. He tended to think all anticlericalism cut from the same cloth. But the route from lollard leveling to late Tudor thinking about the laity passes through an eventful sixteenth century. And that passage was marked by the realm's "divorce" from Rome during the 1530s, proceedings instigated by King Henry VIII and concluded with the counsel of his two enterprising Thomases, Archbishop Cranmer and Vicegerent Cromwell, who took great pains to explain Catholic "abuses" to the commoners.

William Tyndale was perhaps the most conspicuous forerunner of the Henrician reform. His family name suggests origins in the north of England, in the Tyne Valley and Yorkshire where Catholic protest against Henry's "heresy" crested in 1536. But Tyndale was born in Gloucestershire, schooled at Oxford and Cambridge, and in the year the north rose in rebellion, he was executed in Antwerp for being more heretical than Henry. His years at university may have signaled trouble ahead, for he flayed the colleges then, as he did later, for putting off students' biblical studies. Only when they were "armed with false principles," he said, were young men permitted to read the Bible. And by then they were "shut out" of scripture, doomed to miss its sublime truths and instructed to debate concepts and categories better suited to medieval speculation than to personal regeneration.[13]

After Martin Luther published a German translation of the New Testament in 1522, Tyndale contemplated an English one and looked for someone to finance it. He received no encouragement from Cuthbert Tunstall, bishop of London, but Humphrey Monmouth, a merchant suspected of lollard sympathies, heard Tyndale preach, sent him abroad, and paid his

---

12. Bancroft, *Dangerous positions,* 141–42.
13. William Tyndale, *Expositions of Scripture and Practice of Prelates,* ed. Henry Walter (Cambridge: Cambridge University Press, 1849), 291.

expenses. When he got to Luther's Wittenberg, Tyndale picked up William Roye, his garrulous collaborator; in Worms, late in 1525, the two found a printer. Shortly afterward, England's ambassador to Spain, William Lee, warned the government that Tyndale's translation was crossing the channel and reminded his friends at Henry's court "what hurt such books hath done in your realm in times past," referring to sacred texts that the lollards had translated. Thinking of the laity and further defining "hurt," Lee held that heresy had a history of following closely on biblical translation; heresy, he claimed, was "grounded upon bare words of scripture not well taken or understood."[14]

Tyndale's translations arrived in March 1526, and copies were confiscated and burned soon thereafter, Monmouth's among them. Tunstall charged Tyndale with smuggling "alien doctrine" into England; thereupon, the translator turned the bishop's curse on the entire episcopal bench, conceding that his English New Testament looked "alien" (*peregrina*) in England, but only because the sacred text he faithfully rendered knew nothing of bishops' "worldly pomp and honor, superfluous abundance of all manner of riches, and liberty to do what a man listeth unpunished." In other words, the English New Testament showed how alien and estranged from its origins in Christian antiquity the unreformed English church had become.[15]

Pomp, honor, and superfluous abundance were no strangers at court. King and council were uninterested in impoverishing their prelates, it appears, until they proved ineffective in getting Henry what he most wanted. English church officials could not persuade Pope Clement VII to annul the king's first marriage, so Henry VIII prevailed on his bishops to divorce their pope. Legend has it that Tyndale's work played no small part, particularly his treatise on *The obedience of a Christian man*. Henry's lover and, later, second wife, Anne Boleyn, reportedly urged it on the king who grew fond of Tyndale's *Obedience*. Its sustained, devastating criticisms of papacy and episcopacy were impossible to miss. However, since he was almost certainly not thinking of the laity as Tyndale was and as we are, Henry might easily have overlooked *Obedience*'s directive that parishioners take part in parish administration, "every man as he is apt and meet to serve his neighbor."[16]

---

14. Quoted in J. F. Mozley, *William Tyndale* (London: Macmillan, 1937), 65–66.
15. Tyndale, *Expositions*, 337–38.
16. Tyndale, *Doctrinal Treatises*, 212.

Tyndale took up the issues of lay authority and local, congregational self-government more programmatically several years later in his *Practice of prelates*. He added to his rogues' gallery lay and monastic proprietors. They were as bad as bishops, he said, because, as the parishes' absentee, uncaring landlords, they were responsible for all mismanagement. They siphoned off revenues and left too little to attract worthy candidates to the pulpits, let alone keep them there. Tyndale's solution was to change the way that every parish did business: lay churchwardens "ought to take the benefices into their hands, in the name of parishen[er]s, and . . . deliver the preachers of God's word their dwelling and present a sufficient living."[17]

Lay officials, then, would watch over parish finances, look after the poor, and preside when their congregations counseled, censured, and condemned offenders. Tyndale gathered that care for the poor and concern for corruption in the church would inevitably compel the lay wardens, as disciplinarians, to summon their priests and bishops to account, inasmuch as prelates were greedy, "unsatiable beasts." Yet he figured that greed and iniquity had so settled in the system of clerical subsidies that commoners could do little of consequence to set things right. Remedy required the king's intervention and reinvention of the English church. Until then, though, lay participation was advisable. "There are many found among the laymen which are as wise as the officers," and, Tyndale continued, they ought to search their consciences for resolutions to congregational controversy, discipline each other, deliberate on doctrine, and be consulted on the choice of local curates and on the competence of candidates for ordination.[18] Predictably, this "offering" was unwelcome. Tyndale's clerical adversaries thought that they could do very well resolving controversy, interpreting doctrine, enforcing discipline, and selecting personnel without lay participation. As noted, they burned Tyndale's translation of the New Testament,

> calling them heretics execrable
> which caused the gospel venerable
> to come into layman's sight.[19]

---

17. Tyndale, *Expositions*, 336.

18. Tyndale, *Doctrinal Treatises*, 236–41.

19. David Daniell, *William Tyndale, A Biography* (New Haven, Conn.: Yale University Press, 1994), 189–95, quoting from "Read me and be not wroth" in his account of the fires.

Thomas More blamed the victim, alleging that, had the translation been better and the translator less impudent, the reception of both would have been different, far more favorable. More claimed that the church knew best "whyche wrytynge is holy scripture and whiche is not." It would know when and how to make the sacred texts available. But which church knew best, when, and how? For More, it was the *ekklesia*, and when he and other Catholics used the word in canon law and common discourse, it referred to the clergy. The clergy, and not its critics, were custodians of the Bible. Tyndale's translation, though, rendered *ekklesia* as "congregation," "signal-[ling]," William Stafford now says, "a major change: a reevaluation of the laity and the religious, social, and political relocation of the multitude."[20]

Tyndale's congregations possessed "the keys" that Christ entrusted to the apostle Peter (Matthew 16:18–19); congregations, therefore, should be the final arbiters and chief censors in the most serious cases and crises. "Every man and woman that knows Christ and his doctrine has the keys and the power to bind and loose," Tyndale explained. "Every man and woman [is] Peter."[21] Thomas More, thinking of the laity, observed that such "Peters" were unprepared. Tyndale might have agreed yet expected God to prepare the faithful to interpret and practice their faith and, if necessary, to oppose the practice of prelates. Those common people would do well, read and think well, Tyndale was assured, because God willed it. The translator's task was to give them Bibles they could read, vernacular texts, for when "the plaine text" without scholars' glosses was before faithful commoners, "there hast thou . . . great learning, great fruit, and great edifying."[22]

Tyndale's faith in the laity's faith and in God's gift of intelligence to the faithful was the closest he came to answering critics who said his translations of the New Testament put pearls before swine. His "answer" neither consoled More nor appeased the bishops, but it had not been composed to console or appease them. Tyndale's fideism, biblicism, and perhaps laicism as well appear to have been presented, as Stephen Greenblatt now suggests, "to

20. William Stafford, "Tyndale's Voice to the Laity," in *Word, Church, and State: Tyndale Quincentenary Essays*, ed. John Day, Eric Lund, and Anne M. O'Donnell (Washington, D.C.: Catholic University of America Press, 1998), 106; and Thomas More, *Confutation of Tyndale's Answer*, vol. 2, ed. Louis A. Schuster et al. (New Haven, Conn.: Yale University Press, 1973), 706–10.

21. Tyndale, *Expositions*, 234, 284.

22. Tyndale, *Doctrinal Treatises*, 88–89, 306.

uphold individuals in daring acts of dissent."[23] Much the same, of course, could be said about Martin Luther. Tyndale was drawn to his doctrine—and to Wittenberg—and he may well have gotten wind there of Luther's reply in 1523 to the delegates from Leisnig, a small village near Leipzig. The reply was Luther's least obscure statement of the conceit known to students of the Reformation as "the priesthood of all believers." He argued there that laymen required no papal, episcopal, royal, or regional commission to teach, preach, or govern their parishes; it was enough that commoners be Christians of good faith (*keyns anders beruffs*).[24]

Lollards might have read Luther's reply as a manifesto for lay empowerment and agreed that there were no special callings in Christ's time. Had Tyndale known of it, he likely would have noticed how closely its counsel conformed to his own thoughts on lay participation in parish administration. But his king took an early and active dislike to Luther, who returned the disfavor in the early 1520s. Even after Henry VIII broke with Rome, the two men remained unreconciled, and similarities between Lutheran and lollard sentiment hardly endeared Luther or Leisnig to later Henrician reformers, whose caution seemed symptomatic of a growing religious conservatism, both at court and in the country from 1539.[25]

But Luther grew cautious too. For all his early enthusiasm for "Christian liberty" and lay emancipation from "captivity" to the Roman church, he soon recoiled from what could arguably have been identified as the socially disruptive consequences of such freedom. By 1525, peasants unhappy with economic and political inequalities unrelated to the religious reform drew radically egalitarian implications from the reformers' rhetoric. That

---

23. Stephen Greenblatt, *Renaissance Self-fashioning: From More to Shakespeare* (Chicago: University of Chicago Press, 1980), 93–95. Also see Donald Dean Smeeton, *Lollard Themes in the Reformation Theology of William Tyndale* (Kirksville, Mo.: Sixteenth-Century Journal Studies and Texts, 1986), 167–72; Bruce Boehrer, "Tyndale's *Practyse of Prelates*: Reformation Doctrine and Royal Supremacy," *Renaissance and Reformation* 10 (1986): 262–63; and Rudolph P. Almasy, "Contesting Voices in Tyndale's *Practice of Prelates*," in *William Tyndale and the Law*, ed. John A. R. Dick and Anne Richardson (Kirksville, Mo.: Sixteenth-Century Studies and Texts, 1994), 1–10.

24. Luther's reply is printed in *WA*, 9:412. Also see Harald Goertz, *Allgemeines Priestertum und ordiniertes Amt bei Luther* (Marburg: Elwert, 1997), 272–73.

25. For general conservatism, see Christopher Marsh, *Popular Religion in Sixteenth-Century England: Holding Their Peace* (New York: St. Martin's, 1998), esp. 198–99; and Christopher Haigh, *English Reformations: Religion, Politics, and Society under the Tudors* (Oxford: Clarendon, 1993), 152–61.

was how it must have looked to Luther who never repeated his Leisnig advice. On the continent, a second generation of reformers tried to balance lay emancipation with the need for order, solidarity, and patronage. Jean Calvin of Picardy and then Geneva, had more influence than Luther in England under Henry's son and successor, King Edward VI.

Complaints, Commoners, and "Strangers" in the Reign of King Edward VI

From 1541, Jean Calvin of Geneva planned for what political historian Harro Hopfl now calls "a controlled and regulated kind of popular participation" in the administration of that city's churches.[26] And one detects a drift toward lay empowerment in Calvin's apology for reformed faith and practice, his *Institutes of the Christian Religion*, readily available in England from the 1540s and in English from the 1580s. Perhaps some readers looked for—and any of them could have found—the widely respected reformer's explicit prohibition against making clerical appointments without consulting parishioners.[27]

Calvin imagined that parishioners' participation was common in Christian antiquity. He speculated that the apostles Paul and Barnabas "created" officials in each congregation only after the "entire crowd declared its candidate by a show of hands." Calvin acknowledged that laymen later were reduced to onlookers, adding that the restoration of their counsel and consent was a worthy objective for the church's reformed leadership. For then laymen might not simply sift and select candidates for clerical office but serve alongside them as partners, that is, as presbyters or elders and thus as magistrates in "a spiritual polity."[28]

Richard Hooker was skeptical. Two generations after the *Institutes* first appeared, he guessed that Calvin either feigned interest in presbyterial and congregational empowerment or simply lost it, "ripely consider[ing] how gross a thing it were for one of his quality [and for] wise and grave men, to

---

26. Harro Hopfl, *The Christian Polity of John Calvin* (Cambridge: Cambridge University Press, 1982), 159.

27. *Institutes*, 4.4.2.

28. *Institutes*, 4.3.15 (citing Acts 14:32), 4.11.1. Also consult Hopfl, *Christian Polity*, 110–12; and Kaufman, *Redeeming Politics* (Princeton, N.J.: Princeton University Press, 1990), 116–25.

live with such a multitude and be tenants at will under them." Hooker specu-lated, in other words, that Calvin was more autocrat than democrat. He exploited lay respect for his leadership and learning and perpetuated "the secret dependency and awe" that made Genevan citizens his subjects.[29] Was Hooker right? Did Calvin scheme to keep the laity in tow? If that latter question had been asked from 1547 to 1553, under Edward VI, the answer would likely have been "no." Edwardian reformers, thinking of the laity, were less fearful than Hooker would be of becoming "tenants . . . under" lordly lay upstarts. Besides, the Genevan consistory was still struggling at the time for its independence from the city's councils. And, more to the point of this study, Calvin was greatly esteemed by distinguished, prolific refugees from the continent, Peter Martyr Vermigli and Martin Bucer, and by the reformer who invited them to England, Archbishop Thomas Cranmer of Canterbury.

Vermigli drew an inference from the Acts of the Apostles strikingly similar to one Calvin had drawn from the same passage: matters of "weight and importance" ought to be "referred unto the people." Vermigli did not suggest that parishioners should pastor themselves. There was no denying Christianity had been priestless in Christ's time; "godlie men through fear were driven from house to house . . . assembl[ing] togither in secret places by night. But if we would now in these daies worship God after that man-ner," he finished, "we should seeme very ridiculous." Unquestionably, the reformed pastor was indispensable in the sixteenth century, Vermigli con-ceded, therefore, the stipulation "referred unto the people" meant only that the parishioners ought to choose them.[30]

Martin Bucer agreed. Lay-led conventicles were fit for fugitives, but, for discipline and lasting reform, a settled ministry was preferable. Without shepherds, "the sheep of Christ" strayed. On that count, Bucer would have had no argument from Calvin or Vermigli, both of whom he once welcomed to Strasbourg. Calvin left in 1541; Peter Martyr came in 1542. They studied and occasionally preached while Bucer labored to complete the reform of his city's councils and churches and explained that the chief problem with reformed religion there was that its pastors were overextended. He proposed

---

29. *Laws*, "Preface," 2.5.

30. Peter Martyr Vermigli, *The common places of the most famous and renowned divine doctor Peter Martyr*, trans. Anthony Marten (London, 1583), 4.5.9.

that learned laymen be appointed in every parish to assist ministers and that other laymen be chosen to assist the lay assistants.[31] Some years later, after he fled the continent for England, Bucer revisited his organizational strategy, specifying that the lay auxiliaries need not be far advanced in learning to improve the quality of the ministry. Indeed, he had not been across the Channel long (and had only just dined with Cranmer and Vermigli) when he told friends at home about the sad state of reform abroad. England's churches were appallingly understaffed, he confided; the English were superstitious, overly fond of ritual, and deeply suspicious of what they thought to be Cranmer's "too extensive innovations." With so much at stake, then, Bucer might have been tempted to lower the bar and to recruit commoners willing, though unready, to serve as pastors' assistants. But we cannot be sure. He died in 1551, before his hosts had a chance to comment on his proposals, yet after he registered a last observation and complaint that the English church was "in a very feeble state."[32]

Perhaps Bucer's complaints about the "feeble state" of the reformed church and the unpreparedness of its laity reflected what Dairmaid MacCulloch now describes as his festering "sense of grievance." The celebrated Strasbourg reformer expected a degree of deference that the English were not yet ready to concede. Bucer anticipated that he would be consulted often, and his friends on the continent assumed so as well. When he wrote to correct them, his irritation showed. He told William Farel that he condoned neither the retention of Roman ceremonies in, nor the disreputable discipline of, the English churches. And Bucer was equally bad at concealing his anger and impatience from his hosts. Word reached Cranmer, to whom the counsel Bucer offered seemed more like criticism. So Jan Laski, the Polish Protestant who crossed from Emden to England in 1550, became the archbishop's "chief ally among the emigres."[33]

Laski was not blind to what bothered Bucer. The pace of English reform appeared slow to him as well. He commented that Catholic ritual and clerical

---

31. Martin Bucer, "Von der Kirchen Mengel und Fahl," in *Martin Bucers deutsche Schriften*, vol. 17, ed. Robert Stupperich (Gütersloh: Mohn, 1981), 184.

32. *OL*, 2:535–36, 543. Also see Bucer's *De regno Christi*, in *Martini Buceri opera latina*, vol. 15, ed. François Wendel (Paris: Bertelsmann, 1955), 59–62.

33. See Dairmaid MacCulloch, *Thomas Cranmer, A Life* (New Haven, Conn.: Yale University Press, 1996), 469–71; and, for Bucer's complaints to Farel, Constantin Hopf, *Martin Bucer and the English Reformation* (Oxford: Blackwell, 1975), 253–56.

dress were too fondly regarded. But Laski had received Cranmer's permission to implement the reformed religious arrangements he had known and developed abroad. King Edward's council was at first disobliging, when Laski and his friends, French and Dutch Protestants, asked for their own churches. Official reluctance was probably due to Lord Treasurer William Paulet's designs on the property that the refugees wanted. And it shocked no one when the bishop of London spoke at court against the freedom from his supervision that the resident aliens or "strangers," as they were called, looked likely to receive. But within weeks the obstacles were scaled, and Laski was named "superintendent" of the strangers' congregations. By royal charter, they were granted the freedom to use undisturbed (*libere et quiete*) their rites and discipline, "notwithstanding they do not conform to the practices of our realm."[34]

Laski's London parishioners elected lay elders and pastors. No dissatisfaction with that practice was recorded. Apparently, there had been none at Emden. The strangers' church was popular in a more traditional sense as well, for foreigners flocked to worship—"a happy condition" requiring its two pastors to look for help.[35] The first apostles were similarly stretched, Laski said, and they asked the laity for assistance. The request was proper; arrangements were easily made. When the church entered its middle ages, however, the bishops were justified in taking precautions, Laski allowed, because broad popular participation courted disorder. As the strangers' superintendent or "bishop," he himself took precautions and made provisions "to barre out the tumults and dissensions of the people" without prohibiting their choice of leadership. Each congregation still decided what was in its best interests—there was no bending that principle—yet Laski understood that agreement on those best interests or on the best candidates would not be easy to reach. Prayers and fasts might dispose persons to "put all private assertions asyde," but the safest procedure was to commission a conference of elders and pastors (a *coetus*) to receive parishioners' nominees and to elect the most gifted candidate in closed session. The "tumults" having been avoided, Laski risked public discussion once more, the week after *coetus*

---

34. Johannes Lindeboom, *Austin Friars: History of the Dutch Reformed Church in London, 1550–1950* (The Hague: Nijhoff, 1950), prints the charter, 198–203, and Andrew Pettegree, *Foreign Protestant Communities in Sixteenth-Century London* (Oxford: Oxford University Press, 1986), 39–40, discusses Paulet's and Ridley's opposition.

35. *OL*, 1:570–71.

deliberations. Then, parishioners had a final opportunity to supply information that might disqualify any candidate. Laski intended to assure that "non of the congregation . . . be hable justly to complayn" that the *coetus* had prohibited a full and fair review of the options.[36]

Occasionally the *coetus* opened deliberations to its public. The entire congregation joined pastors and lay assistants to hear the deacons present parish accounts, and everyone had a chance to participate in discussions regarding discipline. If historian Andrew Pettegree is correct, Jan Laski was unique among reformers in promoting such "democratic tendencies" but was told that the English considered his churches in London to be models of a perfectly reformed polity.[37] Some reformers likely envied the foreigners' freedom from episcopal interference. They might also have endorsed lay participation in what Bernard Cottret now calls the *moralisation* of reformed Christianity.[38] But what would they have made of the fact that the adult male members of the strangers' congregations could nominate their peers to be elders or pastors and could argue publicly for or against their nominees? A single, persuasive parishioner could effectively veto any candidate. Were the English authorities favorably impressed or fearful? Perhaps all that can be asserted is that Laski, thinking of the laity, expected that under King Edward VI reformed parishes in England would come to look like his strangers' "righte godlie reformed church."[39]

If so, Laski expected too much. His strangers' autonomy may well have misled him as well as others, including historians of the Edwardian Reformation. For, as Basil Hall now says, the French and Dutch reformed congregations under Laski's leadership were "Trojan horse[s] which Cranmer unwittingly had drawn into London." Neither the archbishop nor his suffragans, Hall suspects, were interested in "the positive participation of the

---

36. Jan Laski, *Forma ac ratio, Joannis a Lasco opera*, vol. 2, ed. A. Kuyper (Amsterdam: Leeuwarden, 1866), 66: "ut in coetu demum ministrorum ac seniorum proximo diligens ac gravis accusationum istius modi examinatio fiat." Quotes in the text are taken from the undated sixteenth-century English translation, Bodl., Barlow MS. 19, 25v–28r.

37. Pettegree, *Communities*, 73. Also consult Dirk W. Rodgers, *John a Lasco in England* (New York: Lang, 1994), 29–33; Ole Peter Grell, *Calvinist Exiles in Tudor and Stuart England* (Aldershot: Ashgate, 1996) 147–48; and Susan Brigden, *London and the Reformation* (Oxford: Clarendon, 1989), 464–65.

38. Bernard Cottret, *Terre d'exil: L'Angleterre et ses réfugiés, français et wallons* (Paris: Aubier, 1985), 278.

39. Laski, *Forma*, 10–11.

laity." They were wary of the strangers' innovations.[40] And many strangers were wary as well, presuming that bishops, as hierocrats, would not long tolerate democratic tendencies in their dioceses. John Hooper was peculiar, said the strangers who had been pleasantly surprised when he continued to agitate for further reform of the church after he was named bishop of Gloucester: for "when dainty meat is put unto the mouths [of bishops] it is apt to make them dumb and inactive."[41] Laski and the refugees, however, had high hopes for Hooper and wrote kindly of Archbishop Cranmer as well. He had, after all, supported a statute permitting laymen to exercise ecclesiastical jurisdiction, and he agreed with Laski, Bucer, and Vermigli that administrative policy was formulated with "the consent of the Christian multitude" when Christianity was new. Yet Cranmer had reservations about broadly participatory parishes. He believed Catholic prelates had projected their low opinion of laymen for so long that commoners of the 1540s were convinced of their own inadequacy. Told they were thoughtless, they gave no thought and effort to self-government; therefore, they were not yet ready for lay collaboration in local control and would have to be led until they could be reeducated.[42]

King Edward's councillors had other plans for the church's resources. They seized the bishops' best properties for themselves. Immediately on hearing that the dioceses of Worcester and Gloucester would be combined, the opportunists at court gobbled up two-thirds of what Worcester owned.[43] Lay reeducation would have to depend, then, on local initiative and thus on a settled and learned ministry, though that arrangement was often unaffordable, especially when clerical and lay patrons kept more of their parishes' revenues and spent less on curates' salaries. The predicament registered with Cranmer who dispatched itinerant preachers, but the regime

---

40. Basil Hall, *Humanists and Protestants, 1500–1900* (Edinburgh: Clark, 1990), 198; and Pettegree, *Communities*, 306, for high expectations.

41. *OL*, 2:582. Critics later equated episcopal appointment with the onset of "a drowsye sleape"; see the *Certayne griefes justly conceaved of Bishop Juell*, Bodl., Selden Supra MS. 44, 50r.

42. *Miscellaneous Writings and Letters of Thomas Cranmer*, vol. 1, ed. John Edmund Cox (Cambridge: Cambridge University Press, 1846), 116. Also see Paul Ayris, "God's Vicegerent and Christ's Vicar: The Relationship between the Crown and the Archbishop of Canterbury, 1533–1553," in *Thomas Cranmer: Churchman and Scholar*, ed. Paul Ayris and David Selwyn (Woodbridge, N.Y.: Boydell, 1993), 138–39.

43. Haigh, *Reformations*, 178.

feared that "much contention and disorder might rise and ensue." Hence, the itinerants were taken off the circuit, and the good seeds planted by them were soon "overgrown [with] weads."[44]

Did Cranmer decline to adopt Laski's discipline to prevent "weads" or reactionaries from assuming control of the parishes? Did he want to avoid seeming too radical? At the time, he hoped to summon Lutheran and Swiss reformers to a conference that might rival the Catholics' council at Trent. It was inexpedient for him to advocate levels of lay participation unknown among continental colleagues. They would never agree to come.[45]

On final analysis, though, prospective conferees abroad were likely less on Cranmer's mind than Protestants in England, who did not yet seem capable of resisting some of his very own suffragans and their efforts to draw commoners back to Catholicism. Gardiner of Winchester and Bonner of London, Henrician conservatives, were still influential. In Cranmer's judgment, Gardiner's views on the mass posed a clear and present danger to reformed discipline and doctrine. Truly reformed Christians, Cranmer said, took Christ's cross as their fresh start. They trusted that Christ's sacrifice atoned for their sins, and that trust or faith clothed them in Christ's righteousness. According to Cranmer, Gardiner was too Roman to be truly reformed and wanted to introduce clerical go-betweens who then "divide Christ [from] his people." The masses that Gardiner defended reenacted Christ's sacrifice, as if some clerical "continuance" (or follow-up) were necessary for the cross to have any effect. The commoner who subscribed to such nonsense and who came to depend on clerical intervention rather than faith was more apt to cede authority irresponsibly than to exercise it wisely.[46]

"The old and first church was clearly against" Gardiner, Cranmer insisted; all the more important, then, to repossess it.[47] To that end, the

---

44. BL., Additional MS. 48066, 3r. *TRP*, 1:432–33, declares a moratorium on sermons to avoid the "contention and disorder."

45. MacCulloch, *Cranmer*, 393–94, 448.

46. *The Writings and Disputations of Thomas Cranmer*, ed. John Edmund Cox (Cambridge: Cambridge University Press, 1844), 91–93, 361. For emphasis on personal faith and reception rather than on "priestcraft" or consecration in Cranmer's eucharistic theology, see the *Defence of the true and catholic doctrine of the sacrament*, in *The Work of Thomas Cranmer*, ed. Gervase Duffield (Philadelphia: Fortress, 1965), 80, 150–53; Peter Newman Brooks, *Thomas Cranmer's Doctrine of the Eucharist: An Essay in Historical Development*, 2nd ed. (London: Macmillan, 1992), 92–93; and Christopher Cocksworth, *Eucharistic Thought in the Church of England* (Cambridge: Cambridge University Press, 1993), 28–30.

47. Cranmer, *Writings and Disputations*, 158.

archbishop supported stripping English churches of chantries and parish fraternities. In "the old and first church" there had had been none of that. The apostles had not asked the commoners of Christian antiquity to do penance or fear purgatory or pray to saints. To Cranmer, reform meant scaling back to what prevailed at the start. He was under no illusion that it would be easy. Perhaps he despaired of ever realizing his objectives, for by 1552, rather late in what would be a short reign, he seems to have concluded that English laymen were insufficiently emancipated from superstition to participate meaningfully in parish elections. Regulations he issued that year had nothing to say about the parishioner's right to interrogate candidates for clerical office. Laski was on the commission in some measure responsible for the composition of Cranmer's rules, yet, on lay patronage, he must have been silent—or uninfluential. Caution was the order of the day.[48]

What we know of Cranmer's caution sets him apart from King Edward's first Lord Protector, Edward Seymour, Earl of Hertford and later Duke of Somerset, who appeared to peers to support the commoners' protests against enclosures, landlords, and the like. Diplomat William Paget advised Seymour that he tended to annoy colleagues on the Privy Council: when the people cry "liberty," Paget scolded, "your grace would have too much gentleness," and such gentleness aroused the suspicion of many who "mislike your proceedings" and imagine "you have some greater enterprise in your head that lean so much to the multitude."[49] That leaning made Seymour seem a traitor to the gentry, especially when he denounced enclosures and led the commoners to expect that the hedges would be down in no time. While Archbishop Cranmer, thinking of the laity, looked rather timid, the Lord Protector appeared to play what is now called a "politics of popularity," shoring up his precarious position in King Edward's council by demonstrating his "willingness to accept the commons as contributors in the formation of

---

48. Yet Cranmer's *Reformatio legum* countenanced lay participation in discipline, *Reformation of the Ecclesiastical Laws of England, 1552*, ed. James Spalding (Kirksville, Mo.: Sixteenth-Century Journal Studies and Texts, 1992), 43, 107, 136. For Cranmer's strikes against the church's subparochial, intercessory institutions, see Alan Kreider, *English Chantries: The Road to Dissolution* (Cambridge, Mass.: Harvard University Press, 1979), 186–208; Peter Cunich, "The Dissolution of Chantries," in *Reformation in the English Towns, 1500–1640*, ed. John Craig and Patrick Collinson (New York: St. Martin's, 1998), 157–74; and Eamon Duffy, *Stripping of the Altars: Traditional Religion in England, c. 1400–1570* (New Haven, Conn.: Yale University Press, 1992), 141–54, 368–76.

49. Strype(1), 2.2, 431–33.

policy." And it might have worked, had Seymour not also had to depend on the gentry, as justices, to enforce the very reforms from which they had the most to lose.[50]

Gentry justices were exceedingly slow to comply. Commoners turned levelers and preemptively flattened the hedges. Seymour then appealed to local authorities to suppress disorders their tardiness provoked. Their savagery, though, prompted a violent reaction, riot and greater ruin. The complaints that commoners posted included religious concerns. In Devon and Cornwall they demanded authorities restore "the ancient religion" or, at the very least, suspend reform of the Henrician church until young Edward VI came of age. Farther north, Robert Parkyn reported "many mo schyres rasside upp for maintennance [of] Christ['s] churche," signaling Catholic sympathy there also. No wonder, then, Cranmer was cautious, wary of lay initiative. Yet the commoners' demands in East Anglia tell a very different tale. Rebels there required the removal of unpreaching prelates and urged that parishioners have some say in appointing the replacements.[51]

What we hear from the laity permits us to posit neither a kingdom-wide shift back to Rome nor a fast forward with reform. One conclusion, though, was incontestable by July 1549; Seymour would have to go. John Dudley, Earl of Warwick and later Duke of Northumberland, became Lord Protector. He courted conservatives who imagined Seymour's collusion with commoners had undermined good government. Bishop Gardiner was optimistic. He aimed high and hoped to topple his old foe, Cranmer. Dudley, however,

---

50. Ethan Shagan, "Protector Somerset and the 1549 Rebellions: New Sources and New Perspectives," *EHR* 94 (1999): 46–49; Shagan, *Popular Politics and the English Reformation* (Cambridge: Cambridge University Press, 2003), 275–77.

51. For the "popular Protestantism" of East Anglian agitators, consult Diarmaid MacCulloch, *Tudor Church Militant* (London: Lane, 1999), 122. For the Lord Protector's "mixed signals," see Julian Cornwall's summation, *Revolt of the Peasantry* (London: Routledge and Kegan Paul, 1977), 146. ("Somerset himself contributed the final touch by directing magnates and justices of the peace to repress the disorders . . . and thus achieved nothing, except to provide them with additional opportunities for manifesting their malevolence.") Robert Parkyn, curate of Adwick, near Doncaster, is quoted on the "stirs" of 1549 in A. G. Dickens, *Reformation Studies* (London: Hambledon, 1982), 299. His sentiment is quite compatible with those expressed in Devon and Cornwall where, as Eamon Duffy now claims, religious reforms "seriously undermined [the] communal life" of the West Country. See Duffy's *Voices of Morebath: Reformation and Rebellion in an English Village* (New Haven, Conn.: Yale University Press, 2001), 122–23. It has not gone unnoticed, though, that religious rhetoric was often used to justify socioeconomic protest; consult Robert Whiting, *Local Responses to the English Reformation* (New York: St. Martin's, 1998), 138–41.

was disinclined to roll back reform, and Cranmer sensed it. He and his friends hastened to assure their colleagues on the continent that the new protector's overtures to Gardiner and his partisans on Edward's council were purely political.[52] Yet Dudley proved disappointing to church officials of all stripes. He permitted and perhaps encouraged his allies to steal from the church, so provoking the court preachers that they berated him with some frequency; thus was King Edward told, Dudley incensed by the telling, and Archbishop Cranmer saddled with the critics' candor and the Lord Protector's anger. It seems as if there was plenty of ill will to pass around. Cranmer no longer attended council. His rules for the reformed church were casualties of court intrigue. They failed to win government approval. Larceny, resentments, and riots, along with the disturbing sense that commoners' reeducation had stalled—arguably, all of the above accounts for the laity's low profile in the archbishop's abrogated plans for the reform of parish administration.[53]

It could have been otherwise. Odds that Cranmer and England would have followed Laski's lead might have improved had Edward lived a decade more or had there been fewer stirs and greater calm. For it has been said that the archbishop's books of common prayer (1549 and 1552), by their "studied ambiguity," put "the widest possible limits on [lay] participation." If so, that is, if Cranmer deliberately created conditions for "colloquy" at worship, English officials may have been closer to approving "extensive innovations"—conceivably including a broadly participatory parish regime—than anyone would then have guessed.[54] But calm was in short supply; strife punctuated Edward's short reign from start to finish, and he died before reaching the age of twenty, in 1553. Years later, John Olde and John Scory, in exile, brooding over their missed opportunities, criticized Cranmer for having pulled up short. Yet, while they and other expatriate reformers wondered what might have been, Edward's half-sister and successor, Mary I, was steering the realm back to Catholicism.[55]

---

52. *OL*, 1:353.

53. See MacCulloch, *Cranmer*, 532–34; and David Loades, *John Dudley, Duke of Northumberland, 1504–1553* (Oxford: Clarendon, 1996), 119–24.

54. See John King, *English Reformation Literature: The Tudor Origins of the Protestant Reformation* (Princeton, N.J.: Princeton University Press, 1982), 135–36, for "ambiguity" and "colloquy"; for "innovations," Marsh, *Popular Religion*, 206, quoting Cranmer.

55. See Andrew Pettegree, *Marian Protestantism: Six Studies* (Aldershot: Ashgate, 1996), 27, 43, for Olde and Scory.

Protestant Opposition and Exiles at the Time of Queen Mary

Plans to exclude Mary went rapidly wrong. Immediately after Edward died, she rallied more support in East Anglia than Dudley anticipated, made her way safely to London, then locked the Lord Protector in the Tower. Gardiner's release from prison signaled her aim to return the realm to Rome. The bishop of Winchester was restored to his see just in time to arrange for Dudley's scaffold conversion to Catholicism.

The new queen was quick to make restitution, re-endowing collegiate churches and offering generous annuities to induce councillors to do likewise. Yet there was opposition, notably among influential officials who had grown attached to estates that the two previous governments had confiscated from the church. The new owners must have been encouraged when word got out that "a general dispensation to all holders of church property" would be a precondition for any further fruitful discussion of reunion with Rome.[56] But Pope Julius III and his legate, Reginald Pole, insisted that "holders" return what they, or their forebears, procured as a result of Henrician and Edwardian "depradations." Pole, who was also the queen's principal adviser, soon saw that Rome would have to give ground. Mary had too few accomplices at court willing to turn back the church's property they possessed or to apply their resources to the refoundation of the kingdom's religious houses. And her larger projects were attracting much less local investment than she had expected. Many middlers were prepared to make the small sacrifices necessary to fund a return to Catholicism in their parishes. They paid to restore rood lofts and purchased new rood cloths, surplices, and precious vessels for consecrated oil. Some parishes, however, were slow to redecorate. The early modern religious climate of England, after all, changed so swiftly and so often that the queen's subjects may be excused their doubts whether present arrangements would be permanent. Mary had married King Philip II of Spain soon after her accession, but the couple was childless. Next in line to the throne, Elizabeth, Henry's daughter by Anne Boleyn, was known to favor reform. Mary and Philip contemplated finding her a husband on Spain's Mediterranean coast, yet nothing came of it, in part, because they were afraid she would run afoul of the Inquisition and embarrass them.[57] But

---

56. *CSP,* Spain (1554–58), 65.
57. *CSP,* Spain (1554–58), 92.

with Elizabeth on site, those who welcomed England's new turn to its old religion and those hoping for a reversal must have thought their present settlement temporary.

Pole worked to prove them wrong. Before sailing for England, he opposed lay intervention—royal, parliamentary, and local—in the affairs of the church. Tudor sovereigns had jumped ship, "St. Peter's ship," he explained, blaming Henry VIII's parliaments and Edward VI's advisers for having devised titles and statutes which confused monarchs with priests. If religion changed with every ruler and with a ruler's every whim, there could be no lasting peace. Layman did not belong at the head or helm of a church, Pole argued, and to put a woman there, he added, was unthinkable.[58]

Pole's clericalism led him to discourage the Jesuits' bids to assist with the recatholicization of the realm. He suspected their sermons would rile commoners, who would then bicker about what they only imperfectly comprehended. Solutions in Mary I's England did not depend on importing Jesuits or other preaching orders and on using the printing presses to advance lay "self-education." Pole told his agents to impress the laity with the church's sacraments and ceremonies—to have the parish clergy preside over a return to traditional worship—and praise and reward the "habits" of obedience.[59]

Concessions to proprietary interests made Pole's pills easier to swallow in some circles, though recatholicization was all but doomed after it became impossible for papal legate Pole and the new pope Paul VI to cooperate with each other. The pope started secret negotiations with the French, to the disadvantage of the Hapsburgs. In 1556, Mary's Hapsburg husband, Philip, ordered troops into papal territories. Of course, diplomatic affairs were unlikely to deteriorate indefinitely, but the two years remaining to Pole, his legatine commission rescinded, and to Queen Mary were spent in the shadow of the king's excommunication—their plans wrecked less by lay or Protestant intransigence than by quarrels among Catholic prelates and princes. Still, as Andrew Pettegree now observes, "Protestant dissidence and

---

58. *CSP*, Venice (1534–54), 447–48.
59. Jennifer Loach, "The Marian Establishment and the Printing Press," *EHR* 101 (1986): 139; Thomas McCoog, "Ignatius Loyola and Reginald Pole: A Reconsideration," *JEH* 47 (1996): 269–70.

survival in one form or another was and remained a leading preoccupation of the regime throughout [the] reign."[60]

"Protestant dissidence" around Mary took many forms, from mischief to mutiny and from occasional disrespect to impassioned anticlericalism. Bishop Bonner discovered most of the many forms in his diocese and tried to clear it of troublemakers. Essex was a hive; London, busier still, buzzing with protests against Pole. But Bonner's commissioners were busy as well. They accounted for nearly 70 percent of the significations for heresy sent to Mary's council and chancery. London, the realm's biggest city by far, was filled with youngsters who were born after 1534 and who had no prior or prolonged exposure to Roman Catholicism. Apprenticed yet generally unsupervised, they shared and occasionally expressed contempt for the Marian Catholic revival that was exactly the tinder incendiary reformers required. From the bishop's palace, it looked as if London might soon be burning, although Spanish diplomats, confident in their king's calming influence, saw a different city. They predicted people would conform "in a very obedient manner," after Pole and Rome "dispense[d] the holders of church property."[61] Bonner did not believe it. He sensed that all could not be well in London and Essex until he and his diocesan officials completed their purge (*extirpare, eradicare*), a task that summoned what one critic in exile called officialdom's "discreet severity." Bonner may have liked the term, for when faced with lay and local dissent, "the offyce of charitye," he said, was "to rebuke, punyshe, and correct."[62]

John Foxe despised Bonner's "charitye": "so cruel, so hasty, so inquisitive, so desperate and absurd [that] the like hath not proceeded from any bishop before."[63] Foxe stitched eyewitness accounts and hearsay into his story of the Marian Protestant resistance and scripted Bonner's purges to elicit a variety of readers' responses, from ridicule to revulsion. There was an element of farce in his tale of the bishop's bailiffs who surrounded a Thames-side home but entered a stride too late to catch their prey. Officials

60. Pettegree, *Marian Protestantism*, 155. Also see David Loades, *Mary Tudor, A Life* (Oxford: Oxford University Press, 1989), 122–23, 294–99.

61. *CSP*, Spain (1554–58), 84 and 116.

62. See the *Homilies set forth by the Right Reverend Father in God, Edmund Bonner, Bishop of London* (London, 1555), G1v–G2r; and, for John Scory's remark on "severity," Brigden, *London*, 574.

63. *AM*, 8:452–53.

were foiled and the dissidents were saved by a mariner who noticed that the river route of escape had been left unguarded. A story of Bonner's spies, sent to report on reformers' conversations, ended with their conversion to reformed religion. Authorities seldom got things right, but Bonner was the unrighteous villain Foxe most loved to hate. He was infuriated by what the reformed remnant in the diocese of London had to suffer, and he dramatized their defiance. His many pages on the Marian persecution feature chases, escapes, captures, depositions, and interrogations, although nothing seems quite as poignant as his depiction of the "godly people" who, at risk to themselves, embraced the last martyrs burned in Smithfield in 1558 on Bonner's orders.[64]

From 1563, Elizabethans were treated to similar spectacles in successive editions of Foxe's work. Lay and clerical protagonists passed before readers and into a history of protest which Foxe stretched from the time of the apostles to Elizabeth I's accession. The clerical heroes remained in the realm when Mary's bishops turned them out of their livings. They dodged authorities, led reformed worship, wrote from prison to encourage or console parishioners, and courageously took to the stake. They inspired select commoners to lead in their stead and follow them into danger and to death. The Elizabethan reader learned to despise Marian authorities—Bonner, Gardiner, and others—and to lionize the likes of John Alcock, Ralph Allerton, Richard Woodman, and Edmund Allin.

Layman Alcock slipped into the pulpit after his pastor was taken from their parish in Suffolk and incarcerated. Perhaps he was coached by itinerant preachers en route to or from Colchester, a Camelot of nonconformity barely ten miles south. According to Foxe, Alcock, the lay stand-in, carried on quite creditably and soon won local support. He openly and somewhat successfully, for a time, opposed the priest Bonner sent. Arrested and awaiting execution, Alcock refused to stop ranting against "idolatrous inventions" and the "lewd," "covetous" Catholics reputed to prefer them.[65]

Alcock attacked Catholicism as if he had been schooled with the best candidates for the reformed ministry. Foxe supplied him with a formidable intelligence that resourceful Tudor polemicists would have envied. Layman Allerton's competence was different; if we may trust his depositions and

---

64. *AM*, 8:558–59.

65. *AM*, 8:734–35; and *AM*(1563), 1663–66, for Alcock; for Colchester, *AM*, 8:384.

Foxe's report, Allerton stumbled into the ministry. He chanced on several parishioners from Great Bentley sitting idly, wasting time, so he stopped to read them a few chapters from the New Testament. But there might have been more to it, for Bishop Bonner pressured him to admit and abjure a spate of heretical opinions soon thereafter (1557). Allerton, that is, may have been harassed for consorting with "a company of good men and women" who were trying to interest commoners in biblical study, a company or cell or conventicle known to "fret" the priests in and around London. Others named were laymen. Foxe was impressed by their "diligence," but officials probably were justified in thinking of Allerton's underground, alternative, lay-led "church" as curious, yet dangerous competition.[66]

Alcock and Allerton may not have wanted to call authorities' attention to their evangelizing, but layman Richard Woodman seems to have been spoiling for a public confrontation. He interrupted sermons in Sussex to object to the "detestable doctrine [Marian priests] spit and spew out." He relished chances to chop logic with the best the church could put against him. He argued with them often about the meaning of scriptural passages and about the validity of the sacraments, and when his opponents tried to apply the word "sedition" to his interruptions and arguments, he dug in and claimed he was no more seditious than the apostles had been. When he found himself caught in a contradiction, he took cover behind the accusations that had already been leveled against him: "you said even now, I had no knowledge nor learning."[67]

Edmund Allin's anticlerical eruptions appear more seismic than Allerton's, Alcock's, and Woodman's; his manifesto for lay empowerment was more menacing. Allin's first failing was common enough; at the times appointed for worship, he stayed away from church. His absences angered his parish priest in Kent who, at one service, while elevating the host— "lifting up his Romish God"—surprised parishioners by summoning the truant miller. Subsequently Allin was accused of presiding over his own worship services, preaching and reading to commoners, and insisting that he could do better than the local priests and quite well without them. We learn from Foxe's story that an indomitable Allin cited biblical precedents for lay leadership, referring to Jesus who lectured rabbis on interpretation

---

66. *AM*, 8:405–9; *AM*(1563), 1621–26.
67. *AM*, 8:349–69; *AM*(1563), 1578–87.

and to Moses who recruited laymen to teach religion to the Hebrews. The examining justice, though, was astounded that Allin presumed "to feed God's sheep" when such a sacred obligation had been explicitly entrusted to priests in Christian antiquity and thereafter, in every church, in all Christendom. "Why didst thou teach the people, being no priest," he asked; Allin had an answer:

> Because . . . we are all kings to rule our affections, priests to preach out the virtues and word of God, as Peter writeth, and lively stones to give light to others. For as out of flint stones cometh forth that which is able to set all the world on fire, so out of Christians should spring beams of the gospel, which should inflame all the world. If we must give a reckoning of our faith to every man, and now to you, demanding it, then must we study the scriptures, and practise them. What availeth a man to have meat, and will eat none, and apparel, and will wear none, or to have an occupation, and to teach none, or to be a lawyer, and utter none? Shall every artificer be suffered, yea commanded, to practise his faculty and science, and a Christian forbidden to exercise his?[68]

Had they known of it, Gardiner, Bonner, and Reginald Pole would have thought Allin's answer a nightmarish application of the "general priesthood," that is, of Luther's doctrine of the priesthood of all believers. "To give light to others," indeed! Every benighted Christian's "reckoning" ("we are all priests to preach the virtues and word of Christ") was bound to spread not light, but darkness. Foxe might have agreed early in his career, for he had been a convinced clericalist prior to Mary's accession and had argued that lay initiative, as Allin would later advocate it, was inappropriate. To supply pulpits when incumbents were arrested was one thing; to claim the pulpit as a right and duty was quite another. Foxe was less sure than Laski had been that Christians at midcentury were sufficiently reformed to manage their churches, but he came to admire the courage of Woodman, Alcock, Allerton, and Allin. Persecution changed the martyrologist's mind and made him more of a populist.[69]

---

68. *AM*, 8:321–22.

69. For an analysis of Foxe's *De censura* (1551), specifically its remarks on lay unpreparedness and clerical independence, see Catharine Davis and Jane Face, "A Reformation

But not much of a populist. If Brett Usher is correct, Foxe "camouflaged" the radical implications of the London underground experiments with lay participation in church management, wanting to assure his Elizabethan readers that the Edwardian clericalist consensus on the government of their churches lasted into and through the 1550s. Rather surprisingly, then, Foxe, the chronicler of Alcock's, Allerton's, Woodman's, and Allin's defiance, would have had the Elizabethans believe that Marian Protestants at home and abroad preferred clerical leadership to lay initiative. Perhaps so, though Usher's evidence of a Marian Protestant conventicle that selected and ordained its ministers suggests otherwise. But it is hard to tell what Foxe knew, when he knew it, and whether he "camouflaged" it. And we have no way to determine the level of participatory practices in the London underground assemblies which were impermanent, and what Joseph Martin now calls "incipient" congregations. Experiments in adapting structures to stressful circumstances required space and time to harden into organizational strategies. Bishop Bonner's surveillance afforded the dissidents no space or security; Mary I's short reign left them too little time.[70]

Odds are that organizational innovation was less important to lay participants than fellowship and mutual encouragement in underground churches. For example, twenty or so young merchants, French and Dutch as well as English, met in a backroom of Alice Warner's Stepney tavern to read the Bible to each other, to get news of the Protestant cause on the continent, and to take up a collection for less fortunate dissidents. Warner told Bonner's agents her tenants were leaderless; they referred to each other as brother. She had no clue, she said, which one should be told and trusted to tell the others once she had resolved to deprive the fraternity of her hospitality.[71] Others were more hospitable, but authorities, on the whole, were efficient locating and intimidating persons who sheltered reformed conventicles. Nearly everyone detected for nonconformity during Bonner's first visitation

---

Dilemma: John Foxe and the Problem of Discipline," *JEH* 39 (1988): 45–46, 52–53. Compare Foxe's shift to "the right" with Luther's increasingly conservative and clericalist understanding of "a general priesthood," Goertz, *Priestertum*, 225–32, 290–97.

70. See Brett Usher, "In a Time of Persecution: New Light on the Secret Protestant Congregation in Marian London," in *John Foxe and the English Reformation*, ed. David Loades (Aldershot: Scolar Press, 1997), 233–51; and Joseph W. Martin, *Religious Radicals in Tudor England* (London: Hambledon, 1989), 135–40.

71. *AM*, 8:460.

of his diocese (1554) capitulated and conformed. They undoubtedly mourned the passing of their friends burned for the faith, surreptitiously supplied material comforts—food and linen—to those in prison, and occasionally sent money to fugitives who had left to avoid detection, capitulation, conformity, or death.[72]

Fugitives abroad appealed for help. Many could hardly support their families; who would support their ministry? How could they undergo ordeals of uncertain duration in cities where they had a hard time making themselves understood—Basel, Emden, Strasbourg, Geneva, Frankfurt, and Wesel? Magistrates there were accommodating; they offered "quiet habitation," and all who came, came to admire the discipline of their hosts' reformed churches. But the refugees were struck that no reformer set an acceptable pattern for all others; the local consistories here and there independently struggled to define roles for themselves, their pastors, and their congregations.[73]

The exiles in Geneva looked to Laski rather than to Calvin when they drafted procedures for disciplining colleagues or for electing pastors. Refugees in Wesel did so as well.[74] In Emden, layman John Dowley opposed arrangements that appeared to him to limit congregational participation and restrict lay initiative. At first he only criticized the pastor and several elders of the church for being slow to respond when a plague struck the city in 1558. In their place he and a few friends visited and prayed with the sick. He was told such interference was prohibited "by God's word and common sense." He asked to have the issue raised before the congregation. Instead, the English elders in Emden raised the stakes. They accused Dowley of secession. He turned to the Dutch consistory, asking that his accusers be instructed to delegate authority "to judge or determine" to English parishioners in a general meeting or to a specially appointed commission.[75]

His appeal was not unprecedented. English exiles in Frankfurt asked their congregation to empanel "fit and competent" lay arbiters whenever pastors and elders were "adversarie parts." Dowley's targets-turned-accusers, "adversarie parts" from the start, refused to relinquish authority and submit

72. Pettegree, *Marian Protestantism*, 100–102, 116–17; Brigden, *London*, 624–28; and Marsh, *Popular Religion*, 187–88.

73. Christina Garrett, *The Marian Exiles: A Study in the Origins of Elizabethan Protestantism* (Cambridge: Cambridge University Press, 1938), documents who went where.

74. LPL, MS. 2523, 4r.

75. Dowley's complaint is printed in Pettegree, *Marian Protestantism*, 172–82.

his complaint to parishioners or to a Dutch jury. Dowley seems to have stunned them with his contention that laymen could call on fellow laymen to judge their judges—to evaluate the ministry and the accuracy of any minister's accusations. "I wished to commit my case wholeheartedly to the entire church," Dowley summed up; "my opponents did not." And his summation, alas, is as close as we come to closure. No resolution was reported. Still, even if an endgame in Emden might be ascertained, it could have no greater bearing on our thinking of the laity than the precedent Dowley might have cited, had he known of it.[76]

English exiles in Frankfurt were thrilled with arrangements made for them and wanted to share "the great benefit" with their countrymen elsewhere on the continent, to compose a still larger "gatheringe together off oure dispersed brethren."[77] They were bouyant during the first few months and looked to weather the Marian interim without terrible hardship. The two schisms that rocked their congregation could not then have been predicted, but they were remembered better than the bouyancy twenty years later when John Field and Thomas Wood wrote the story of the "troubles begonne at Franckford."[78]

The first and more widely known set of troubles concerned the liturgy and need not detain us. The second set started over money. Refugees succumbed to what might now appear to have been minor irritations. Living off largesse took a toll on trust and community morale. The fugitives found it difficult to agree how to allocate the little they had. John Ponet, one of two former bishops among them, endeavored to preserve peace. He implored English exiles to "feight [as] a throupe together," to survive and serve their common cause, "the learned with their pen, the riche with their substance, the poor . . . dispersinge thinges that may edify." Yet the fugitives, impoverished by flight, were not content peddling pamphlets ("dispersinge"). They mistrusted wealthy countrymen, "the rich [still] with their substance," no matter how philanthropic they were.[79]

---

76. Pettegree, *Marian Protestantism*, 179, and *Troubles*, lxxi–lxxii, for the Frankfurt precedent.

77. *Troubles*, xxi. Also see CCCC MS. 435, B4v, C3v, for Henry Knowles' subsequent remarks on Frankfurt's kindnesses, "beyond compare."

78. For Field and Wood, in this connection, consult Patrick Collinson, "The Authorship of *A Brieff Discours off the Troubles Begonne at Franckford*," *JEH* 9 (1958): 188–208.

79. E. J. Baskerville, "John Ponet in Exile: A Ponet Letter to John Bale," *JEH* 37 (1986): 442–47, prints Ponet's encouragement.

For a time Richard Chambers was the refugees' chief purser and almoner. He gave liberally of his savings as well as of the donations he received from the exiles' friends still in England. Yet he was resented for having nearly complete control over the distribution of funds. His companions in Frankfurt asked for "a deaconshipp appointed more uprightly and according to the rule described in the Acts of the Apostles." Robert Horne, their pastor, believing Chambers capable and compassionate, had no plans to oblige, so his parishioners appointed commissioners, whose charges were to establish the desired "deaconshipp" and revise the church's discipline accordingly. Parishioners then summoned pastor and purser to discuss the changes. Frankfurt magistrates urged reconciliation to no avail. Horne left the congregation and city with Chambers, who claimed later that he had no objections to lay initiative (he was a layman, after all) and to a more broadly based diaconate. "Where the discipline of Christe is used in juste causes, it is to be regarded," Chambers conceded, going on, though, to trump his "regard" with a crucial provision or qualification, "but your unorderly absuinge off it against me . . . I esteem not."[80]

Chambers' critics were in a hurry. The congregation's disputes over discipline and over the distribution of funds in Frankfurt could not last long without affecting the supply from England. The exiles understood that "it woulde fall owte to the great hurt off the poore yff godly men being offended with oure dissentions . . . withdraw nowe their liberalitie."[81] Refugees, therefore, hastily patched together a "discipline of Christe," which called for the annual election of elders and deacons. Incumbents were supposed to resign two weeks before a mid-March census and vote. Pastors would not have to stand for reelection each year yet were to be examined annually by as many as eight men chosen by parishioners to interrogate, correct, and, when necessary, remove them. Once elected and corrected, pastors and elders disciplined the other members of their congregation. The elders possessed "the authoritie of the churche" to redress all grievances and to punish what was "not publickely knowen." The entire congregation became involved again only when offenders exhibited contempt for elected officials. The insolent were ordered to appear before a general assembly to repent their contempt along with their original trespass.[82]

---

80. *Troubles,* lxxxii–lxxxiv, clxxxiv.
81. *Troubles,* xcv–xcvi.
82. *Troubles,* xcv–xcix, cxxviii–cxxx, and clxxvii.

Should pastors and elders fail for any reason to call parishioners together, the congregation, according to its new "discipline of Christe," must summon itself to discuss and vote on matters of importance. Decisions of the majority were binding on all and were subject to no review. To Christians who preferred degree to democracy, the discipline in Frankfurt must have seemed unpleasantly prole or grimly portentous, because if those arrangements were adopted elsewhere, neither pastors nor elders nor synods of the same could henceforth dictate *de jure* to clamorous congregations of reformed refugees.[83]

But the refugees headed home shortly after Queen Mary and Cardinal Pole died within hours of each other late in 1558. It might have seemed providential afterward, but the deaths caught Edmund Grindal by surprise. He had been anticipating an imminent return during the previous four years, and had only just started learning German, resigning himself, that is, to a longer stay. Anthony Gilby and John Knox, leaving Geneva for England, hoped all colleagues would drop their disagreements on the continent; no smoldering grudges should return with them. Their new queen would certainly appreciate a united front, a reformed consensus, and she would thus more readily request their counsel and reward their courage.[84] And she did, although Gilby and Knox were not principal beneficiaries. Horne was named bishop of Winchester. Grindal advanced consecutively to the sees of London, York, and Canterbury. And John Jewel was made bishop of Salisbury by 1561. Gilby wanted no part of diocesan administration. He settled as a pastor in Leicestershire, dubbed "bishop" by those who remembered his conspicuous condescension to comrades-in-exile, Horne, Jewel, Grindal, Sandys, Curteys, Aylmer, Pilkington, and Parkhurst. For they eventually accepted the hierocratic elements of England's reformed church, reassimilated, and replaced the "mitred bishops" of *"Mariana tempora."*[85]

Did they remember the experiments with lay participation? In 1564 Grindal recalled the debt he and fellow fugitives owed their continental colleagues. He prodded repatriated, well-positioned reformers to commemorate

83. For the "overt radicalism" of the refugees' politics, see Jane E. A. Dawson, "Trumpeting Resistance: Christopher Goodman and John Knox," in *John Knox and the British Reformation*, ed. Roger Mason (Aldershot: Ashgate, 1998), 137–46; and Knappen's comments in *Tudor Puritanism*, 156–58.

84. *Troubles*, clxxxviii.

85. See John Charldon's *A sermon preached at Exeter* (London, 1595), D8v–E1r, for criticisms of the "mitred" replacements.

the "liberalitie" they had experienced abroad so that it be "nott altogether buried in oblivion."[86] But oblivion was the safest place for memories of con-gregational initiatives and parish regimes made possible by recent persecu-tion and displacement. Polities developed "under the cross," in exile, must have seemed wildly improbable once reformers were back in the realm. Into the 1560s, reassimilation was the order of the day, more timely and prudent than a radical restructuring of the established churches.

---

86. BL, Lansdowne MS. 7, 133r.

THREE

Into the 1560s

Elizabeth I's "Alteracion"

✠

Queen Elizabeth I first reigned over a Catholic kingdom. The prompt and continuing obedience of her subjects was prerequisite, if she and her councillors were to preside over a re-reformation. "Papist" clergy had to leave. They were predators; the realm's commoners had been their prey. Marian exiles were to be welcomed back, although the new government, thinking of the laity, suspected that the laity might be led astray by outspoken reformers as well as by incorrigible Catholics.

But the laity likely had more confidence in itself, in its ability to resist any side's seducing. Commoners had experienced competent lay leadership in their parishes for generations, and they knew their lay colleagues were competent. Obviously, discontinuities were to be expected. The times would test leadership at every level. The regime's initiatives to remove England's "many papists" from their cures and to rid the realm of "cloked papistrie" resulted in vacancies. Diocesan officials appointed lay lectors to assist when there were too few pastors to fill the pulpits. Every parish's churchwardens, however, were the most striking examples of what lay authority and local control might mean. Wardens must have been as disoriented as other onlookers by recent changes in regime and religion, yet they continued to act as their parishes' chief financial officers. Their ledgers reveal little about them, save their trades. Nonetheless, we know that they were elected by congregations, collected and spent parish revenues, and usually disciplined offenders, "presenting" them to appropriate courts and occasionally referring issues for congregational deliberation. Wardens were slandered by some they disciplined and described by parishioners in arrears as little more than cashiers or as "base" and "low," yet one might reasonably infer from their trades they were "drawn from the broad middle section of English society."[1] Hence, they proved to most commoners, if not also to church and court authorities, that a commoner could be both manageable and managerial.

Lay wardens had long served England's churches, but their competence in practical affairs appeared to matter less to a reformer like John Jewel than their theological illiteracy. Catholicism left them to "drown in darkness," Jewel charged, claiming that reform might save them by making their worship comprehensible and their Bibles accessible. Advocates of greater lay say in parish affairs pressed Jewel and other exiles-turned-bishops for more than comprehension and education. Yet advocates and diocesan officials alike, thinking of the laity, were unsure how much authority "simple people" might be prepared to handle without driving the reformed English church into "troublesome dissensions."

"The Unsettled Settlement"

Beneficiaries of Queen Mary I's religious settlement were unlikely optimistic as 1558 drew to a close. Elizabeth came with December, and her government's proposals for religious reform and conformity looked to turn the clock back to the early years of Edward VI's reign. Of course no one could be sure exactly what shape the new queen's re-reformed church would ultimately take. And she was advised against major changes ("no inovacions";

---

1. John S. Craig, *Reformation, Politics, and Polemics: The Growth of Protestantism in East Anglian Market Towns, 1500–1610* (Aldershot: Ashgate, 2001), 43.

"no tumult"). Nonetheless, Mary's bishops presumably sensed their days in the shade were done. Beyond that, though, clarity was hard to come by.[2]

What the new administration did best was to keep onlookers off balance. Elizabeth, her privy council, its commissioners for ecclesiastical causes, many local justices, and numerous members of the first parliament tilted uncertainly toward reform. Commoners strained to see what was coming, looked for omens, consulted sorcerers. Beached whales, monster births, freakish weather, and fires foretold military catastrophes or political shifts— no boon to a new government. Queen and regime therefore tried to outlaw "enchantments" and "conjurations," although, as historian Alexandra Walsham concludes, "print invested orally transmitted wonder tales with a permanence and authority which enhanced their premonitory quality." Officials, thinking of the laity's susceptibilities, worried that seers and tellers were playing to the exotic imaginings of the realm's doomsayers and, worse still, that tales of destabilizing changes prompted what they predicted.[3]

Omens were manipulable. The same sign might move Christians either to repent their sins or to resent their sovereign. A fire in London that nearly destroyed St. Paul's Cathedral in 1561 was said to have signaled divine displeasure, but with what was God displeased? With the faith of ostensibly faithful (and reformed) Christians? With the queen, the court, and officially sanctioned religious reforms? Elizabeth altered her half-sister's religious arrangements, but the new settlement had not settled well with all her subjects; for years after her accession, the unhappiest of them were heard, as was commoner Richard Shaw in Wigan, to denounce the regime's tactics and the realm's "newe religion." Were dissatisfied laymen looking for "an alteracion" of their queen's "alteracion"?[4]

James Pilkington, not yet bishop of Durham, was having none of that. He saw through the smoke at St. Paul's and argued that only "evil-tongued" and ill-intentioned critics of the English Calvinists and their queen "impute

---

2. CCCC, MS. 543, 32v, for the advice. Hindsight, of course, supplies a much clearer view of Elizabeth's reformed religion: her acceptance of solafideism, preferences for "theological ambiguity" and "reverential ceremony," "horror of novelty," and aversion to being instructed from the pulpit. For all of this, see Susan Doran, "Elizabeth I's Religion: The Evidence of Her Letters," *JEH* 51 (2000): 699–720.

3. Strype(1), 1.1:87–88; Norman Jones, *The Birth of the Elizabethan Age: England in the 1560s* (Oxford: Blackwell, 1993), 42–47; and Alexandra Walsham, *Providence in Early Modern England* (Oxford: Oxford University Press, 1999), 220.

4. CRO, EDA 12/2/75r.

this token of God's deserved ire" to the reform. The fire was a "general warning," Pilkington acknowledged, but it did not counsel returning to Rome. Instead, it signaled that institutional change, however propitious, had not yet encouraged widespread personal regeneration. Pilkington blamed the blaze on Christians' imperfect repentance, remedies for which he identified as self-examination, candid confession, sensible behavior, and a whole-hearted observance of "the fine religion nowe set furth," the "newe religion" that Shaw and others deplored.[5]

But setting forth that "fine newe" religion was difficult. Reform bills passed in the Lower House of Elizabeth's first parliament only to face an uphill run through the Upper, where the bishops Mary appointed refused to confirm their new queen's supremacy over the church, opposed having the liturgy in English, and resisted changes in clerical dress. The convocation of Canterbury clergy informed the Commons and the court in 1559 that the government of the church belonged to bishops and pastors, *non ad laicos*, that is, it belonged to the very prelates who objected to the regime's apparent fondness for a religion "lately brought in and allowed no where nor put in practyse but in this realme onely, and that but of a smale tyme."[6]

The queen and council struck back. They removed the obstructionists for "ignorance and malice," accusing them of sabotaging the start-up deliberations with religious reformers and undermining royal supremacy and religious uniformity.[7] The Marian bishops were "deprevyd," Henry Machyn reported, calling the roll for posterity in his diary and identifying the reformed preachers at St. Paul's Cross in London who undertook to explain to passersby the new queen's "alteracions" and deprivations.[8] Edwin Sandys and John Jewel, two June preachers who had recently returned from the continent, were soon appointed to the sees of Worcester and Salisbury, respectively. Parker, the new archbishop of Canterbury, appears to have offered no objections. He had not been abroad with them, but, as Sandys appreci-

---

5. Pilkington, "The True Report of the Burning of the Steeple and Church of Paul's in London," in *Tudor Tracts, 1532–1588*, ed. A. F. Pollard (London: Constable, 1903), 407–8.

6. Bodl., Tanner MS. 302, 26r; *Proceedings*, 20; *Concilia*, 180; and CCCC, MS. 121, 172–75.

7. See William Dey's account of the Westminster disputation's first day, CCCC, MS. 118, 384. Also see *ZL*, 1:79.

8. See *The Diary of Henry Machyn*, ed. John Gough Nichols (London: Camden Society, 1848), 200–201; and Henry Norbert Birt, *The Elizabethan Religious Settlement* (London: Bell, 1907), 36–38.

atively remembered, Parker was most welcoming when the Marian exiles returned to the realm: "you have streatched forthe your hande further than all the rest."[9]

But the reformers' ready explanations and the work of eager, new diocesan administrators did not seem to save their sees from being "set religiously adrift." Even where bishops were resolute, parishioners were wary. In London, churchwardens at St. Lawrence Jewry authorized only that their rood loft be "cut lower" in 1563. To be sure, elsewhere, things proceeded quickly. At St. Ewen's in Bristol, laymen completely dismantled their rood loft that same year and swiftly sold the lumber, but, as late as 1569, in the diocese of Chichester, "the tymber of them that be taken downe lieth still in many churches redy to be set up agayne."[10]

Did the timber that "lieth still" signal commoners' hopes for the restoration of Catholicism? Was Queen Elizabeth a less than thorough religious reformer because she suspected popular devotion to Catholic ritual, ornament, and clerical dress was deeply rooted (and because she mistrusted her ability to turn English soil)? The realm's historians, during the seventeenth century, celebrated the last Tudor for lifting "the yoke of Antichrist," yet they also regretted that the churches' full recovery had to be deferred to a more suitable season.[11] They echoed the precisionists of the 1560s who

---

9. LPL, MS. 959.2, unfoliated, for "streatched." Patrick Collinson, *Archbishop Grindal, 1519–1583: The Struggle for a Reformed Church* (Berkeley: University of California Press, 1979), 90–91, 96, claims Jewel and Sandys accepted episcopal office to prevent "faint-hearted Protestants" from being appointed. "Faint-hearted" is Pilkington's characterization; he agreed to serve, as did Edmund Grindal, who said he wanted to keep "semi-papists" from the sees. Advocates of lay participation were likely to hope for more, of course, and they might well have been encouraged had they guessed that a few exiles-turned-bishops contributed to a "Declaration of Protestants to the Queen on their first coming over," a document calling for parishioners' involvement in the choice of pastors (CCCC, MS. 121, 152–53).

10. See the "Disorders in the Diocese of Chichester," appended to Archbishop Parker's 1569 *sede vacante* visitation records, PRO, State Papers 12/60/71. For St. Ewen, BRO, P/StE/ChW/2, 16; for the loft at St. Lawrence, London, Guildhall MS. 2590/1, 14. Caroline Litzenberger, *English Reformation and the Laity: Gloucestershire, 1540–1580* (Cambridge: Cambridge University Press, 1997), 104–5, 162–63, discusses the dioceses "adrift." Few dispute Robert Whiting's claims (*Local Responses*, 130–31) that "convinced Protestants" were a minority in 1560; Eamon Duffy, commenting on the price paid for the Prayer Book and psalter that year (*Morebath*, 143), says that "cost as much as conservatism kept . . . compliance slow."

11. David Underdown, *Fire from Heaven: Life in an English Town in the Seventeenth Century* (New Haven, Conn.: Yale University Press, 1992), 59, quoting John White's *The Troubles of Jerusalem's Restauration*, delivered in 1645 and printed the next year.

clamored for what a number called the completion of reform. That same number also censured the new government for being too tolerant of residual Roman Catholicism. Impatience, caution, change, uncertainty, present from the start, were all parts of an unstable early Elizabethan mix. No wonder, then, historian Norman Jones now writes at length about an "unsettled settlement of religion," reporting "Protestant discontents" and "Catholic confusion" through the 1560s, at "the birth of the Elizabethan age."[12]

Elizabeth's government employed many midwives. It delegated royal prerogatives and issued letters patent to an assortment of commissioners for ecclesiastical causes—prelates, lay lawyers, and privy councillors, traveling in circuits, often accompanied by local notables. In 1559 one commission worked the northern province; five, the southern. Commissioners for the southwest left London in early August, reached Exeter before the end of September, and returned to London the first week in November. They and others so charged restored priests deprived during Mary's reign and ordered the abjurations of those who preached in favor of papal authority, declared the value of charitable work, pilgrimages, and auricular confession as the means to justification, and advocated prayer in Latin. Altars en route were removed "against their visitation." Commissioners could not guarantee discipline and conformity, but one assumes rood lofts and timber readied for their reconstruction would have been more conspicuous, had they made no circuits. As permitted by their letters patent, moreover, they transferred their powers to local, lay officials who thereafter interrogated nonconformists and enforced Elizabeth's settlement as best they could.[13]

Or did they? It seems now, as it must have then, that all the queen's men were not always on the same page. Her council had to count on its commissioners for ecclesiastical causes to assure her subjects conformed religiously; commissioners relied on the cooperation of local deputies. Early on, Elizabeth's closest advisers realized the system or network might be undermined by its members' different commitments to reform. The regime knew it had to come up with and to control a supply of committed, loyal, reformist

---

12. Jones, *Birth*, 17–86. Also see Susan Brigden's chapter on the 1560s, "Perils Many, Great, and Imminent," in *New Worlds, Lost Worlds: The Rule of the Tudors, 1485–1603* (London: Lane, 2000), 213–38.

13. For the itineraries and other documents related to the southwestern and southeastern circuits, see C. G. Bayne, "The Visitation of the Province of Canterbury, 1559," *EHR* 28 (1913): 638–41, 648–49, 672–74. Also consult Roland G. Usher, *Rise and Fall of the High Commission*, reprint ed. (Oxford: Clarendon, 1968), 16–17, 45–46, 64.

preachers, if ever it were to preside over a loyal, lay consensus. Accordingly, the authorities turned their attention to the universities where many clergy were trained. At Cambridge, "Cloked papistrie" was detected into the early 1560s.[14] Oxford, however, proved the more daunting challenge. On his return from exile, John Parkhurst found "few gospellers" yet "many papists" at its colleges.[15] The heads of six of them were sent packing; six senior fellows at New College, the foundation more Marian than most, were imprisoned. Yet the council's commissioners met with stiff resistance, *constantia*, commented Nicholas Sander, a fellow at New, before leaving the realm to join Catholic alumni abroad. Sander alleged that intimidation, flattery, and finally bribery got the commissioners some grudging consent, but it was negligible, at best, he said, when compared with the steadfast opposition. The commissioners left disappointed, without administering the government's oath of obedience and with an almost desperate plea that Oxford fellows, at the very least, attend their recently re-reformed churches.[16]

The next year, Oxford was "yet under the papistical yoke," according to James Calfhill, subdean of Christchurch.[17] Bishop Horne thought so as well. He appointed a special commission to monitor college reform. But for all his efforts, some Catholics continued to take refuge in Oxford into the 1560s and until the Jesuit missions to England intensified the court's crackdown on the resident "papists." Much later, historians of the university held that the persistence of Catholicism at the colleges was symptomatic of "the precariousness and transitional position of church affairs" in the kingdom.[18] Sander would have said "precarious" not "transitional." He figured that it was only a matter of time before commoners would carry the realm right back to Rome. He predicted local justices of the peace would be in the lead, and that would have made sense. They staffed several of the queen's commissions, conducted inquiries for other commissioners, and interrogated suspected nonconformists. David Loades describes local justices as "the real workhorses" of the late Tudor regime. If queen, council, and

---

14. CCCC, MS. 106, 529.

15. *ZL*, 1:29.

16. *Miscellanea*, 20, 43–44, for Sander's 1561 letter to Cardinal Moroni.

17. BL, Lansdowne MS. 981, 73r.

18. See Hastings Rashdall and Robert Rait, *New College* (London: Robinson, 1901), 114–15; and C. M. Dent, *Protestant Reformers in Elizabethan Oxford* (Oxford: Oxford University Press, 1983), 145–47. But Horne told Parker that there was no "disorder" in his diocese in 1565, CCCC, MS. 114A, 435–36.

reformed bishops had their way, justices would become local overseers of reformed religious conformity. But if Sander had his way, they would eventually unfurl their true, conservative colors and lead England back toward Catholicism.[19]

Into the 1560s, in some places Sander's way looked the likelier of the two that opened from Elizabeth's settlement into the future. Edward Fleetwood, pastor at Wigan, recalled long afterward that church officials in Lancashire and Cheshire had been frustrated for decades: whenever the diocesan authorities presented papists for punishment, justices let them off. Local justices were "backward," Fleetwood complained; they winked at nonconformity, and their "gentle dealing" served only to increase Catholics' contempt for the new regime's reformed religion.[20] But ten years later, the justices in those parts remembered things very differently. They put their predecessors on the court's side of reform, mentioning a loose confederation of justices and pastors, "some among us forty years preaching," cultivated a cluster of "unfayned professors of the gospel" on tough terrain, which, in 1559, was "overgrowne with popery and prophaneness."[21]

Were the justices "backward" or advanced? Resistant or acquiescent? Can the two recollections be reconciled? "Gentle dealing" may have been the rule early, given the "precariousness" of reform, notably in the north of England. But by 1564, bishops everywhere were fed up. They answered an inquiry from the privy council calculated and circulated to elicit their concerns with the level of cooperation they had been getting from justices of the peace. The bishops said that some local justices were "fit" and "favourers of religion and godlye orders." But others were "fainte furtherers" whose dereliction of duty, "moche marke[d]" by the humblest commoners, was more than an annoyance. It was dangerous to discipline. Worse, bishops confirmed, there was no shortage of "very supersticious," "extremely perverse" justices in nearly every diocese. After the survey returns were reviewed, many delinquent and "perverse" justices were dismissed, but only after a second purge, five years later, did relations between bishops and the bench improve.[22]

---

19. *Miscellanea*, 44; David Loades, *Tudor Government: Structures of Authority in the Sixteenth Century* (Oxford: Blackwell, 1997), 118.

20. BL, Additional MS. 48064, 68v.

21. PRO, State Papers, 14/10/62.

22. Mary Bateson, ed., *A Collection of Original Letters from the Bishops to the Privy Council, 1564* (London: Camden Society, 1893). Justices were directed to assemble "with as

So the justices in 1604 might well have been justified celebrating their predecessors' collaboration with reformers. Local justices were put on notice in 1564—and particularly from 1569, they understood—that they must become "fit," not "fainte," "favourers" and "furtherers." Yet during the early 1560s, many, if not most, of them likely hesitated or even retarded the pace of reform, as Sander, Fleetwood, and the bishops reported. Sander expected the local justices to draw back the vast majority of the queen's subjects—no more religiously uncertain than the pope, he claimed—draw them back, that is, from the precipice Protestants would throw them over. The reformers responsible constituted no more than a small group of schismatics (*grex parvus*), Sander said, assuring friends in Rome that they might think of the late Tudor laymen as allies.[23]

Four hundred years later, John Neale came upon Sander's set, dubbed it "puritan," and insisted that returning refugees with several like-minded friends in London constituted that "strong . . . party at work on behalf of reformed religion," which "inspired" the Lower House of the new queen's parliament to press her and her council for more than they would otherwise have conceded in 1559. It was "a runaway" Commons, Neale said; radical former refugees urged it on, and Elizabeth's council could only brake it by appealing to the Upper House. If he is right, queen, court, and Commons were overwhelmed by Sander's "flock." But he was wrong. In the 1950s Neale's became the definitive picture of parliamentary management, yet it has since been painted over and replaced. Historians of religion and law now suspect that Neale's and Nicholas Sander's successfully strident radicals were not all that radical, strident, or successful. The returning exiles seem to have been "generally temperate establishment men." Yet one is left to wonder: if Neale overrated the puritan vanguard and inflated the importance of the extremists whom Sander had reported into being, then who took the lead in 1559?[24]

---

much spede as possible" to subscribe to the prevailing religious settlement in 1569, after several "stirs" in the northeast (PRO, State Papers 12/60/18). But during the 1580s, Fleetwood was sure government intervention was needed to reduce the effects of the closeted Catholicism of certain uncooperative justices (BL, Cotton MS. Titus B II, 239r–40r).

23. *Miscellanea*, 24, 45.

24. See John E. Neale, "The Elizabethan Acts of Supremacy and Uniformity," *EHR* 65 (1950): 324, for a succinct restatement of his hypothesis. But, for "temperate establishment men," see Winthrop Hudson, *Cambridge Connection and the Elizabethan Settlement of 1559*

John Calvin of Geneva guessed correctly. Late that year he wrote a short letter of congratulation and encouragement to the queen and her closest adviser, William Cecil. Calvin's sentiments were predictable; he pressed them to give thanks for their recent success by implementing further reform. He also assumed Elizabeth and her council were out front, with commissioners, justices of the peace, and the Commons in tow.[25] Norman Jones inventories the results: a "clearly defined supremacy," "properly established uniformity," and "pleasant increase in the queen's revenues" from her bishops' estates and defunct chanceries. Elizabeth and Cecil, then, were driven, in 1559 and into the 1560s, neither by "those that be swifte [and] goe before the lawe or beyond" it nor by "those that be too slow." Queen and regime, instead, proceeded with a momentum of their own making—carefully, sometimes slyly. Commoners strained to see what direction their government might be going, while it watched them for signs of disaffection.[26]

The returning exiles were closely watched and still bear watching. Much as their fellow citizens, they tried to ascertain what tack the new regime was taking. They also tried to influence the course and speed of reform. Grindal said he contended "long," "earnestly," yet unsuccessfully for a quicker pace, but failures did not deter him from diocesan administration. He was bishop of London before long and until 1570.[27] Possibly he, Horne, Jewel, Parkhurst, and others sensed that Cecil and the queen wanted to keep potential French and Spanish Catholic aggressors guessing while the new government settled into place and before proceeding too far and too conspicuously with their religious reform. Or did the impatient exiles-turned-bishops think the early Elizabethan church was, as historian Patrick Collinson imagines it, "like an old apartment block which had not been repaired for years [and] which still contained too many of its old tenants . . . [who] made too few concessions to their new landlord or lady who, on the contrary, made all too

---

(Durham, N.C.: Duke University Press, 1980), 5–6, 93–99, 143–45; N. M. Sutherland, "The Marian Exiles and the Establishment of the Elizabethan Regime" *ARG* 78 (1987): 283–84; and Norman L. Jones, *Faith by Statute: Parliament and the Settlement of Religion, 1559* (London: Humanities Press, 1982), 46–47, 61–64, 169–85.

25. *CR*, 17:418–20.

26. Jones, *Faith by Statute*, 134–37. For the "swifte" and the "slow," see Nicholas Bacon's speech, opening parliament in 1559, *Proceedings*, 51.

27. *ZL*, 1:10–11.

many concessions to them"?[28] Maybe so; it is hard to tell what was going through the minds of the queen's new bishops. I suspect, though, that John Jewel was in earnest when he explained to Peter Martyr Vermigli in 1559 that the queen and council were advancing "piously," "firmly," yet "prudently."[29]

For her part, Elizabeth reacted angrily when criticism went to the bone. Alexander Nowell, new dean of St. Paul's Cathedral, laced up his courage and, in what another described as his "very good sermon" at court, expressed dissatisfaction with the pace and "prudence" of reform. The queen interrupted to inform him that his words were "skant wyl lyked of the hier powers." She left before Nowell could apologize or elaborate, and her leaving made it abundantly clear to her new bishops as well as to the dean that they had little choice, save to wait.[30]

The queen's caution and criticism slowed the advocates of broad popular participation in parish and parliament. Word was that the Commons might then become a purer form of "democracie" than allowed at the time, but there looks to have been little agitation to that effect.[31] Privy councillors kept control, in part, because they had hardly any faith in the electorate. They thought that commoners were easily gulled by the chief villains of the day, "merchants of mischief" and "selfish men who create scarcity amid plenty." They dazzled and duped ordinary people. Rogues were too agile for "the multitude," too quick and cunning to be outflanked. The gravity of greater men—and that alone, as the "greater" themselves let on—prevented greed from lifting English society off its moral and legal foundations.[32]

---

28. Patrick Collinson, "The Religion of Elizabethan England and of Its Queen," in *Giordano Bruno, 1583–1585: The English Experience*, ed. Michele Ciliberto and Nicholas Mann (Florence: Olschki, 1997), 9.

29. *ZL*, 1:161.

30. Elizabeth Gilgate's letter to her brother notes Nowell's "very good sermon" and the queen's angry response: Bodl., Ashmole MS. 1729, 163.

31. See John Aylmer, *An harborowe for faithfull and trewe subjectes* (London, 1559), H3r, and, for relevant remarks on Aylmer, Anne N. McLaren, *Political Culture in the Reign of Elizabeth I: Queen and Commonwealth, 1558–1585* (Cambridge: Cambridge University Press, 1999), 66–69.

32. For Thomas Lever's arraignment of the "merchants of mischief," see Arthur B. Ferguson, *The Articulate Citizen and the English Renaissance* (Durham, N.C.: Duke University Press, 1965), 290–91, and for Lever's "experiment in distributive sovereignty," Malcolm Hardman, *A Kingdom in Two Parishes: Lancashire Religious Writers and the English Monarchy, 1521–1689* (Madison, N.J.: Fairleigh Dickinson University Press, 1998), 55–62. For conciliar control of Commons, consult Geoffrey R. Elton, *The Parliament of England, 1559–1581* (Cambridge: Cambridge University Press. 1986), 321–22; Michael A. R. Graves,

Moreover, councillors believed commoners were unpredictable, or, to be precise, predictably inconstant and unruly. Parliament heard from its speaker in 1567, Richard Onslowe, that leadership in the realm must never be hostage to the "greate variance, parciallitie, strifes, and partakinges" of the people. Better, Onslowe said, to select candidates for the commoners, present them to freeholders and borough freemen, and presume that the presentation was equivalent to confirmation.[33] Precisely that line was taken from 1559, when parliament heard that "alwaies uppon a little libertie [ordinary people] are readie to rebell and dare doo any thinge, and every man follow his owne waye."[34] Three years later, Thomas Norton and Thomas Sackville informed the queen similarly and instructed her accordingly:

"For give once sway unto the people's lusts
To rush forth on and stay them not in time,
And as the stream that rolleth down the hill
So will they headlong run with raging thoughts
From blood to blood, from mischief unto moe,
To ruin of the realm, themselves and all,
So giddy are the common people's minds,
So glad of change, more wavering than the sea."[35]

What was to be done with those "giddy" commoners "so glad of change"? Clearly, they would have to be persuaded that change was no longer in their best interests, once the queen's "alteracions" were established by statute. Persuasion would take preaching, and the provision of preachers was a job that predictably fell to the queen's new bishops. They were parts of the government's management strategy—and significant enough parts

---

"Managing Eliabethan Parliaments," in *The Parliaments of Elizabethan England*, ed. David Dean and Norman Jones (Oxford: Blackwell, 1990), 37–63; and Norman Jones, "Parliament and the Political Society of Elizabethan England," in *Tudor Political Culture*, ed. Dale Hoak (Cambridge: Cambridge University Press, 1995), 232–36.

33. *Proceedings*, 169. Onslowe illustrated the dangers of democracy by citing the "moste holieste elections" of popes, which turn "utterlie unhollie [and] unquiet with greate parte takinges"; but, for the infrequency of contested elections in England, Mark Kishlansky, *Parliamentary Selection: Social and Political Choice in Early Modern England* (Cambridge: Cambridge University Press, 1986), 10–12.

34. *Proceedings*, 10.

35. *Gorboduc or Ferrex and Porrex*, ed. Irby B. Cauthen (Lincoln: University of Nebraska Press, 1970), 61.

that Cecil and Elizabeth made no secret of their intent to manage the episcopal managers. Christopher Haigh says that the government "bullied" its
bishops.[36] Archbishop Parker sensed as much at times and complained that
contempt for high ecclesiastical office had spread from the court into the
whole country, where no one thought a bishop "worthye to eate venyson."[37]

Contempt was a matter of concern into the 1560s. The queen and council wanted compliant, not "giddy" or insolent, sneering subjects. Parliament,
fashioning the realm's new political and religious order, was told returning
exiles were "persuaders of rebellion."[38] Abbot Feckenham endeavored to
capitalize on the anxiety. He explained to members that Catholicism "dothe
brede more obedyent, humble" subjects than did reformed religion.[39] But
James Pilkington countered that Rome was widely known to have bred obedience by intimidation; papists "built their kingdom more in one year with
fire and fagot than gospellers will do in seven." If haste mattered more than
depth of feeling, Catholics had the edge, Pilkington granted, but he also
claimed that "gospellers" generated loyalties that would last. Fear breeds
obedience and humility only as long as fearsome figures hover as tyrants
over their precincts and peoples. By contrast, the reformed preachers empower rather than intimidate the faithful, encouraging them to search for
and discover divine mercy at work in their souls—and the divine will at
work in their ordered societies and those who ruled them. Doubtlessly, it
would be easier and politically far more advantageous in the long run, to
supply sermons than to compel conformity, loyalty, and humility. "When
preaching fails, the people perish," Pilkington finished, writing of the country's ruin as the alternative to its religious reform.[40]

Grindal was more explicit and less gloomy when he later explained why
those parishes with "continual preaching" during the 1560s responded so
swiftly with troops when queen and regime were threatened in 1569. He featured the contributions from "one poor parish in Yorkshire," Halifax, yet he
fathered as grand and as groundless a generalization as Feckenham had ten
years before. Then archbishop of York, Grindal insisted that reformers
rather than Catholics bred obedient subjects. "Obedience proceedeth of

---

36. Haigh, *Elizabeth*, 43.
37. BL, Lansdowne MS. 6, 131r.
38. CCCC, MS. 121, 142–3; and Strype(1), 1.1:116.
39. Strype(1), 1.2:436.
40. Strype(1), 1.1:271–72.

conscience," he reasoned; "conscience is founded on the word of God, and the word of God worketh this effect by preaching."[41]

Did Grindal convince the court? Not likely. For one thing, the queen never warmed to reformed sermons as her half brother Edward had. Yet more to the point in the 1560s, neither she nor Cecil trusted that "continual" preaching would breed better subjects as long as so many of the realm's most ardent preachers refused to subject themselves to their bishops. Diocesan and government officials alike were increasingly troubled by the more radical, "forward," and puritanical reformers, and their troubles will soon concern us. Indeed, we will shortly learn how suspicious both sides became, conformists and nonconformists, thinking of the laity. But first we must learn something about what laymen thought of themselves, specifically how comfortable commoners were with lay leadership in their parishes.

Lay Leadership in Reformed Parishes

Reformers of all stripes were preaching-obsessed in the 1560s. They supposed sermons were sure antidotes for residual Catholicism. The bishop of Chester directed the laymen in his diocese "duetifullie [to] make their repaire at all tymes when, and as often as, any sermon shal be preached within three miles of their dwelling houses to the church where the sermon shal be made."[42] The bishop of Winchester preached often and tirelessly recruited and examined others to fill the pulpits in his diocese. He translated several of Calvin's sermons, capping his efforts to assure that the newly reformed and faithful "flie idolatrie" and neither dishonor God nor defile themselves "with any manner [of] superstition."[43] And reformed laymen as well acknowledged the importance of the pulpit. London draper Richard Sandell provided funds in his will of 1567 for eight sermons in his parish church and for six more in the three Essex parishes where he owned property.[44]

But preachers were more conspicuous agents of religious reform than were lay financiers. The English reformation was clerical in both origin and

---

41. *Remains*, 380.
42. CRO, EDA 12/2/123v–24r (1564).
43. See Horne's translations of *Two godly and learned sermons made by that famous and worthy instrument in God's church, John Calvin* (London, 1564), E4v–E5r.
44. London, Guildhall MS. 9051/3, 204r.

orientation, according to historian J. J. Scarisbrick, who claims that congregations were "captive" to a Protestantism which tethered "layfolk around increasingly impressive pulpits." The commoners were worse off, Scarisbrick continues; they were more servile under Protestantism with its "ministry of the word" than in Catholic churches where stunning sights, sounds, scents, and gestures filled their senses and enchanted their lives. Inside "the average [reformed] parish church" altars became tables, and "tables . . . seemed to be turning against the average layman." Beat Kumin agrees that reformers were creating a new clerical aristocracy, and he mourns, with Scarisbrick, the loss of chantries and parish fraternities, subparochial institutions that appear to have reduced the social distances between priests and parishioners. Kumin is sure that the reformed gentry and the reformers they supported created an English Protestant clerical order more remote from the commoners than the order and hierarchies maintained by the priests and bishops of Catholic Europe.[45]

The early reformers' complaints about the arrogance of medieval prelatical culture, complaints rehearsed in the previous chapter, suggest that the enchantment and intimacy Scarisbrick and Kumin admired were less well liked than they think. Perhaps, as they say, the reformation dreadfully exaggerated distances—those between priests and people and between the elites and the commoners—yet that, too, is contestable. Data collected by Ian Archer attests that reformers' emphasis on the pulpits did not destroy parish solidarity. Frequent sermons seem to have drawn together the laity in inner-city London parishes of fewer than a hundred households. Archer's conclusions are telling: dissolution of subparochial institutions had few, if any, seriously disabling effects on the "levels of religious observance" in London and on the cohesiveness of the larger extramural parishes that remained "important unit[s] of identity, creating ties among members, rich and poor."[46] And such ties ostensibly were strengthened by what Gareth Owen found on a previous outing, namely, the growing lay preoccupation with ministerial quality in London, where religious reforms provided the context in which

45. Beat A. Kumin, *The Shaping of a Community: The Rise and Reformation of the English Parish, 1400–1560* (Aldershot: Scolar Press, 1996), 179–80, 231, 242, 258; and J. J. Scarisbrick, *The Reformation and the English People* (Oxford: Blackwell, 1984), 162–65.

46. Ian W. Archer, *The Pursuit of Stability: Social Relations in Elizabethan London* (Cambridge: Cambridge University Press, 1991), 87–92.

"parochial determination to impose image[s] of 'the faithful pastor' upon the clergy" found broad support.[47]

But that was London. Elsewhere in England pastors were in shorter supply. Archbishop Parker was repeatedly told that there were far too few reformed preachers to fill all the vacancies in Canterbury province. John Bruen called "that want" "pittifall"; sheep without a shepherd, he grieved, "are as men cast out of God's sight."[48] To some reformers, pluralism seemed to be a solution, but Thomas Lever protested, as did other relatively radical returning exiles, that parishes were poorly served by a pastor serving more than one. Lever had not returned to England to compromise the reformed ministry, he intimated, though his responsibilities as archdeacon to have congregations at least minimally supervised compelled him, in effect, to drop his opposition. He tried, nonetheless, to make the bitter pill of pluralism a bit easier to swallow by seeing to it that pluralists not rush from one parish to the next in the same day. Lever would have them at least seem unhurried and thus save the appearance of pastoral care.[49]

Archbishop Parker experimented with alternatives to pluralism. He relaxed the standards for ordination, but the haul of rough and altogether unready recruits for the parish ministry posed new problems; therefore, he licensed—and allowed his suffragans to license—laymen to read the prayer-book services. Some were hired to help nonresident pluralists cope with their cures. In Rochester one was appointed in each of the two parishes served by a single blind curate. Of the seventy parishes with lay lectors or readers in Parker's diocese of Canterbury, only seven had resident clerics. Curates frequently visited thirty others; the remaining thirty-three were vacant—aside from the laymen licensed to serve.[50]

Parker's experiment might have been seen and spurned as a Protestant throwback to the minor orders of the medieval church, yet Thomas Lever took to it. He frowned on pluralism, mistrusted holdovers from the last

---

47. See Gareth Owen's "Tradition and Reform: Ecclesiastical Controversy in an Elizabethan London Parish," *Guildhall Miscellany* 2 (1960–68): 63–70.

48. BL, Harleian MS. 6607, 49v. Also see Ralph Houlbrooke, *Church Courts and the People during the English Reformation, 1520–1570* (Oxford: Oxford University Press, 1979), 187–89, for the diocesans' reports to Parker.

49. London, Inner Temple, Petyt MS. 538/38, 71v–72r.

50. BL, Lansdowne MS. 6, 141v, for Rochester. For Parker's experiment, consult Rosemary O'Day, *The English Clergy: The Emergence and Consolidation of a Profession, 1558–1642* (Leicester: Leicester University Press, 1979), 129–31.

regime, and found newly ordained Coventry clerics too indolent and un-skilled to do much good. It looked to Lever that Marian priests-turned-Protestants and recent reformed recruits had neither calling nor compulsion to preach. They just "seek to have some portion and profit of the ministerie by reading onelie." He preferred lay lectors, "men such as live honestlie in any vocation" and assist with church services.[51]

Congregations chose their lay readers. Parker's "order for serving cures now destitute" urged only that nominees be "honest, sober, and grave" and that bishops or their chancellors exercise "oversight." Diocesan officials were directed to call for and to canvass testimonials.[52] If results of the canvass-ing survived, we could learn whether the overseers actually intervened and screened for excessively reformist or for residual Catholic sentiments. But we may infer that barriers to the appointment of commoners, if obstacles anywhere, were not hindrances everywhere: Archdeacon Pulleyne seems to have made no fuss in Colchester when cobbler Peter Hawks and alehouse keeper John Watson were selected to serve.[53] Alas, few others are known by name and trade, and we know too little about them to say much more than that they read. Parker probably wanted it that way; he meant to keep the lec-tors' profile low. His was a provisional measure. Lay readers were prohib-ited from attending to their succession. When sickness required them to resign, they should "leave it to the sute of the parishe to the ordenarie for assignynge some other able man," and they should always be ready to step down and "geve place upon convenient warning" whenever parish patrons provided a more comprehensive clerical presence.[54]

In 1562 Parker's experiment was discontinued. Perhaps he imagined his suffragans were close to a better solution to the problem of pulpit supply. Or did he resign himself to lowering the bar and to having them ordain less scrupulously yet again? Late Tudor puritans suspected that standards had plummeted and that 1562 marked something of a watershed. They urged officials to suspend and replace unpreaching pastors ordained and settled

---

51. London, Inner Temple, Petyt MS. 538/38, 71v.

52. Strype(1), 1.1:276–77.

53. Mark Byford, "The Birth of a Protestant Town: The Process of Reformation in Tudor Colchester, 1530–1580," in *Reformation in English Towns*, ed. Patrick Collinson and John Craig (New York: St. Martin's Press, 1998), 38.

54. BL, Additional MS. 19398, 59; Strype(1), 1.1:225–26.

since then. Norfolk layman Arthur Heveningham spurred his fellow parishioners to get involved: "those that be under dum ministers ought to labour by all godly meanes to get unto them learned pastours."[55]

And parishioners were not without "meanes." Some of the more resourceful men of the parish had considerable leverage as their churches' chief financial officers, succinctly described at St. Margaret Pattens in London as "wardens of the goodes, workes, rents, and ornaments."[56] Ordinarily, they were uncompensated, but at Christchurch in Bristol, they annually withdrew twenty shillings for themselves and their deputies during the 1560s and 1570s "for the gathering of rentts and the making of this book." "This book" was the ledger that gave the totals for each year's expenses and income; inventoried the parish's revenue-producing properties; recorded the costs of, and assessments for, special parish projects; and named all debtors and creditors. That twenty-shilling charge in Bristol was the equivalent of what an unskilled laborer was paid in the 1570s for thirty-five days of work.[57] Wardens' contemporaries usually put them at the same socioeconomic level as those laborers or just above it, viewing them as no better than parish cashiers, calling them "simple," "low," "base," and "lewd." To be sure, ledgers contain traces of that "simplicity." Wardens for 1565 fumbled with their figures at St. Michael's in Chester, canceling and recomputing totals, casting themselves as dunces and casting doubt on the entrepreneurial good sense of parishioners who chose and trusted them. But ten years later wardens twice went out of pocket there to advance a substantial amount to the parish. Admittedly, ready reserves and the willingness to cover costs in a crisis may not necessarily preclude incompetence. Wealthy parishioners capable of comfortable adjustments to circumstance were perhaps as base and simple as their critics imagined. We shall never be certain, yet we are able to enter into evidence enough from churchwardens' accounts to suggest that the insults of those in arrears and the uncharitable remarks of occasional observers have relatively little value. They neither describe the wardens nor represent lay thinking about them.[58]

---

55. BL, Egerton MS. 2713, 210v; BL, Lansdowne MS. 42, 207r–208r; and the *Booke of certaine canons concernynge some parte of the discipline of the churche of England* (London, 1571), canon 6, prohibiting the appointment of lay lectors.

56. London, Guildhall MS. 4570, 34r.

57. BRO, P/Xch/ChW/1(a), 141r, 215r.

58. CRO, P/65/1, 32r, 66r, 69v. John Craig cites warden-bashing in his study of Suffolk, "Cooperation and Initiatives: Elizabethan Churchwardens and the Parish Accounts at Mildenhall," *Social History* 18 (1993): 362–63.

Granted, wardens' status and competence cannot be compassed with a one-fits-all generalization. Churchwardens were a motley crew. In Nottinghamshire they were on the "low rung" of ladders that incumbents scaled to get onto aldermanic benches; early sixteenth-century wardens, social-climbing in the countryside, succeeded to manorial offices. Thomas Ardern in Kent, however, amassed a small fortune and was a leading member of the Faversham town council before he was named churchwarden and, within months, mayor.[59] There is no telling the respectability or the reserves of the saddler, baker, brewer, grocer, and haberdasher who came to court in the 1550s when a judge summoned wardens, past and present, from two parishes in London to settle a disputed lease. But it would seem that craftsmen and artisans, "mean" when seen from above, nonetheless acquired a stake in the management of their parishes' properties and the ways and means to make a difference in parish affairs.[60]

Beyond this appearance of solvency-and-then-some, the wardens' personal purses are closed to us. The epithets "low" and "base" look to have little or no descriptive value. Scholars once took them seriously, probably because they supported then current theories about the eventual regentrification of parish management during the 1580s. But historians now place early Elizabethan churchwardens between the base and fancy-bred. Some soundings taken over the last twenty years by four of the most perceptive students of local variation in Tudor culture—Eamon Duffy, John Craig, Eric Carlson, and Martin Ingram—suggest that lay wardens were "of essentially middling status," increasingly recruited from "the middle to upper strata of parish society," where commoners measured prestige, in part, by public service. The receipts from St. Ewen's, Bristol, illustrate such talk of "the middle" and "middling," depositing John Thomson, parish warden in 1565 and 1566 and town barber, exactly at the median when assessments from two to twenty shillings were collected for the pastor's and parish clerk's wages. Into the 1560s, the laity, thinking of the laity in positions of leadership,

59. For Ardern and Faversham in the 1540s, see Lena Cowen Orlin, *Private Matters and Public Culture in Post-Reformation England* (Ithaca, N.Y.: Cornell University Press, 1994), 30–33; for Nottinghamshire, David Marcombe, *English Small Town Life, Retford, 1520–1642* (Nottingham: University of Nottingham Studies in Local and Regional History, 1993) 52–33; and, for the middlers and manorial offices (reeve and bailiff), Katherine French, *The People of the Parish: Community Life in a Late Medieval English Diocese* (Philadelphia: University of Pennsylvania Press, 2000), 85–86, 90–91.

60. London, Guildhall MS. 9531/12/2, 431r.

recognized its Thomsons as ordinary or average laymen with an impressive range of managerial responsibilities.[61]

Wardens were assessors and collectors; they put most of their fellow parishioners, including former wardens, much of the time on the "payment due" or income side of their ledgers, which show rents and rates, though seldom record responses, other than payment or nonpayment. We cannot discern, then, how cheerfully John Sherlock of Chester acquiesced to the steep 50 percent hike in his assessment for the parish clerk's wages from 1563 to 1565 or whether there were objections to the garden tithes at St. James, Bristol, when fees in the early 1570s ranged strangely.[62] But it looks as if churchwardens were a parish's frontline when the bills came due and when calculations were challenged. And they were its likeliest emissaries when a delegation was needed to deal with nonparishioners, as when wardens of St. James were commissioned at a special parish meeting to bargain with, and posibly browbeat, outsiders illicitly grazing their horses in meadows owned by the church.[63]

More pleasant duties probably included discussing legacies with pious parishioners, whose bequests ranged from trinkets to tenements. Rent from the latter often provided a parish's most reliable income. At St. John the Baptist in Bristol, even "the house wherein the parson dwell[s]" had been donated and helped pay the church's way, though rent was not raised from 1561 to 1580. Wardens might find themselves in a delicate position as agents of the landlord parish confronting the pastor and beneficiary of early modern rent-control.[64] Yet presumed problems of that kind paled before the everyday challenges of stewardship. Gifts from the living, for example, were obviously less predictable than legacies. Accounts regularly report a few pence from passersby. Only luck might land parishes more than a penny in their poor box, yet wardens were expected to help luck along. At St. Lawrence

61. BRO P/StE/ChW/2, 19, 27, for Thomson. Also see Duffy, *Morebath*, 30–32; Craig, *Reformation*, 42–44; Craig, "Cooperation and Initiatives," 363–64; Ingram, *Church Courts*, 123; and Eric Carlson, "The Origins, Function, and Status of the Office of Churchwarden, with Particular Reference to the Diocese of Ely," in *The World of Rural Dissenters*, ed. Margaret Spufford (Cambridge: Cambridge University Press, 1995), 194–95.

62. Bristol, BAO P/StJ/ChW/1(a), 20r; and, for Sherlock, Chester, CRO, P65/8/1, 20v, 30v. Parish clerks typically were appointed by pastors but paid by parishioners as canon law stipulated.

63. BRO, P/StJ/ChW/1(a), 28r.

64. BRO, P/StJB/ChW/1(b)i, 134, 176.

Jewry, London, they were stationed at the doors in 1564, not simply to tally attendance but to encourage donations.[65] Churches depended more than before on the doorway donations, bequests, and fees for space in parish tenements, shops, pastures, pews, and gardens, for Elizabeth's "alteracion" took a noticeable toll on the fairs and fun that brought laymen and their money to church. Raising money became quite a chore as the costs continued to mount. Indeed, wardens could not cut some of their parish's expenses. They were required, for instance, to pay impropriators—persons who purchased shares of the rectorial tithes—before applying parish revenues to running and repairing the church. At St. James, Bristol, for instance, two lay patrons received returns on their investments (more than three pounds in 1575) before the groundskeeper, Pierce Banks, got his hard-earned four shillings.[66]

In due course, the pastor at St. James was paid his salary, which had been raised the previous year to nine pounds. Pastors' salaries were ordinarily the big-ticket item, although accounts rarely disclose how the sums were settled and adjusted. We have evidence from St. Michael's in Chester that such decisions were relegated to a committee composed "by common election," a panel of wardens and former wardens.[67] And we know that parishioners were not always prompt with payment. Pastor Eusebius Paget was known to have reminded reluctant laymen that the Bible provided for tithing. Payment, he claimed, was a "signe" of "the inwarde honour due unto" God.[68] Other reformers ruefully asserted their rights to maintenance, but their churchwardens, administrators pro tempore, were paymasters and neither advocates nor agitators. The proportions lost to impropriators or retained by rectors were fixed by others or by custom. The wardens' lot was to spend what was left after impropriations were deducted, to spend the parish revenues on a variety of other needs.[69]

They looked to the wages and welfare of the pastor and parish clerk. They compensated others who worked around the church: groundskeepers and bellringers, whom wardens at St. Thomas, Bristol, kept well paid,

---

65. London, Guildhall MS. 2590/1,16.

66. BRO, P/StJ/ChW/1(a), 38r.

67. CRO, P/65/8/1, 66r, 72v; and BRO, P/StJ/ChW/1(a), 31r, for the pastor's salary at St. James.

68. Euesbius Paget, *A godlie and fruitfull sermon* (London, 1583), A5v–A6r.

69. Consult Patrick Carter, "Clerical Polemic in Defence of Ministers' Maintenance during the English Reformation," *JEH* 49 (1998): 239–48.

fed, and gloved.[70] Routine parish projects obliged wardens to hire assorted others—masons, carpenters, tilers, and packs of unskilled workers—all of whom, thinking of the laity, drew on their direct experience with lay leadership. But there were limits to what churchwardens might order up. Construction fashionable during the later Middle Ages was scandalously inappropriate for reformed parishes: adornment of images and altars that survived into the 1560s or maintenance of lights. And reformed parishes raised no new chapels dedicated to saints.[71] To be sure, the fabric required constant upkeep, and occasional extensions were undertaken. Wardens reported spending for labor and material in different ways. At Saints Philip and Jacob, Bristol, they entered one sum "for makyng of the pewes and all stuff that went to ytt"; elsewhere, and more conscientiously, paymasters itemized "all the stuff," recording what suppliers charged them "for nayles occupied about the pewes" and painstakingly identifying the different kinds of nails their workmen used. At St. Oswald's in Chester, church-wardens detailed the reconstruction of the parish gates and grates—every expense from the cost of cutting and carrying timber to the charges for land-scaping once the work was done.[72]

Not all repairs could be foreseen. Wardens were no prophets. They could not infallibly predict and plan for storm damage and vandalism. Yet nearly all their accounts attest the expectation that the poor would always be with them, always on the wardens' watch and inventoried with annual parish expenses. Almstakers were usually unnamed and alms left unexplained, but every so often, an entry mentioned the misery, as when Joan Bles, "having foure small children on her hand, two . . . beinge very sike and her selfe very poor," twice got assistance at St. Botolph within Bishopsgate in 1575.[73]

Payments to poor Bles and those for pews and nails were likely made without consulting parishioners. Yet ledgers suggest that congregations approved other appropriations. The wardens at St. John the Baptist in Bris-tol, for example, sent money for the "reliffe of the prisoners in Newgate" after that gift was "agreyd by the consent of the parish." An entry for 1565 at St. Werberg in the same city surprisingly specified parish endorsement of

---

70. BRO, P/StT/ChW/13, 4v–5v.

71. Duffy, *Morebath*, 182; French, *Parish*, 147–48.

72. CRO, P29/7/1, 4r; BRO, P/StP&J/ChW/3(a), unfoliated, entries for 1564 and 1575; and BRO, P/StT/ChW/12, 5v. Also consult BRO, P/StT/ChW/1(a), 264r, for figures for a larger, public works project.

73. London, Guildhall MS. 4524/1, 25r.

an unspectacular concession permitting the pastor to keep what was paid him for funerals and weddings. Also in Bristol, wardens at Christchurch advanced their stipendiary priest one third of his annual salary "at the parishe commandment."[74] Perhaps notations of this sort—"agreyd by consent" or "parish permit"—routinely signaled solidarity rather than reported the results of actual conversations. Or maybe congregations' consent was perfunctory. After all, the sums mentioned were relatively insignificant. Yet, if there were need, broadly participatory deliberations could have been held and parishioners polled when the congregations assembled to receive, and conceivably to read, their wardens' entries for the previous year and to elect their new financial officers. All we know with confidence, though, is that after ledgers passed to the new wardens, everyone present adjourned for "a drinking," expenses for which were paid from parish funds and duly recorded.[75]

Arguably, parishioners "not part of the wardens' remit" and therefore "invisible to us" exerted tremendous influence at such meetings. Select vestries, which are said to have developed from the 1560s, would have been increasingly responsible for relaying parish "commandment," "permit," counsel, or "consent." And those panels "institutionalized the controlling role of elite families . . . by guiding and eventually replacing the general meeting" as Elizabeth's reign wore on. David Loades now seems correct on that count, but into the 1560s, parish panels were not self-evidently and socioeconomically elitist. Their forthright conversations in Chester immediately followed worship and were open to all parishioners. At Saints Philip and James, Bristol, the frontbenchers on the panel were certainly lay activists, but not necessarily members of a superior caste. Thomas Thomas, twice named churchwarden during the 1560s, appears to have been no more than a middler.[76]

---

74. BRO, P/StJB/ChW/1(b)i, 25r; P/StW/ChW/3(a), 28r; and P/Xch/ChW/1(a), 264r.

75. For example, BRO, P/StT/ChW/12, 6r.

76. BRO, P/StP&J/ChW/3(a), unfoliated, entries for 1564 and 1567. For democratic and oligarchic elements in Chester, where there were ample opportunities for commoners to participate in different strata of parish administration, see Nick Alldridge, "Loyalty and Identity in Chester Parishes, 1540–1640," in *Parish, Church, and People: Local Studies in Lay Religion, 1350–1750*, ed. S. J. Wright (London: Hutchinson, 1988), 108–9. The controlling role of elite families is discussed by Loades, *Tudor Government*, 189, and Kumin, *Shaping*, 251–54; for "invisible" influence," see Duffy, *Morebath*, 20–21.

When, in 1571, Archbishop Parker authorized parishes' select committees to proceed with parish administration, he specified no single organizational strategy. He instructed them to proceed as convenience and custom dictated. In effect, he countenanced the practices commended by his predecessor, Thomas Cranmer, who had advised "wardens be chosen by a majority of the parishioners."[77] And the language of ledgers suggests that vestrymen and wardens assumed that they were accountable to that majority or any other which developed as they conducted parish business. For Cranmer's advice (or, to be precise, his regulation) seems to have been in force into the 1560s. Parishioners at St. Lawrence Jewry, London, removed an uncooperative warden in 1567 "because he wold not supplie his place accordyng to the order takyn by the parishe," which then elected Thomas Aldersay to complete the term of his impeached colleague. Parker commanded nothing—and the earliest Elizabethan vestries demanded nothing—that would have abrogated a congregation's "order[ing]" and electing its churchwardens.[78]

But wardens, as the parish managers, answered as well to higher-ups in the church hierarchy, and sometimes the answers expected of them turned wardens against the interests of their parishioners who, for example, were pleased to have a preacher and cared little about his licensing. Diocesan officials cared more (because Parker did) and directed churchwardens to inspect the licenses of itinerants and those of resident pastors as well. Some wardens in Chichester failed to reply. One pair returned a less than emphatic "licensed to preach he is, we think," hoping their hunch might stand or fearing what inquiries might reveal. Church courts in Bristol, much as Parker, wanted no hunches; in 1564 they ordered the wardens of Redcliffe to inspect licenses and permit no one to preach unless he behaved impeccably, taught conformably, and produced documentation of his appointment.[79]

Parker and his suffragans, repeating the instructions of their medieval and earlier modern predecessors, also directed wardens to monitor the behavior of their peers. Churchwardens were to present lay offenders at regular intervals to justices who assisted diocesan authorities and to the com-

77. *Synodalia*, 122–23, for Parker; for Cranmer, *Reformatio legum*, 139.

78. London, Guildhall MS. 2590/1, 25.

79. For Chichester, BL, Additional MS. 39454, 4v, and, for Redcliffe, BRO, EP/J/1/6, 143. On the question of licensing, Parker was unequivocal: *Synodalia*, 125: *nisi quem episcopus institutione sua approbaverit.*

missioners for ecclesiastical causes named by the queen's council. If the lay presenters filed charges or presentments properly—but accused wrongly— they could not be prosecuted for defamation, but the informants who alerted wardens to, and misled them about, any alleged impropriety were likely to be sued. That risk possibly discouraged talebearing, and authorities may have intended the disincentive. For the courts were clogged with litigation that began with parishioners' accusations, from the tiresome to the terrible— wardens being obliged by their oaths of office to make a presentment whenever a reputation was assailed and preliminary investigations failed to exonerate. True, parliament heard words to the effect that churchwardens were often quick to acquit and slow to denounce their fellow parishioners.[80] Commissioners in the diocese of Chester heard as much as well and dis- patched the dean of their cathedral chapter in 1564, an enforcer to urge on the local enforcers in nearly a dozen parishes.[81] Ordinarily, however, the wardens were left to do their jobs, sniffing out nonconformity and attending to a myriad dreary delinquencies. Robert Holland, Anna Booth, and Roger Nixon were reported for coming to church *tarde et raro;* Tristram Coke, for boozing and brawling at a wedding.[82] But what happened at weddings seems to have been less important to parish and diocesan disciplinarians than what went on before and after in bed, which is to say that the brawls worthy of the local wardens' and the courts' best efforts were thought to be the reformed church's pitched battles against sexual impropriety.

Reading the *detecta* and depositions, one gets the impression that the wardens relentlessly prosecuted adultery. Infidelity was more than mischief to them. When she left her husband for a lover in 1571, Jane Easton was told that contempt for the marriage vows was contempt for the sacraments and sanctions of the church.[83] Joanna Ridgeway and her "illicit consort" illus- trate the point; they shamelessly met for sex on Sundays in their Chester parish church, according to the visitation correction book for 1563.[84] War- dens, courts, and commissioners appreciated that there were degrees of depravity. Alongside the scandalous combinations of contempt, concupis- cence, and adulterous love, occasional ante-nuptial incontinence seemed but

---

80. *Proceedings,* 202.
81. CRO, EDA/12/7, 76v–80r.
82. CRO, EDA/12/3, 15r; and CRO, EDV/1/11, 5r.
83. CRO, EDC/5, 11.
84. CRO, EDV/1/5b, 2r.

a tickle. Young and impatient couples were frequently allowed to confess their incontinence privately to their pastors and occasionally to their wardens. Adulterers, though, were seldom spared "the full rigour of a public penance."[85] So when parishioners arrived at church in Olveston near Bristol one Sunday in 1566 to find two of their neighbors standing by the pulpit— she with "a sheete about her and the man, a blankett," all the churchgoers knew immediately what a few might have already suspected.[86]

Adulterers' proximity to the pulpit assured that they and their shame were conspicuous, yet the commissioners in Chester stipulated, as though it needed saying, that Roger Siddall be stationed "where he may best be seen of the congregation." Scaffolding was subsequently raised to display Roger Byrne.[87] Penitents were only required to stand for the reading of the homily on adultery, but Edith Clark was told in 1560 to stay standing "all the time of the divine service."[88] Byrne stood only while the gospel was read, yet his ordeal had taken him through the streets of Chester the previous week— barefoot and wrapped in a white sheet. He had to walk to the marketplace, acknowledge his adultery there, pay to repair the steeple at St. Peter's in the city, drop more money in the poor box, own up to his adultery again in church, and "abstayne from the unlawfull companie of" his consort.[89] Courts excommunicated unrepentant adulterers; commissions had power to keep them in prison but rarely did. The few offenders who professed their innocence in the face of compelling contrary evidence, as did George Rather, might be marched into the market square by jailers to hear the wardens read the charges against them to a curious crowd.[90]

Public shaming ought to interest historians thinking of the laity, though they tend to concentrate on protest or riot, to be relatively unconcerned with the early modern mob as "an agency of order," and to consort with those ritual theorists who find crowd mystique more fascinating than crowd control.[91] But Elizabethan crowds did control delinquency, as Lawrence Stone

---

85. Ingram, *Church Courts*, 236.
86. BRO, EP/J/1/6, 348.
87. CRO, EDA/12/3, 18v–19r; EDA/12/4, 5r.
88. BRO, EP/J/1/5, 93.
89. CRO, EDA/12/3, 23v.
90. CRO, EDA/12/2, 113.
91. For help with the historiography, consult Mark Harrison, *Crowds and History: Mass Phenomena in English Towns, 1790–1835* (Cambridge: Cambridge University Press, 1988), 3–46.

now suggests; parishioners confronting adulterers in churches or in the market squares, he says, turned out to be "a powerful means of enforcing public standards of morality." The landed aristocrats, of course, persevered promiscuously and had the clout necessary to hold off, buy off, and write off censure, yet market crowds, congregations, and conscientious lay wardens seem to have unnerved and deterred middlers with reputations to make or maintain.[92]

It soon becomes clear that reformed parish regimes colonized much of what was left of late medieval parish administration. But to identify continuities is not to deny that wardens' leadership and "laudable discretion" during the 1560s anticipated, in some respects, what presbyterians envisioned in the 1570s: "a lawful and godly seigniory in every congregation."[93] But concentrating on continuities is less important, for our purpose, than trying to see what the early Elizabethan laity saw when it contemplated management strategies, that is, as it watched wardens work, year by year, to fix rates, collect rents, and catch rogues. It would have been noticed, for instance, when the churchwardens amicably served alongside pastors and deferred to diocesan authorities or ecclesiastical commissioners. Yet wardens would also, and often, have appeared to be local advocates of the laicization of parish government. And they demonstrated that middlers were neither as unmanagerial nor as unmanageable as Richard Bancroft, Matthew Sutcliffe, and Richard Hooker, among others later claimed. "Lewd," "low," "base," and "simple" not only fail to describe lay wardens accurately, as we have already remarked, but the epithets now seem also to misrepresent what most fellow parishioners thought of the lay managers, the results of whose work, according to Nick

---

92. Stone, *The Family, Sex, and Marriage: England, 1500–1800* (New York: Harper and Row, 1977), 144–47, yet Stone also writes there about "ineffectual" courts, "ineffectual," because "shame punishment" depended on culprits' voluntary compliance and on a demographic stability that was soon lost. Houlbrooke, *Church Courts,* 12–16; Marsh, *Popular Religion,* 111–12; and Diarmaid MacCulloch, *The Later Reformation in England, 1547–1603* (New York: St. Martin's, 1990), 141, offer less ambivalent remarks about the courts' "powerful means" and "consumer satisfaction." On aristocracy and adultery, note Richard Greaves, *Society and Religion in Elizabethan England* (Minneapolis: University of Minnesota Press, 1981), 229–36.

93. See *The Admonition Controversy,* ed. Donald Joseph McGinn (New Brunswick, N.J.: Rutgers University Press, 1949), 470, for "godly seigniory"; and Ingram, *Church Courts,* 46, 161–62, 328, for the wardens' "laudable discretion" and influence on religious conviction and identity formation.

Alldridge's studies of Chester, "gave back to laymen what they had lost by the suppression of the guilds and fraternities."[94]

Those results would be better remembered by historians had the preaching-obsessed puritans' obsession not eclipsed most of what went on around their sermons. John Whitgift said puritans wanted parishioners to hang on every word that they heard from the pulpit to the exclusion of all else, and the archbishop's charge stuck.[95] Emphasis on preaching—and historians' emphasis on that emphasis—have all but obscured the consensual character of prayerbook worship (and of parish life). Learning how wardens worked among the "giddy common people," however, has enabled us to repossess parts of that life and to discover what laymen, thinking of lay leadership, thought important and necessary, namely, solidarity and solvency. The parishioners and pastors alike trusted their lay churchwardens to achieve and preserve both.[96]

"Hot Troublesome Dissensions": John Jewel's "Simple People"

Expressions of such trust in commoners were not uncommon among reformers on the continent. Often, though, confidence in lay leadership and local control was offset by worries that the secession, known now as the reformation, would spawn additional partitioning, that secessions would splinter what there was of the Protestant consensus, if the laity had too much choice. It would have terribly unsettled reformed religion everywhere if a rupture with Rome seemed to preclude Protestants from ever again coming to terms with each other, if protest and schism looked to be contagious. One Calvinist emphatically, but not influentially, answered "no."

Jean Morely studied in Paris and Zurich, visited Wittenberg, then settled in Geneva in 1554. When Theodore Beza published his *Confession of the*

---

94. Alldridge, "Loyalty and Identity," 93–94, 117.

95. *Whitgift* 2:493.

96. John Craig, "Cooperation and Initiatives," 372–78; John Craig, "Reformation Politics and Polemics in Sixteenth-century East Anglian Market Towns" (Ph.D. diss., Cambridge University, 1992), 56–58; and Sharon Arnoult, "Spiritual and Sacred Public Actions: *The Book of Common Prayer* and the Understanding of Worship in the Elizabethan and Jacobean Church of England," in *Religion and the English People, 1500–1640: New Voices; New Perspectives*, ed. Eric Joseph Carlson (Kirksville, Mo.: Thomas Jefferson University Press, 1998), 32–39.

Christian Faith a few years later, Morely was likely among its more avid readers. He was acquainted with Beza and must have gathered that the *Confession*'s take on the polity implications of the priesthood of all believers would be widely read and well respected. From studying classical and Christian antiquity, Morely had already developed opinions about the best way to govern parishes, and from what we know of those opinions, we may assume that he was pleased when Beza held, in principle, that the laity should elect its pastors. Yet Beza disappointed Morely by calling it imprudent to institutionalize broad lay participation. The run-up to elections brought out the worst in commoners. The wicked exploited the weak; the fractious created factions. The principle, Beza concluded, was impractical. Morely disagreed. Into the 1560s, he may have been the only high-profile Protestant to think that reformed Christianity was ripe for direct democracy, to believe that troubles which ordinarily attend power-sharing were not to be feared because the recent reformation had assimilated all the faithful to God's will.[97]

Beza was unconvinced, as were clerical colleagues at the French synods that circulated catalogues of errors and forced concessions from Morely by 1566. The commoners' consent was good enough, he grudgingly allowed; instead of raising their hands or voices, reformed parishioners might "vote" by failing to object to a candidate.[98] Morely reconsidered again in 1572. He talked with reformers in Swansea when he came to England and was led to think an uncompromised version of his plan for democratic parish regimes might be hospitably received by the realm's bishops, but he was wrong. Had they not ignored him, he would certainly have been opposed as he was in France. For by the 1570s, authorities in England feared lay deliberation leading to votes on personnel or policy would prompt what Bishop Cox of Ely called "tumultuary conduct" and could destroy the peace of every parish.[99]

There is no sign that John Jewel, one of Cox's most prolific episcopal colleagues, took notice of Morely's visit or, for that matter, knew much, if anything, about Morely's controversially democratic notions during the 1560s. When Jewel returned from exile to become bishop of Salisbury, he occasionally glanced across the Channel, writing to friends in Zurich. More often, however, when he glared in that direction, he saw Rome and red. For

---

97. See Phillipe Denis and Jean Rott, *Jean Morely et l'utopie d'une democratie dans l'église* (Geneva: Droz, 1993), 149–50, 191–98.
98. *Synodicon in Gallia reformata*, vol. 1, ed. John Quick (London, 1692), 56–77.
99. ZL(ET), 180.

Jewel soon became the government's chief apologist for the reformed religious settlement. Queen and regime engaged him to dispute from pulpits and in print the Catholic assertion that religious order depended on "the blessed succession of the bishop of Rome," which, it turned out, provoked some of Jewel's best writing. The succession of offices, he said, was only an administrative convenience. Faith came "by hearing" and not by lining up with long-dead prelates in what the Catholics called an "apostolic succession." God's word, Jewel went on, could be heard by anyone who listened for it, cleric or commoner. Hence, priests in holy orders should make no exclusive claims to holiness and to religious truth. Quite the contrary, he insisted, popes, bishops, and priests were purveyors of a self-serving lie, the rancid idea that their restricted access to "the gift of God's truth" had been sound doctrine from the start.[100] They forgot to mention, Jewel said, that the first evangelists got their "gift" to give it to the commoners of Christian antiquity. He reproved Catholic clergy of his time for having given so little by comparison—and for having insisted that it be given in Latin, which left the uncomprehending "simple people" of the realm "drown[ing] in darkness."[101]

William Fulke, lecturing at Cambridge during most of Jewel's pontificate, echoed the bishop's sentiments. "Simple people" were all but excluded from worship—Latin prayers making it impossible "for the heart to thinke that which the tongue soundeth." For how could souls be consoled when, as petitioners, they repeated promises of repentance without being able to understand the words?[102] Jewel suspected a plot: because the commoners depended on clerical mediation all the more when the words of their prayers and word of God's unconditional love were kept from them. Jewel insisted that every "amen" ought to signal informed consent. No commoner need become a logician, though each should know enough to steer clear of the idolatry of the Catholic mass. Vernacular prayers enabled "simple people" to appeal "directly" through Christ to God. Routing appeals through Catholic priests and saints, he decreed, was unnecessary and unscriptural.[103]

The Catholic rejoinder, in effect, was that the warped minds of simple people were incapable of thinking straight and that the reformers misled

---

100. *Jewel,* 3:347–49.
101. *Jewel,* 2:778.
102. Fulke, *Text,* 296r.
103. *Jewel,* 1:524, 2:65, 92, 703–4.

them, trying to convince commoners that they had the intelligence and the right to define doctrine. Reformations, according to some of the realm's unreformed, made the profoundly ignorant proud rather than learned, dangerously independent, not deferential. Cuthbert Scot, Marian bishop of Chester, told of an English nobleman who believed Christ was present at communion but who refused to worship him there. That refusal, Scot claimed, was tantamount to treason. It was as if subjects who profess to honor their monarch dressed in fine robes (as the nobleman professed to honor Christ in glory) nonetheless declined to honor her when she wore a plain coat. Scot must have planned his analogy to impress the queen and regime, not just with lay illogic but also with the likely political repercussions of lay willfulness.[104]

He was deprived of his see and fell silent, but other Catholics escaped to the continent and made sure England heard more about the perils of lay ignorance and independence. Thomas Harding, Oxford professor of Greek before Elizabeth's accession, counseled that little truth could survive "all sorts of people" talking about the truths of their faith. He cited the Waldensians and sixteenth-century sectarians who started by reading the Bible in their vernaculars yet were soon redrafting Christian doctrines to reflect their strange ideas about poverty or sanctity. Harding noted that the sectarians ended by opposing all lawful authority. The lesson was not lost on Jewel who knew how easily people could be seduced. He stayed behind in Mary's England long enough to see them abandon reform and return to the Catholic mass. In 1559, on his return from the continent, however, he had agreed to expand the commoners' part in worship, put altars "in the midst of the people," and conspicuously reduce the distance and differences between priests and parishioners. Yet Jewel was never more the advocate of lay empowerment than when he rejected Harding's warning that it was "dangerous and hurtful" and patently not necessary to salvation to let laymen loose in and with their Bibles.[105]

Harding had not meant to keep all laymen from reading. He would have permitted those who knew Hebrew, Greek, or Latin to study sacred texts, for the educated were a cut above the "all sorts" who, he thought, were prone to heresy and living sordid lives—commoners who were uncontrollably

---

104. Bodl., Tanner MS. 302, 29r; *Jewel*, 2:550–52.
105. *Jewel*, 1:98; 2:689.

contentious. Jewel struck repeatedly at Harding's caricature. Had the church at Corinth kept its "all sorts" from communion, the apostle Paul would have been even angrier with the Corinthian authorities, Jewel conjectured, and his mission would have failed miserably. Had the fourth-century Church in Milan denied its "dangerously" contentious (and incontinent) laymen access to scriptures, the celebrated Augustine might never have been permitted to read his way to conversion.[106]

And were Harding's colleagues, learned exegetes all, that superior to Jewel's "simple people"? Visit Rome, Jewel slipped in, and one learns that intelligence keeps few prelates from sinking to deplorable depths of depravity.[107] But there, as elsewhere, commoners "reason of the . . . nature of mankind a great deal more skillfully than Plato or Aristotle." Jewel was exaggerating, of course, recycling the exaggerations of Jerome, Theodoret, and Chrysostom, who inflated lay competence in late antiquity. Applying their remarks to his century, Jewel dreamed into existence resourceful "tailors, smiths, or cloth-workers," in early modern Salisbury or London and "women who live by their labor, sewsters and maidservants [and] husbandmen and ditchers and herdmen" who "understand the principles of our religion" better than Harding's prelatical friends. Jewel declared that lay literacy and discretion exceeded all the estimates of the opposition; the "vulgar people and such [whom] M[r] Harding calleth swine and rude and rash people and curious busy-bodies were able not only to understand scriptures, but to judge of their preachers."[108]

Harding's "rude and rash people" were an unruly lot. The history of the Christian traditions taught him that commoners argued with their priests and with each other whenever biblical passages were presented as topics for discussion. Jewel replied that schism almost always originated with clerical elites, for "fantastical imaginations of opinions and sects pertain to the learned sort and nothing to the lay-people." He then amended "and nothing"; heresy's pull on the laity in the sixteenth century, as before, was as irresistible as gravity's, because Catholic clergy had not allowed laymen to read scripture, preferring to keep them ignorant and overly impressionable. The Catholics dreaded debate, he added, and dread made Harding a horrible his-

---

106. *Jewel,* 2:676.
107. *Jewel,* 2:685–86.
108. *Jewel,* 2:696, 4:796–97.

torian, unable to distinguish between controversies that crippled Christianity and those that were inconsequential or, as it happened, advantageous.

> But having this eloquence and skill so largely to amplify these small [sixteenth-century] quarrels of so little weight, what would [Harding] have been able to do if he had been in the primitive church and had seen all these hot troublesome dissensions that then were able to shake the world? What clouds might he then have cast to scorn at Christ and to bring his gospel out of credit? Doubtless, as he saith now, all these diversities spring only from Doctor Luther, so would he then have said all these former diversities and sundry forms of heresies sprang only from Christ. And hereof he would have concluded, as he doth now, that the rude and rash people should in no wise be suffered to read the scriptures.[109]

Jewel believed that the commoners of Christian antiquity read sacred literature from the time it was available. He figured that Augustine and other venerable early church authorities urged the laity to pore over and talk over canonical texts both at home and in church, expecting that the exercises might make "rude and rash" people less so.[110] With discussions came disagreements in which Peter and Paul, Paul and Barnabas, Cornelius and Cyprian, Jerome and Augustine, among others, proved that discord did not inevitably destroy discipline. The churches learned to reconcile differences and distinguish right from wrong applications of the good news they received. Jewel concluded, then, that Elizabethan commoners might read their Bibles to their hearts' content. They should participate in religious deliberations, he added, much as Christians participated at the early church councils, laymen who were welcomed by the apostles and, later, the bishops who valued their contributions: the first lay and clerical leaders of Christian antiquity knew from experience how often "simple people" judged "more uprightly" than the wise and worldly.[111]

---

109. *Jewel*, 2:687–88.

110. *Jewel*, 2:670, 3:86. Tessa Watt, *Cheap Print*, 329–30, explains that "peasant reading" was "intensive reading" in which the text was read and reread to aid memory rather than to acquire new information.

111. *Jewel*, 3:93, deferring to Cyprian on lay participation at church councils, and 4:897, on lay judgment.

When Jewel returned from exile, he may have hoped for broad lay participation in deliberations leading to the reform of the realm's churches. He said that he anticipated a more rapid, thorough reform than Elizabeth and Cecil had been prepared to sanction. Jewel waited, was named bishop of Salisbury in 1560, and served there until his death in 1571, embracing the aims of the religious and political establishments that embraced him. So when his evidence for popular participation in early Christians' councils displayed a cutting edge into the 1560s, he intended it to cut Catholic—and not English reformed—episcopal colleagues. When he conjured up commoners speaking articulately at a church conference, he was not proposing to open the meetings over which he and other diocesans and deans of their cathedral chapters had been presiding. He was imagining what right-minded laymen might contribute to the Council of Trent. He wrote tirelessly against the Catholic clerical bureaucracy but wrote nothing that can be construed as a call for the laicization of the reformed church. True, Jewel became more circumspect as time passed. He sensed that the laity was bewildered in the 1560s by the sudden and disorienting changes of the previous decade. He boasted to Harding of the good sense of their reformed countrymen: "the simplest may soon espy your doings," Jewel told him, all the while wary, though, that on his side of "soon," Harding might trip up such "simple unlearned people" and take them back.[112]

Jewel wanted to be sure the simplest could "espy" what Catholics were up to. The commoner who knew why Jericho was overthrown—why the old faith in England had been beaten—might more easily resist appeals for its restoration. Bishop Pilkington of Durham, Jewel's fellow exile while Mary reigned, concurred; he told the Earl of Leicester in 1564 that the differences between "papistry" and Protestantism must be made clearer in the 1560s than they had ever been. Yet Pilkington and Jewel acknowledged that complications attended this challenge. It would amount to more than careful catechesis. Too few pastors served too many parishioners who were mystified by the recent changes in religion and regime.[113] "For lack of instruction," commoners "know not whither to turn them," because "they know neither what they leave nor what they should receive." Indeed, Jewel knew there was no quick fix. His advice to friends on the episcopal bench

---

112. *Jewel*, 3:54, 3:102, 4:773.
113. BL, Lansdowne MS. 7, 212r.

was to "to build up the church of Christ" and to build from the second story down, that is, to recruit and retain competent resident apologists and place a persuasive preacher in every pulpit.[114]

Without that second story of energetic resident preachers, English commoners might easily be lured back to Catholicism. Or, what was equally serious, the laity might be drawn to impatient, imprudent ministers (*temere nimis*) who "rashly" pressed for the government's reform of the realm's churches to take a different course. And Bishop Horne of Winchester believed that the radical reformers, amplifying "the importunate clamors of the multitude," were likely to try to force the queen's new bishops to seize the bridge from her council and to steer the English church into one of the less promising channels cut by the Swiss reformers. Such mutiny, he said, would only "shipwreck" the English reformation. Queen and council should be coaxed, not coerced.[115]

Horne's prediction and counsel were often repeated, and the repetition enraged puritans who accused Elizabeth's first bishops of betraying reformed religion—of equivocation, procrastination, and collusion with conservatives at court. Patrick Collinson now seems more understanding: Horne, Pilkington, Jewel, and Grindal—maybe even Parker—were "amphibians," Collinson says; they were relatively thick-skinned prelates, "partaking of both official and unofficial reforms," working for both, for a time, without working against either.[116]

But Collinson's amphibians looked equally at sea, not equally at home, with puritan critics and at court. The bishops were not invited to join the queen's council in the 1560s. They were told what to do to discourage "diversitie, varietye, [and] singularitie" and not asked what needed doing.[117] Furthermore, Parker was unhappy with the regime's responses to his campaign for uniformity. Ostensibly to oblige the queen and council, he circulated rules for clerical attire, yet he found officials at court unappreciative and uncooperative. His clergy, by contrast, responded more demonstrably,

---

114. *Jewel,* 2:983–84, 1023–24.

115. *ZL,* 1:248–49.

116. Collinson, "The Elizabethan Church and the New Religion," in *The Reign of Elizabeth I,* ed. Christopher Haigh (Athens: University of Georgia Press, 1985), 177; and, for corroboration, consult David J. Crankshaw, "Preparations for the Canterbury Provincial Convocation of 1562–1563," in *Belief and Practice in Reformation England,* ed. Susan Wabuda and Caroline Litzenberger (Aldershot: Ashgate, 1998), 60–93.

117. BL, Lansdowne MS. 8, 12r.

particularly the reformed pastors who resented his efforts to end bishops' tolerance of "low-key nonconformity." Parker felt friendless whenever he crossed the Thames from Lambeth to London and Westminster precisely while he was making new enemies in the country. He explained to Elizabeth that the nonconformists rallying support for their resistance to his rules in 1566, were, in effect, "wounding" her subjects. The criticism of his regulations and of diocesan officials enforcing them could only lead to popular disaffection and episcopal despair.[118]

The critics claimed otherwise. They were dissatisfied with the church, they admitted, but not with the government. Queen and council could count on their allegiance, though they would not be treated as cadets, snapped to attention, to an unconditional or unquestioning obedience to their archbishop's new rules and to their bishops' orders to enforce them. Let diocesan officials reason with them, they urged, for they would listen to reason (*ratione persuaderi et instrui cupimus*). Yet they confided as well that they could not imagine anyone rationally, defensibly defining the differences between the Jewish customs that Jesus had repudiated and the residual Catholic customs and costumes that Parker and his suffragans had lately prescribed.[119]

Thomas Lever signed the critics' remonstrance. He was concerned that the laity could not distinguish between the "outward habits and inward feeling of popery": whatever bishops might say or mean, their retention of popish attire and rituals led people to expect a restoration of Rome's hold on the English churches. His informants told him that Catholics were playing to that expectation as early as 1560, promising that a reunion with Rome was just around the corner, so little of the Catholics' customs and costumes having changed then (and thereafter).[120]

Contests between Catholics and English Calvinists continued through the 1560s and beyond. Both sides said they were thinking of the laity, and the claims can be verified easily. To Catholics and Calvinists alike, each commoner was territory to be fortified and fought over. Jewel's "Jericho" would have to be overthrown, parishioner by parishioner, reformers estimated, and

---

118. *Correspondence,* 284; and for "low-key nonconformity," see M. E. Perrot, "Richard Hooker and the Problem of Authority in the Elizabethan Church," *JEH* 49 (1998): 33. For Parker's troubles at court, see Jones, *Birth,* 63–64.

119. LPL, MS. 2019, 1v–2r.

120. *ZL,* 1:84–85.

its ruins scattered so there could be no rebuilding, no Roman Catholic reconquest. For their part, Calvinist nonconformists urged their bishops to be more responsible and less respectful of the old ways and wardrobe, particularly of the "popish" "garments dedicated to idolatry."[121]

One "Grief" complained "rudelye yet trulye" that John Jewel approved the "implements and trappinges of Antichriste," that he was leading England back to Rome or—equally as fiendish—idling while reformed yet conformist Christians "contented themselves with a corrupt manner of the service of God." The aggrieved let on that they had been present at ordinations where Jewel and his episcopal colleagues borrowed Catholic benedictions and exhorted new priests to "receive the Holy Spirit" as if only the ordained were so inspired or "graced." Bishops, it seemed, wished to preserve the chasm between commoners and clerics. Officials' wardrobes and words, the "Grief" asserted, perpetuated a lay servitude to the clergy and offended all "Christian eyes and ears."[122]

Into the 1560s, conformists and nonconformists vigilantly attended to those eyes and ears, wanting to control the laity's views of clerical reality. They fretted about commoners who "know not whither to turn them," as Jewel said, and who could be turned back to Rome, into schism and sects, or around in circles. Jewel and other moderate reformers among the realm's new bishops were miles from Morely. They had not advocated broadly participatory parish regimes. The prospects for a more rapid reform of polity, which was dear to them, were bleak. Nonconformists accused them of selling out the reforms that they once thought possible. No wonder, then, that they appeared irritable to friends.[123] Only Pilkington of Durham was ready to appease outspoken critics of "popyshe apparrell" and of Parker's efforts to lace up the unwanted vestments. Apparel was very much beside the point, Pilkington noted; the war over what to wear would have been eminently forgettable, a teapot tempest, were it not for the spectacle of the puritans and Parker exchanging insults. The rancor "rejoyceth the adversaryes" of reformed religion. Why should Catholics in the realm and abroad not rejoice when the queen's new bishops thought it necessary, Pilkington said, to "stop the mouths of so many grave, learned, and godly zealous preachers"?[124]

---

121. "Articles, letters, and examinations of Maister Robert Johnson," in *Register*, 116.
122. Bodl., Selden Supra MS. 44, 48v–49v, 52r.
123. *ZL*, 2:151 (*animi exacerbati*).
124. BL, Additional MS. 48064, 173v–74r.

This personnel problem seemed so intractable. Even Parker thought it tragic to "stop the mouths of" "so many worthye men" when there was such a "scarcytie of teachers" in the realm. Yet Pilkington, Parker, and their associates were obliged to strive for religious uniformity. Elizabeth expected it, and they could not risk disappointing her. She was a "godly captaine," supreme governor of the church. Preachers who advocated "diversitie and varietye" displeased her; hence they displeased her lieutenants and had to be disciplined and, if obstinate, deprived. Bishops occasionally winked at nonconformity, but it was impossible to overlook the most incorrigible pastors' insistence that they had the right to pick and choose which prayerbook prescriptions were worth observing. Moreover, the refusals to subscribe to Parker's rules at mid-decade alerted all bishops that the church's "second story" was as likely to alienate as to educate the laity. Indeed, the nonconformists' most persuasive and virulent preachers could, if they desired, keep tenants below from thinking well of the executives above.

The bishops were besieged. Jewel probably disclosed more about the predicament than he knew when he wrote to friends in Zurich of the lack of goodwill. *[Q]uisque in sua specula,* each bishop in his turret or watchtower presided apart from the others and from "the simple people." Yet the altitude from which bishops looked over their clergy and looked after lay education strangely suggests a bunker mentality.[125] To be sure, parish accounts prove that wardens dutifully bought copies of Parker's rules and bishops' visitation articles. And wardens usually passed along to diocesan courts the congregations' complaints about clerical nonconformity. But dissidents deprived of their pulpits frequently resurfaced as lecturers or deputy curates in other parishes. They were not easily detected and silenced. Some parishes preferred them. Parishioners at St. Margaret Pattens in London pensioned a pastor to make room for Nicholas Standen, who, with John Field and Thomas Wilcox, organized clerical resistance in the city and dared counsel all diocesans to "come to a better frame of mind," readmit conscientious clerical objectors to their livings, and remedy the "scarcytie" in the kingdom by taking back suspended clerical colleagues and by appointing to the ministry laymen "suited to it."[126]

---

125. *ZL*, 1:40.

126. Peel, 2:70. For Standen at St. Margaret's, see H. Gareth Owen, "The London Parish Clergy in the Reign of Elizabeth I," (Ph.D. diss., University of London, 1957), 483–84.

Nonconformists were as interested in staffing as were the bishops who opposed them. Thinking of the laity, the dissidents insisted that commoners were still too "rude and rash" into the 1560s to do much good without close clerical supervision. Their understanding of reformed religion was as yet imperfect. Indeed, reformed pastors were right, according to nonconformists among them, to be more concerned with lay gullibility than with lay government. And they would be right as well to object to Parker's commending "garments dedicated to idolatry" because that "popyshe apparrell" bedazzled ordinary people who were still too "simple" and "unlearned" to know that clothes did not make a Catholic.

Into the 1560s, diocesan officials and dissidents proceeded cautiously, as did the government. Bishop Jewel argued for lay literacy; clerical nonconformists said that commoners might be "suited to" ministry; middlers continued to manage the parish, documenting, if not asserting, lay authority and local control. Many of the ingredients for a populist initiative were within reach, but not the recipe for a broadly participatory parish regime; Morely's was lost. Yet things would soon change.

FOUR

Populist Initiatives and Government Reaction

Into the 1570s

✚

At issue, into the 1570s, were the first Christians' polities and practices. Were they democratic? Frequently or seldom so? And were they at all relevant to the reformed churches in England? The partisans of participatory parish regimes—Thomas Lever, William Fulke, John Field, and others—contended that the apostles had favored local autonomy and lay authority. "That old and true election . . . by the congregation," they added, "ought to stand" in the sixteenth century. Their critics disagreed.

The critics, that is, challenged both the idyllic scenes of lay participation its partisans sketched from scripture and from other early Christian literature as well as the political wisdom of empowering commoners in the 1560s and early 1570s. For those were treacherous times. Anxiety was as yet unrelieved. Elizabeth's "alteracion" did not yet seem irreversible. Government and diocesan officials suspected that conformist behavior, such as it was, disguised subversive opinion, both Catholic convictions and radically re-formist views. It was only prudent, therefore, to prefer peace to broad lay participation, and nothing demonstrated that preference into the 1570s better than the suppression of prophesying.

Prophecies were market-day sermons and conferences meant to im-prove the quality of clerical exegesis and preaching. Commoners apparently had been getting involved in the discussions, possibly commenting on doc-trine and discipline or, at the very least, comparing clerical comments and choosing favorite preachers. Prophecies or "exercises," as they were also called, had much to recommend them. Poorly educated pastors learned from intelligent and seasoned colleagues. People in poorer parishes, coming to market, had opportunities to hear some of their region's best preaching. But impressionable and "changeable people" could also get "carried away" when radical and impatient preachers directed "ill words" at conformists and com-plained of the pace of reform.

The government feared as much. In 1576 Grindal, archbishop of Can-terbury, tried to save the exercises, promising to cork the radicals and con-trol the crowds. But the regime and some of his own suffragans doubted that he had the cleverness to do so—and perhaps the will as well. The govern-ment ordered the "exercises and prophesinge, used as well by the laie and unlearned people," discontinued. Prophecies seemed to queen and regime more circus than solemn. Yet, to partisans of prophesying and advocates of lay participation, government officials supporting suppression and especially the bishops enforcing it appeared to want their commoners to be "as dumb asses [that] saye never a word." They, the authorities, seemed to prefer a "papal hush" to reformed conversation. But, said the advocates, to silence the laity was unscriptural, demeaning, and demoralizing, and discussion among the simple people—even some discord—was "necessarie" if their reformed religious truths were to be sifted and take hold.

"That Old and True Election . . . by the Congregation"

In 1567, when Bishop Grindal of London suspended several of the city's pas-tors for refusing to wear prescribed vestments and to conform to other prac-tices of the realm's re-reformed church, more than a hundred commoners rented the Plumbers' Hall and assembled there to worship without benefit of authorized clergy. They explained their *de facto* declaration of independence to the commissioners appointed to investigate, mentioning that they had consulted the Bible and found nothing to persuade them to accept the prayerbook prescriptions their suspended pastors criticized. Commoners at Plumbers' Hall objected to kneeling and crossing in the book's liturgy. They complained of the continued use of some clerical vestments, which, along with the objectionable gestures, seemed to them more Roman than right. They hoped to worship as the first Christians did and wanted to implement "a discipline according to the word of God." One commissioner asked how they expected to determine what was "according to the word of God" without theological training. Robert Hawkin and William White answered for their friends. Laymen were capable of comprehending scripture, they said, citing biblical study in "the best reformed churches" among the Scots and Swiss. Hawkin and White pointed out that England was flanked by notably well-informed reformers who believed their respective commoners were discerning and capable company. And the two from Plumbers' Hall added that, by contrast, the commissioner's question and condescension seemed as smug as the complaints of Catholics who presumed only one church, their church, should "judge" the word of God.[1]

Grindal, however, knew smugness when he saw it, and, for arrogance, he said, none surpassed Hawkin and White: "I never saw any behave themselves so unreverently." The bishop reminded those two and their constituents at the Hall that Bullinger of Zurich, who presided over one of the "best reformed churches," once counseled Christians in England to be "conformable" and submit to their bishops, "for order and obedience sake." The Plumber's Hall congregation was patently and inexcusably *dis*obedient; Hawkin and White were shamelessly defiant at what was meant to be an inquiry into their concerns and competence. Grindal had nothing to add to that inquiry's findings: the dissidents "made assemblies, using prayers and preachings, yea ministering of sacraments," and the congregation's spokesmen all but espoused disorder, insolently defending the indefensible and intolerable, lay and local self-determination.[2]

Truth be told, though, Grindal would have known that certain parishes had acquired a degree of self-determination and defended it successfully against episcopal protests. The courts recognized that exemptions from

---

1. *Remains,* 214.
2. *Remains,* 202, 207.

episcopal oversight, which certain religious foundations enjoyed for centuries, had been transferred at their dissolution to clerical and lay patrons willing to pay for them. The government further acknowledged that those patrons or their heirs might legitimately donate their rights to congregations, which thereafter might select stipendiary curates. The lay assertiveness of such "donative curacies" seems antibureaucratic, if *anti* anything, but not anticlerical, although the privilege and local autonomy hardly endeared those curacies to clerical conservatives. "A benefice donative," Richard Cosin said contemptuously, was "a mere lay thing."³

Six of twelve parishes in Ipswich were donative curacies, and magistrates there appointed a separate minister to oversee municipal preaching and pastoral care. At St. Andrew's, Norwich, parishioners selected their pastors. In Tewkesbury, the borough officials purchased the town's abbey church and had the wardens report directly to bailiffs. Elsewhere, the borough officials were busy as well, particularly after King Edward VI dissolved chantries and confraternities. The officials bid for confiscated lands, tenements, and endowments and bought up the rights to present candidates to local livings. Some proprietary urban corporations apparently got and exercised more power over their preachers than lay elites ever had. City fathers had more control over the choice and conduct of pastors, that is, than parish elites formerly had over guild chaplains and chantry priests.⁴

At Bury St. Edmund's, magistrates in league with other parishioners appointed nonconformists as pastors of the town's two parish churches. When opposition to those incumbents mounted, into the 1570s, municipal

---

3. See Richard Cosin, *An apologie of and for sundrie proceedings by jurisdiction ecclesiastical* (London, 1591), 39; and the lectures John Doderidge delivered at New Inne, 1602 and 1603, and published as *A compleat parson or a description of advowsons* (London, 1641), especially 2–3, 11, 62–63.

4. Patrick Carter, "Economic Problems of Provincial Urban Clergy during the Reformation," in *Reformation in English Towns*, 147–58; Tittler, *Reformation*, 133–34; and, for "more inclusive administrative control" over late medieval municipal parishes, Dietrich Kurze, *Pfarrerwahlen im Mittelalter* (Cologne: Böhlau, 1966), 442–50. For the abbey church in Tewkesbury, *Tewkesbury Churchwardens' Accounts*, ed. Caroline Litzenberger (Stroud: Bristol and Gloucestershire Archaeological Society, 1994). For donative curacies in Ipswich, see Diarmaid MacCulloch and John Blatchley, "Pastoral Provision in the Parishes of Tudor Ipswich," *Sixteenth-Century Journal* 22 (1991): 472–73. For St. Andrew's parish in Norwich, Kenneth Shipps, "Lay Patronage of East Anglian Puritan Clerics, Pre-revolutionary England" (Ph.D. diss., Yale University, 1971), 267–68; and Patrick Collinson, *Elizabethan Puritan Movement* (Berkeley: University of California Press, 1967), 341–43.

officials turned for counsel to nearby Cambridge.[5] Delegates there to discuss the legitimacy of lay initiative with the likes of Laurence Chaderton or William Fulke, valued members of their respective colleges and soon to be college heads, must have heard of—and might have heard—the lively university debates about the localization and laicization of parish administration. The provocation was a set of lectures on the Acts of the Apostles that Thomas Cartwright delivered soon after being appointed Lady Margaret Professor of Divinity. During the 1560s, along with Fulke, he spoke against the surplice. Early in the 1570s, he claimed the first Christian missionaries had sanctioned local autonomy, broad lay participation, and lay leadership.[6]

His lectures are lost. John Whitgift, master of Trinity College and vice-chancellor of the university, responded to them. Cartwright then responded to the response. The pamphlet punch-up went several rounds and lasted nearly seven years, concentrating after 1572 on the alternative strategies for church management developed in two *Admonitions* to parliament, about which we will shortly have more to say. For now, it is important to remain at Cambridge, to learn what Cartwright and Whitgift can teach us about polity disagreements.

Cartwright's lost lectures no doubt stressed the importance of biblical and early church models. Protestants had by then been known for two generations to presume that what once was ought yet to be. Christians' first councils, for example, seemed exemplary, though Thomas Godwyn put reformers on notice that councils often failed to constitute a unified witness. The rulings of one could contradict those of others. To the argument that councils showed that early churches determined what a sacred text

---

5. Craig, "Reformation Politics," 81–104; Diarmaid MacCulloch, "Catholic and Puritan in Elizabethan Suffolk," *ARG* 72 (1981): 269–72.

6. See John S. Coolidge, *The Pauline Renaissance in England: Puritanism and the Bible* (Oxford: Clarendon, 1970), especially 69–76, for useful comments on puritan "primitivism" and biblical literalism. Also consult Diarmaid MacCulloch, "The Change of Religion," in *Sixteenth Century, 1485–1603*, ed. Patrick Collinson (Oxford: Oxford University Press, 2002), 105, which refers to arguments that claim to identify "God's *jure divino* plan" for parish polity as the presbyterian "game." Cartwright and others playing that "game" were indeed men "from relatively humble backgrounds" and "educated above their station." As their conformist colleagues adopted aristocratic values, "manipulating the language and moral sensibilities" of a society they suspected and perhaps despised, Cartwright, Fulke, and a few others, Peter Lake now says, were thinking about the laity more adventurously; see Peter Lake and Michael Questier, *The Antichrist's Lewd Hat: Protestants, Papists, and Players in Post-Reformation England* (New Haven, Conn.: Yale University Press, 2002), 590–91.

meant and how it might apply to circumstance, Godwyn replied emphatically that such determinations and applications hardly amounted to "sovereignty over scripture." Besides, he continued, the first Christians, unlike their partially reformed sixteenth-century descendants, were "plentifullie endued with the spirite of God."[7] Cartwright's pamphlets continually referred to the earliest churches, as he would have done while lecturing on Acts. Those congregations, he trusted, consulted with the itinerant apostles who designated local leaders. How unapostolic and how unwise, then, for Elizabeth's bishops to think so little of the local laity and think so well of their own powers of discernment to make appointments without checking parish opinion and without building a congregational consensus. The bishops acted as though they possessed "all the gifts needful," insight and foresight to match pastors with parishes perfectly. Whitgift, slightly missing the point, objected that the earliest Christians had not actually elected their pastors. When the apostles thought it "convenient" to ask the laity to endorse nominees, they simply did so to avoid any suspicion of favoritism and bias; no "general rule" followed, according to Whitgift. But Cartwright generalized with abandon: "the examples of all the apostles in all the churches and in all purer times," he insisted, argued incontrovertibly for local and lay discretion. The practices of seeking congregational consent and awaiting it "ought to stand."[8]

Whitgift answered, recycling the customary doubts about lay discretion: "tumult, disorder, [and] confusion" follow whenever parishioners assemble to discuss parish leadership. Jean Morely, confronted with observations like Whitgift's in 1562, responded that huge crowds had gathered without incident to hear and discuss the sermons of Chrysostom and other celebrated preachers of Christian antiquity. But Cartwright took a different tack, and, like Morely later in the 1560s, he did not insist on the finality of parish elections. He allowed that a panel of presbyters (lay elders) might set aside the election results without reconvening the congregation. Yet Cartwright added, as if he had immediately repented the provision, that, notwithstanding the presbyters' power to set aside or override, the parishioners' counsel and consent should always be sought and could be had, he con-

---

7. CCCC, MS. 340, 171–72.

8. Donald J. McGinn excerpted and organized topically the exchanges between Whitgift and Cartwright in *The Admonition Controversy*. For this example, see 445–46, but also consult *Whitgift*, 1:296–300.

tinued, during an "ordinary meeting for the service of God and without any of those things which [Whitgift] imagineth."[9]

To seek congregational consent was to accept and respect the liberty Christ left all Christians and to show that the Christian faith generated "a new understanding," as the apostle said that it should (Romans 12:2–3). Cartwright, asserting as much, was implying that reformed Christians could also show what had gone wrong with unreformed Christianity. They, and not their Catholic or conformist critics, would thereby demonstrate how to draw proper polity implications from their new understanding. It was essential, therefore, that reformed parishioners not forego deliberations even when the candidates for their pulpits were unimpeachable. Interrogations were indispensable all the same. Parish presbyters should offer candidates "to the examination," if only to signal to would-be pastors and parishioners alike that everyone's belief and behavior were "in the compass of the church to judge of."[10]

Cartwright was driven from Cambridge for "oughts" of this sort. Whitgift left to become bishop of Worcester. The issues that had them quarreling, however, continued to be debated at the university. In 1573 William Redman, fellow of Trinity College and later bishop of Norwich, proceeded on "the grounds very learnedly set down by Mr. John Whitgift," Henry Howard wrote William Cecil, enclosing a synopsis of the "proceedings," which puts Fulke and his arguments in an unfavorable light. But Howard's precis also suggests Redman tended to split hairs once he set to work on an aphorism Fulke introduced into the debate: *quod omnes tangit ab omnibus debet*, "whatever matters to all ought to be decided by all." Fulke was quoting Pope Leo I, who had countenanced popular participation in fifth-century episcopal elections. Fulke found that remark tremendously useful, although he hardly admired the source. Still, the pope's statement meant to him that important issues were to be resolved by parishioners, voting publicly, rather than by remote or resident clerical officials. Redman enlightened him. Leo I's statement signified something quite different, he said, explaining that the need to consult or to reach consensus had applied only when the matters at hand were important to commoners as individuals, *ad singulos*.

---

9. Compare Cartwright's comments, *Admonition*, 455, with those of Morely in his *Traicte de la police et discipline chrestienne* (Lyon, 1562), 33–34, 112–13. Also see *Whitgift*, 1:455.

10. *Admonition*, 421–23.

Any matter important to everyone as a congregation or collective, *quasi ad universos,* had been in the first and fifth centuries, and ought to be in sixteenth-century England, determined by the clergy, without lay participation.[11]

A series of objections and responses apparently related to another university conversation shows Redman's colleagues trying to prove that the venerable bishops of Christian antiquity ruled their churches as collectives, to prove, that is, that bishops never paused to fashion consensus or even to sift parishioners' opinions. One critic of broader lay participation insisted that to have consulted the laity would have been to have disobeyed a direct order from the apostle Paul to make arrangements for, not to discuss arrangements with, the churches in Crete.[12]

Yet there was no denying that Paul, Timothy, Titus, and many other early Christian leaders summoned parishioners for something other than worship. The New Testament supplied examples, not the specifics. But critics of broad lay participation warned against making too much of the summonses and the meetings that resulted. The Jews and early Christians had not gathered to speak and be heard but to listen and be reprimanded (*non esse consultum sed admonitum et reprehensum*). The authorities rebuked sinners "in the presence of all," who were rather like props, put on notice by the public scolding. The wicked were publicly humiliated "so the rest may stand in fear." Deliberations as well as discipline were staged for lay edification, staged *coram omnibus* but not *ab omnibus,* in the presence of the "plebes" yet without inviting or welcoming their participation. True, the commoners of Christian antiquity came to the conference or council, held in Jerusalem, as reported in the New Testament's Acts of the Apostles, but only the odd leveler dared to propose that laymen were able to discuss the necessity of circumcision or the nature of Christian mission with panels of apostles and other church authorities. Yet at adjournment, according to Acts (15:22), "it seemed good to the apostles and elders with the whole church to choose men from among them and to send them to Antioch with Paul and Barnabas." It did not seem nearly as good to Whitgift and Redman, along with the other Cambridge critics of lay participation.[13]

11. BL, Cotton Titus MS. C VI, 19v, 22r. For a discussion of several of Fulke's sources, consult Françoise Ganshof, "Note sur l'election des evêques dans l'empire romain au IVᵉ et pendant la première moitie du Vᵉ siècle," *Revue internationale des droits de l'antiquité* 4 (1950): 485–87.

12. Bodl., Selden Supra MS. 44, 75r–76r, citing Titus 1:5.

13. Bodl., Selden Supra MS. 44, 67, 69v–70v.

The Cambridge critics had to admit the occasional involvement of "the whole church," though Redman insisted that congregational participation was incidental in the first century and could be eliminated in the sixteenth "without offense." What would the women of his time think if they were asked to wash the feet of church officials simply because the women of the first century washed the apostles' feet?[14] Everything described in the Bible was not prescribed. Scriptures reported the situational as well as the standard. Perhaps the first missionaries thought that it was convenient at times to invite parishioners' participation to assure compliance by airing and publicly overcoming dissent. But Redman, stating the obvious and laying the last stone, specified that compliance in Tudor England was assured by the queen as the supreme governor and by her Christian magistrates, so Fulke need not bother with counsel or consent. *Nihil a plebe*; nothing remained for the commoners to do, but obey.[15]

In 1573 Andrew Perne, long-time master of Peterhouse, joined the chorus against lay participation in parish elections. During the 1560s, he successfully objected to the involvement of junior fellows in a college election, preferring and preserving "the quietness and commoditie" of his college, he claimed, from the opinions of its young scholars.[16] Plenty of preferences for quiet were expressed in other discussions of parish discipline. Whitgift, Redman, and Perne doubted that parishioners' voices had much to contribute to good government. Critics of broad participation argued that commoners were incapable of orderly deliberations and lasting agreements; it seemed unlikely they could agree among themselves (and less likely that they would agree with their leaders). Ballots begot brawls; *ex suffragis rixae tumultus*. Laymen were so insatiable, advised Redman and Perne, that the slightest effort to consult them in the selection of their pastors "inflamed [their] cupidity" and ended with their discontent, factions, tyrannies, and ruin. There had never been, nor would there ever be, much careful, politically refined, and disinterested thinking from the laity. One would have to be mad to suppose the base would ever elect the best.[17]

But it was known to have happened. God worked wonders, as when Ambrose was elected bishop of Milan in the fourth century. Partisans of the

---

14. BL, Cotton Titus MS. C VI, 22r.
15. BL, Cotton Titus MS. C VI, 20v.
16. BL, Lansdowne MS. 7, 161r.
17. Bodl., Selden Supra MS. 44, 76v; and BL, Cotton Titus MS. C VI, 21v.

declared candidates at the time had threatened to disrupt deliberations in the city basilica, so Ambrose, then provincial governor, arrived to assure order. But the crowd, on hearing a child's voice designate the politician-peacekeeper as the next bishop, forced him to accept the office. The partisans of local control and broad lay participation might have referred to this episode and used it as a precedent for parish elections; or perhaps their Cambridge critics only anticipated they would. In any event, those critics (pre-emptively?) let it be known that the Milanese had bungled the business, electing their man before the local clergy had an opportunity to baptize him and admit him to holy orders.[18]

The critics avoided blaming Ambrose. He was, after all, an icon of episcopal authority. Cyprian, a third-century bishop of Carthage, was an easier target, though less dependably autocratic than the legendary bishop of Milan. Cyprian had explicitly urged parishioners to examine candidates for the ministry and to voice or vote their consent. He volunteered that the rituals of public examination and acclamation expressed God's will—*vox populi, vox dei*. Elizabethan critics of participatory parish regimes admitted Cyprian's suggestion seemed to endorse lay involvement, but they also argued that *assensum* and *suffragia*, acclamation and choice, were distinguishable. Cyprian wanted the parishioners to inquire about a candidate's talents and virtues, yet after interrogation, they were obliged either to consent or protest. They had no right (and chance) to propose alternates—alternatives to the candidate or to the procedures. Yes, the councils of Carthage over which Cyprian presided used the term *electio* in their canons: *Sine plebis electione non potest assumi titulus epsicopi ergo plebis electio est necessaria*. But "election" then meant acclamation. Hence, Redman could go on to declare that Tudor practice into the 1570s corresponded quite well with what Cyprian and his colleagues commended, for when the appointments were announced in an Elizabethan parish, the silence signaled there were no objections. The silence was tantamount to acclamation or congregational consent, Redman held, transforming a likely embarrassment into a lovely precedent. But Perne took a different approach. He held that Cyprian's councils of Carthage were provincial synods; so, even had they countenanced what the partisans of broad popular participation could call elections, the edicts that resulted imposed

---

18. Bodl., Selden Supra MS. 44, 76v. For historical considerations and historiographical reflections, see Kaufman, "Diehard Homoians and the Election of Ambrose," *Journal of Early Christian Literature* 5 (1997): 421–50.

no necessity on the European churches of the time or on reformed churches of Perne's time. Advocates of consent and participation were bold, resourceful, yet foolish, citing a regional irregularity as though it might pass as a rule.[19]

William Fulke was not troubled by regional specificity. An election anywhere in Christian antiquity proved to him that the church's venerable "fathers" once tolerated variation and broadly participatory practices. They would not have done so, he argued, had they known that commoners' participation displeased God. And, he went on, who in the reformed churches of the sixteenth century could claim to be in a better position than the trustworthy, tolerant officials of the first to know God's pleasure? Fulke scolded the opposition for doubting the apostles' judgment and for explaining away scriptural passages and Cyprian's purposes, both of which let the laity make significant choices about leadership.[20]

Fulke was "frivolous," Henry Howard reported, counting Redman and Perne among those "wise men" at Cambridge who had contempt for "playne democratia." Even if a case could be made that the apostles let commoners elect pastors, "wise men" would forbid it, Howard said, noting Fulke was driven by a "desire of innovating" rather than by any creditable "zeal to further or advance religion."[21]

Nonconformists were similarly accused during the 1560s and early 1570s. Critics said they were indifferent to the progress of reform. Their innovations or experiments could not "advance" Protestantism; they discredited it. Thomas Lever wrote several "notes for some reformacyon of the ministrye" to declare that progress would depend on lay participation in parish elections. Lay proprietors tended to place their friends and favorites in pulpits. Diocesan officials looked the other way, not wanting to anger the affluent and influential, Lever went on, so the better check and balance was lay and local oversight, if not the direct congregational selection and pulpit supply. He proposed that the parishes could be spared irresponsible incumbents, the effects of irresponsible and unresponsive patrons, if parishioners could, at the very least, veto obviously unsatisfactory nominees.[22]

---

19. BL, Cotton Titus MS. C VI, 20v. For Cyprian, acclamation, and the councils of Carthage, see Jakob Speigl, "Cyprian über das *judicium Dei* bei der Bischofseinsetzung," *Romische Quartalschrift für christliche Altertumskunde und Kirchengeschichte* 69 (1974): 37–41.

20. BL, Cotton Titus MS. C VI, 21v–22r.

21. BL, Cotton Titus MS. C VI, 19v.

22. London, Inner Temple, Petyt MS. 538/38, 71r.

Lever left his "notes" unfinished and undated. We cannot tell exactly how they fit with Fulke's proposals, yet the idea that parishioners should interrogate and approve their would-be pastors looks to have been catching on. *The holie discipline of the church,* circulating among presbyterians in 1573, required that candidates serve parishes for some months, a period of probation that should culminate with a public examination. A rationale for both probation and examination was articulated the year before by the second of two *Admonitions* to parliament, which optimistically anticipated the time when protocols would assure that laymen "may be acquainted with [the would-be incumbent's] gifts and behaviour and geve their consentes for his stay amongste them."[23]

The first *Admonition* made a more comprehensive case for the commoners' "consentes." It was drafted by Thomas Wilcox and John Field after their allies in parliament failed to persuade queen and council to prohibit kneeling at communion and the clerical use of the surplice. The proposals to prohibit died on Cecil's desk in 1571.[24] The council then directed its ecclesiastical commissioners to withold licenses to preach from nonconformists, some of whom said subsequently that the government's attempts to extort conformity stirred the very resentment and resistance the commissioners were told to contain.[25]

Field and Wilcox proved the point. They went on the attack, posting several targets—"advowsons, patronages, impropriations, and bishoppes' authoritie." The objective was to "bryng in that old and true election, which was accustomed to be made by the congregation." They averred that, without broad participation, placement resembled an auction of sorts: each aspiring pastor could "picketh out for himself some good benefice . . . and obtaineth that next advouson by money or by favour and so thinketh hym-

23. W. H. Frere and C. E. Douglas, eds., *Puritan Manifestoes* (New York: Franklin, 1954), 96–97. The second admonition often, yet contestably, is attributed to Thomas Cartwright (see, for example, A. F. Scott Pearson, *Thomas Cartwright and Elizabethan Puritanism* [Cambridge: Cambridge University Press, 1925], 73–74). For the probation and examination prescribed by *The holie discipline,* see Oxford, Queen's College MS. 280, 164r.

24. Geoffrey R. Elton, *The Parliament of England, 1559–1581* (Cambridge: Cambridge University Press, 1986), 207–9; Thomas Freeman, "The Reformation of the Church in this Parliament: Thomas Norton, John Foxe, and the Parliament of 1571," *Parliamentary History* 16 (1997): 131–47; and Michael A. R. Graves, *Thomas Norton, the Parliament Man* (Oxford: Blackwell, 1994), 191–95.

25. BL, Additional MS. 28571, 74v–75r.

self to be sufficiently chosen." Compare such "unlawful sutes" with early Christians' practices: "now every one picketh out for himself [though] *then* election was made by common consent of the whole church." *Then*, congregations "had authoritie to cal" and cull their ministers. Field and Wilcox were sure that "*then*, no minister [was] placed in any congregation but by the consent of the people."[26]

The opposition denied what Fulke, Field, and Wilcox were making of the first and fourteenth chapters of the Acts of the Apostles, the basis for their *then*s. Nothing was written there, the critics said, that suggested elections in the first century had been routine rather than rare. Moreover, they challenged the *Admonition*'s assumption that sixteenth-century commoners were as ready and able to recognize and elect worthy candidates as advocates of broad participation willed them to be. Critics alleged that, in both policing and polling, the ordinary parishioner's impartiality and intelligence were suspect, at best. Could proles dispassionately weigh a neighbor's sins when that weighing brought their own sins to mind? And could they be severe and effective judges when, as sinners, they hoped others might spare them? Would they be strong enough to be stern, when they knew that reprisals were possible? And how long, if at all, if they had power over their pastors, would parishioners put up with clergy who censured to correct them and refused to credit their excuses? The critics of lay participation needed no field research to compose answers to such questions. They argued that giving power to the people would be a gigantic mistake.[27]

John Barstow, lay political analyst, thought the problem was one of "training up" an electorate. Nothing could be accomplished beyond recall without commoners' consent, he admitted, yet he was skeptical that commoners could ever learn to value and selflessly fulfill a citizen's duty. Barstow's *Safegarde of society* recycled an ancient remedy in 1576. He learned that the ancient Egyptians annually required subjects to "give a straight accompt of howe they lived." Officials then reviewed the accounts and executed all who had lived wickedly or lied. Hence, "training up" their "commonaltie" amounted to paring it down.[28] The Elizabethans apparently showed no enthusiasm for "training" or winnowing an electorate with Barstow's

---

26. *Manifestoes*, 36 (emphasis added).
27. Bodl., Selden Supra MS. 44, 67r, 71v.
28. John Barstow, *The safegarde of society* (London, 1576), 79v–80r, 88r, 107v–8r, 110r.

blade. It was not only that Egyptian measures seemed extreme and bloody, but also that the reformed partisans of broad lay participation trusted God to "train" or prepare the laity for parish elections and administration. They believed, as, in theory, all English Calvinists did, that God's covenant with Christians was both absolute and conditional. But the advocates of local control and lay authority added a twist: the faithful would be saved, they said, on the condition that they fashion and maintain a polity that proved God's faith in each member's morality was not misplaced. Only then might reformed Christians hold up their end of the bargain for salvation. They agreed with Barstow: the faithful should be "trained up," but they figured God could be counted on to do the training. The covenant, therefore, could be called absolute, for its completion (lay training and lay management) depended on the deity's "all-sufficiency." What God wanted and required, God provided. God wanted the late Tudor laity to participate in parish administration as had the commoners of Christian antiquity. Participation in the first century was a model for what was required of the sixteenth. Given that conclusion, which the advocates had teased from the apostle Paul's pastoral letters and from the Acts of the Apostles, reformers with presbyterian or populist projects relied on God either to "train up" the laity or raise up worthy delegates in parish consistories to rule for and with the congregations.[29]

The Calvinists known now as presbyterians sensed that the relationships between consistories and congregations would take some planning. The second *Admonition* directed that parishioners "shall consent upon and chuse" representatives variously called seniors or elders or presbyters who were to keep the congregation apprised of all the consistory's "doings." When elders decided to excommunicate an unrepentant parishioner, they were to "shew the grevousnesse" of the offenses and ask for "the assent of their whole congregation . . . bicause they may not usurpe authoritie over the whole church." The parishioners for their part, though, may not overrule what elders "do well" and "put any of them out, but upon just cause proved either in that consistorie or in some one of the councils."[30]

The standard presbyterian view was that the consistory in each parish ought to judge the parishioners' complaints against each other. If the fair-

---

29. Coolidge, *Pauline Renaissance*, 127–32.
30. *Manifestoes*, 118–20.

ness of local leadership was called into question, a regional council or synod reviewed the charges and, ideally, resolved the crisis. Reformed partisans of broader lay participation believed that "the right and ready way to resolve all doubts and questions in religion" led to and through local congregations, "from one or few to moe." Yet they anticipated mayhem and also opened a route "from [the] moe to the moe godly and learned" that drew difficult cases to conferences or synods. Thomas Cartwright admitted in 1591 that presbyterians ceded very little authority to the laity, despite arguments that several of them made for lay counsel and consent twenty years before.[31]

This striking admission is worth pondering. It corroborates Patrick Collinson's claims that presbyterians' regional clerical conferences were "elevated above" congregations, that "generally the tendency in the Calvinist churches was to progress (regress?) from a lay to a clerical idea of eldership." Collinson's survey of the Elizabethan puritan movement features the presbyterians' efforts to make the choice of incumbents and the discipline of delinquents sensitive to local circumstance, but it also acknowledges that the few times they were tried, the presbyterians' experiments were clerically dominated. Parishioners managed to partner with pastors, yet the consistories and congregations usually came uncoupled; the partnerships parted company with what Collinson calls "the rank and file." Chroniclers of "withdrawal" whom we met in the first chapter would say that such parting or departure was decisive, disconnecting the godly few from the grubby multitude and "narrowing" what might otherwise have been a broadly participatory parish regime.[32]

Broadly participatory parish regimes, then, were the "what might have beens" of the 1570s that so alarmed critics of lay empowerment then and into the 1580s and 1590s. Whitgift, Perne, Redman, Bancroft, Sutcliffe, and others feared destabilization, and they were certain that it would either precede or follow lay elections. So their "church policy," from the start, was to have pastors decide whether, when, and how an election ought to occur:

---

31. BL, Additional MS. 48064, 221v; Bodl., Selden Supra MS. 44, 73r, 77v; *Manifestoes*, 111. *The holie discipline* puts lay elders at regional and national synods (Oxford, Queens College MS. 280, 116r–18v), but Cartwright's admission suggests that Matthew Sutcliffe correctly characterized presbyterian laymen as "cyphers in the synode"; *A treatise of ecclesiastical discipline* (London, 1590), 196.

32. Collinson, *Elizabethan Puritan Movement*, 106–7, 299. For "narrowing," see Tittler, *Reformation*, 242–43.

omnes apostolicae actiones ostendant electionum curam pastoribus incumbere.[33]
And conformist authorities were not about to encourage any pastor's affir-
mative as to the "whether." Thomas Cartwright survived twenty years of
such sentiments as well as countless interrogations, a few suspensions, and
two periods of exile before disclosing in 1591 that he and fellow presbyterians always set the strictest limits on lay participation. Perhaps he had forgotten Fulke, Field, Wilcox, and Lever? Or did he question the usefulness
of remembering them; that is, did he think nothing was to be gained by
recalling democratic alternatives to the patronage practices that prompted
debates in the early 1570s?[34]

Cartwright's memory might make an interesting topic, but it is not our
topic at the moment. In the next chapter we shall ask why presbyterians like
Fulke, Dering, and Cartwright surrendered their populist ambitions late in
their careers. Here, though, we only urge that historians of Elizabethan religious reform not be as forgetful as the reformers they study. For work on
late Tudor clericalization or "confessionalization" will remain incomplete
until it attends more closely to what so frightened the critics of broad lay
participation and local autonomy. The provisional conclusions of that work
hold: parish presbyters appear to have perpetuated local oligarchies and puritans to have increasingly shown contempt for popular culture. Yet as we
rediscover what puritans, presbyterians, and conformists were thinking of
the laity, we may be able to think more intelligently about those three sets of
reformers.[35]

Admittedly, the evidence for what they were thinking is difficult to tease
from the customary sources for the reformers' doctrines and discipline, and
some of the best evidence has been overlooked. Henry Howard's nearly
illegible precis of a Cambridge "divinity disputation" settled in a rarely cited
site in his correspondence. A much-mutilated Oxford commonplace book
inventories objections to lay participation in parish elections and suggests
a second university dispute, yet the transcript leaves important questions

---

33. Bodl., MS. Selden Supra 44, 75v.

34. BL, Additional MS. 48064, 221v.

35. For "confessionalization," in this connection, consult my contribution, "Recon-
structing the Context for Confessionalization in Late Tudor England: Perceptions of Reception Then and Now," in the volume honoring Bodo Nischan, edited by John Headley and
Hans J. Hillerbrand (forthcoming from Ashgate); but also see Caroline Litzenberger,
"Defining the Church of England: Religious Change in the 1570s," in *Belief and Practice*,
137–53.

unanswered: "who," "when," "where." We can draw on those sources to sup-
plement what we learn from the first *Admonition*, the presbyterians' occasional remarks, and the critics who supplied the occasions. Rarely, though
often enough to keep us on the scent, an episode or remark patently fore-
grounds the puritans' nostalgia for "that old and true election." When, for
example, ecclesiastical commissioners summoned Edward Dering to find out
whether he believed the reformation introduced the "right ministery" into
their realm, he responded that "if by a right ministerey is meant the order
which the apostles instituted, this is not ryght." "Then," Dering added
(referring to first-century polity and echoing Lever, Fulke, and Field), the
pastors "were chosen by consent of many."[36]

The dearth of evidence, of course, may reflect the regime's effectiveness in suppressing dissent. The council's commissioners were especially
vigilant after 1570, when papal excommunication put the queen in jeopardy
and her sentries and counsellors on their guard. Intelligence officers reported
priests and Jesuits "in great numbers verie busie within the realme." The
government was told a plot was "almost in full ripeness" in 1571, while the
parliament debated the fate of conspirators who caused havoc two years
before.[37] When a member of the Commons said that citizens ought to be
asked their opinions on conspirators' culpability, his colleagues balked. They
preferred to preserve secrecy and warned each other that "words tollerable
in this house are not sufferable at Blunte's Table," the London tavern where
many members boarded. In 1572 the Commons reprimanded Arthur Hall
after he was heard repeating "out of the House" what he had spoken and
heard within.[38]

Insecurity goes a long way toward explaining intolerance, but, as we
have seen, Elizabeth's officials were insecure from the start—increasingly
intolerant of "low-key" nonconformity, yet always hard on outspoken dissent. In 1567 Speaker Richard Onslowe predicted to the Commons that
government would promote "great variance" and "strife" if it allowed a ref-
erendum.[39] He knew what was widely known since the queen's first parliament, that "variance" or "diversitie" greatly displeased her and her council.
Historian Patrick Collinson, whose familiarity with the pleasures and inse-
curities of that time is unsurpassed, has lately, perceptively sketched the

---

36. Bodl., Selden Supra MS. 44, 32r.
37. Bodl., Tanner MS. 80, 74r–76v.
38. *Proceedings*, 360–66, 392.
39. *Proceedings*, 169.

predicament of the 1560s and 1570s. He confirmed that "the failure of the state church to define and underwrite Protestant orthodoxy" quickly led to a "confused struggle over the material liturgical symbolics of religion," namely, ornaments and clerical vestments. He also concluded that the struggle somehow "released" a "social energy" into the next decade's discussions of patronage and church discipline. What Collinson meant by "social energy" is uncertain, but we are now better able to appreciate how failure, confusion, ambiguity, and agitation for further reform and broadly participatory parish regimes appeared to authorities responsible for containment.[40]

Encountering opposition, they doubled their efforts to set the religious settlement on secure footing and clarify what was impermissible; nonetheless, they welcomed and capitalized on one ambiguity. The apostle Paul instructed the whole congregation in Corinth to combat evil, leaving technical or political considerations unspecified. Paul permitted the laity to discuss the general trajectory of parish policy, that is, yet he believed the whether, when, and how of implementation ought to be clerical calls.[41] Not so, said those in favor of broadly participatory regimes. Paul put the principle in play and urged everyone to work harmoniously. He had not thought to comment on implementation, because he assumed that commoners and clerics necessarily (or providentially) would come to depend on each other. And such co-dependence, *alter moderatum alteris,* saved parishes from both tyranny and mob rule. The critics, of course, recoiled from the breathtaking statement that pastors depended on the people, *nec ministri sine plebe.* They were convinced that replacing hierarchy with reciprocity would make pastor, policy, and implementation hostage to the parishioners' every whim.[42]

We might wager with some confidence that, while the conformist critics raged against democratization and laicization, the virtues of reciprocity, collaboration, and co-dependence were acknowledged and appreciated more readily elsewhere, particularly where churchwardens worked alongside their rectors and curates. There, as Christopher Marsh now says, the wardens "operate[d] with considerable flexibility," competence, and tact.[43] But I am

---

40. See Collinson's "Comment" on Eamon Duffy's paper in *England's Long Reformation, 1500–1800,* ed. Nicholas Tyacke (London: UCL Press, 1998), 80.
41. Bodl., Selden Supra MS. 44, 73v–74r.
42. BL, Cotton Titus MS. C VI, 21v: *nec plebs potest quisquam sine ministris, nec ministri sine plebe.*
43. Marsh, *Popular Religion,* 70–72.

not aware that wardens ever surfaced in arguments for lay initiative and leadership. They should have been the perfect answer to the premise of lay unpreparedness, for wardens were enterprising and largely successful managers. Perhaps, though, they too closely resembled presbyters to become posterboys for the campaign for broader and more direct parish democracy? The puritan advocates of participatory regimes must have understood that their case for lay and local control had to share space on the platform with calls for parish presbyteries. Into the 1570s, conceivably, the more populist reformers wondered whether the acceptance of their arguments for consent and control was closely, remotely, or even inversely related to the triumphs of their presbyterian colleagues. If the presbyters' gains meant parishioners' losses, populist puritans would have been reserved about the churchwardens' places (as elected officials or competent lay managers) in their thinking of the laity.

We have been left too little to get far beyond this sort of speculation. Arguments for lay and local control rarely extended from the reconstruction of purportedly scriptural precedents to the parishioners' and pastors' experiences in exile and at home, with consistories or with lay churchwardens. That deficit is difficult to explain. Other facts established so far are ready now to be filed. From the 1560s and into the 1570s, bishops might have helped develop a participatory parish polity, but they did not. They were the *ex officio* officials and beneficiaries of a government that detested "diversitie" and assumed that what it detested would follow from local autonomy and lay leadership. Hence, agitation for broader lay participation never amounted to a movement. We have had to reconstitute what there was of it from the shards of argument that still survive. And we are learning that what Edwin Sandys had said of all presbyterians in 1574 had applied far better to the populists among them who were thinking most favorably and democratically of the laity: *non multum efficiunt,* they did not get much done.[44]

The suppression of prophesying sealed their fate.

Prophesying and the People

Prophecies, also called exercises, opened with consecutive sermons on the same scriptural passage. Ordinary people in town for business or for market-day amusements paused to listen. And possibly a number of them used what

---

44. *ZL*(ET), 184.

they heard from the preachers "for the stirring up of fayth and repentaunce," as the organizers hoped they might.[45] But the chief purpose was to have preachers learn from criticisms they received once the public proceedings adjourned and the exercises reconvened as clerical colloquies. Prophesying was defended as in-service training for the clergy with little or no university education. Yet, into the 1570s, advocates and adversaries of the prophecies were forced to do some serious thinking about the laity. Prophesying drew crowds, and crowds tempted critics of royal and diocesan administration. The queen and council suspected that sermons or the discussions that immediately followed them would touch off protests against the religious settlement, the terms of which were unpopular in some quarters. To reassure the court, the partisans of the prophecies insisted that the laity only listened, but after inquiry and considerable debate, the government suppressed prophesying in 1576.[46]

Arguments for and against suppression supply nearly all the evidence we have for the late Tudor exercises, yet it is hard to tell whether anything written at the time was unleavened by the fictions contrived and circulated to save or stop them. To save them, one side appears to have understated the nature and extent of lay participation; to stop them, the other side seems to have exaggerated both. Still others, wanting to defend the prophecies without necessarily compromising lay contributions, celebrated the laity's initiative and pointed to the apostle Paul's directive that all Christians in Corinth prophesy. Yet "all" could not have meant the whole congregation, according to one argument copied into an Oxford commonplace book: the apostle wanted only the few, to whom God gave the requisite gifts, to pronounce on doctrine or discipline. True, a great many prophets once ranged across Israel (*copia prophetarum*), but, at the time, there had been little time left: the covenant had to be renewed, and the law construed before Jesus and the gospel completed divine revelation. Time passed, things changed, and one thing

---

45. BL, Egerton MS. 2713, 210v; BL, Sloane MS. 271, 6v.

46. Patrick Collinson's studies of prophesying are exemplary. For its spread and popularity, see his "Lectures by Combination: Structures and Characteristics of Church Life in Seventeenth-Century England," *BIHR* 48 (1975): 182–213, reprinted with additional figures in his *Godly People: Essays on English Protestantism and Puritanism* (London: Hambledon, 1983). Collinson, though, trusts defenders of prophesying when they underscored its conservative character, and he infers from the puritans' persistent hostility to separatism in the 1570s that there were no opportunities at the exercises for the free, lay expression of "radical discontent" (Collinson, *Religion of Protestants*, 258–60, 275–76).

clearly changed for the worse, the argument concluded: laymen grew too stupid to prophesy. Exercises baffled them, exciting passion yet inviting confusion. Prophesying in the sixteenth century, unlike that in ancient Israel or in first-century Corinth, generated heat but not light, "perturbation," not "edification."[47]

Bishop Cox of Ely had unkinder words for commoners. He knew that "some exercise" was necessary. "When the greater ignorance, idelness, [and] lewdnesse of the greater number of poore blinde prestes in the clergye shalbe depely weyed and considered," the only alternative to in-service training was to start again from scratch. And that, for Cox, was unthinkable. Continuing with the prophecies as then practiced, though, was dangerous. Laymen were often stirred or incited to ill effect (*exagitare*; *ventilare*), passing along their passion and muddle to those "poore blinde prestes."[48]

Rallying support for the prophecies, layman Thomas Wood thought differently about the laity. He maintained they were beneficiaries. Critics might contend that the commoners were misled, but, Wood countered, "the harts of . . . godly men," "knowe what singular benefitt doth dailie growe by such most godly exercises." Arguably, he intended "singular benefitt" to refer only to the education that preachers received and to the consequent improvement of the quality of their ministries. And that "benefitt doth daylie growe" by trickling down to the laity.[49] But it is equally likely, if not likelier, that Wood referred to benefits deriving from direct lay participation in prophesying. To establish as much, we ought to review the controversies that led to their suppression. The benefit to us should be a better understanding of what the early Elizabethan partisans and critics of broadly participatory parish regimes were thinking of the laity.

The story starts during the reign of King Edward VI. The first reformed Christians to prophesy in England were refugees who filled the Dutch and French "stranger" churches in London. Laski, their "bishop," believed the exercises to be the perfect occasions for airing and answering questions about

---

47. Bodl., Selden Supra MS. 44, 64v–65r, citing 1 Corinthians 15:5 and 1 Samuel 10:9–11.

48. BL, Additional MS. 29546, 48r; BL, Lansdowne MS. 25, 61r.

49. See *The Letters of Thomas Wood, Puritan, 1566–1577*, ed. Patrick Collinson (London: Athlone, 1960), 10. Also review the concise formulation of the "trickle down" claim in the document composed for, or by, Grindal, *Quod propheta sit retinenda*, LPL MS. 2007, 144v: *usus prophetiae: ministros aptiores reddit ad docendum ignorantiam simul et ignaviam propellit.*

doctrine and discipline. They encouraged fugitives united only by the ordeal of exile to exchange views and build consensus. Prophesying was most useful, Laski said, in strengthening his church's defenses against predatory separatists waiting to exploit the refugees' unspoken complaints and unasked questions with their radical, heretical, "anabaptisticall" notions.[50]

The French discussed the Bible at their exercises. The Dutch regularly scheduled times for commoners' comments on the previous Sunday's sermons. Some of the strangers' hosts and observers were impressed, and the refugees welcomed their interest. In 1551 they proposed holding some exercises in English. No source tells us if they did, but pastors later complained that parishioners "refuse contemptuously their own churches" in London to attend those of the refugees, which had been dissolved during Mary's reign yet refounded when Elizabeth succeeded her.[51]

Changes in reign affected not only continental Calvinists in England but native reformers as well, many of whom left the realm after King Edward's death in 1553 to return after Queen Mary's, as already reported here. John Knox was pastor in Berwick before he fled to Frankfurt, but he continued north to Scotland when he recrossed the Channel five years later. There he directed laymen to assemble with their reformed pastors and form "cumpan[ies] of interpretouris." He called their exercises "prophecieing" and was alert to the problems likely to plague companies' conferences. To keep competing interpreters from generating rival factions, Knox published prohibitions against invective. Nonetheless, he would not have "prophets" be other than candid. On occasion, he said, they must censure complacent colleagues, especially Calvinists who were settling to the south for a partially reformed church. Among them were Knox's fellow exiles, who, he complained, were more interested in keeping the peace than in promoting reform. While he was designing a truly reformed church in Scotland and develop-

---

50. Laski, *Opera*, 2:102–3. Also note the reference to lay participation in a letter from Martin Micronius, one of Laski's clerical colleagues in London, to Bullinger and Zurich, *OL*, 2:575. But by the 1550s, the laity no longer participated in the Zurich *Prophezei*, for which, J. J. Hottinger and H. H. Vogel, eds., *Heinrich Bullingers Reformationsgeschichte*, vol. 1 (Frauenfeld: Beyel, 1838), 117.

51. Bodl., Wood MS. F.30–32, 87; *OL* 2:587; and, for skepticism about the importance of strangers' experiments, Peter Fairlambe, *The Recantation of a Brownist* (London, 1606), E3v–E4r. Also, in this connection, see Philippe Denis, "La Prophetie dans les eglises de la reforme au XVIe siècle," *Revue d'histoire ecclésiastique* 72 (1977): 300–303.

ing opportunities for lay participation therein, former exiles and other of the queen's new bishops, according to Knox, were timid and had been "turned."[52]

He might have illustrated the conservatism of those English authorities by alluding to their attempts to have fugitives from the continent restrict lay participation in their prophecies. It was acceptable, and even agreeable, to find Henrick Moreels, who installed and cleaned carpets, deferentially discussing divine attributes with learned refugee pastors and laymen. Few denied the advantages of that type of exchange. But it was another thing altogether to let the discussions in weekly exercises deteriorate into theological free-for-alls. In 1561 Dutch refugees introduced rules to assure commoners were courteous and not combative. Knox had done so as well, but in London those measures were small yet significant steps in the direction of lay silence.[53] That direction would have pleased Bishop Grindal who was bothered by the fugitives' freedom. He was especially displeased when, during the Dutch exercises, an eccentric named Velsius expressed, *aperte* and impertinently, his odd notions about the deification of human nature. Grindal protested both the performance and the strangers' liberties that allowed it to play.[54] And soon afterward he helped Nicholas Des Gallars, who had opposed Morely in France, suspend protocols favoring participatory practices and press for a more "aristocratic and clerical government" of the refugees' London churches.[55]

Grindal witnessed lay participation in congregational elections and discipline when he was in exile. He confided that he had a high regard for the English Calvinists advocating lay initiative, but he nonetheless refused to subscribe to their cause. And he chafed at their insults, which, on occasion,

---

52. *The Works of John Knox*, vol. 2, ed. David Laing (Edinburgh: Bannatyne Society, 1848), 242–45, citing 1 Corinthians 14:29–31. For Knox's debts to Laski, see Janet G. MacGregror, *The Scottish Presbyterian Polity: A Study of Its Origins in the Sixteenth Century* (Edinburgh: Oliver and Boyd, 1926), 53–54, 76–77, 133–34; and Denis, "Prophetie," 313–14.

53. Aart Arnout van Schelven, ed., *Kerkeraads-Protocollen der nederduitsche Vluchtelingenkerk te London, 1560–1566* (Amsterdam: Historisch-Genootschap, 1921), 247, 251, for restrictions; 384–85, for Moreels.

54. PRO, State Papers 12/28, 29r–30r.

55. For Des Gallars' provisions *de exercitatione prophetica*, see BL., Additional MS. 48096, 7–8; Owe Boersma and Auke Jelsma, ed., *Unity in Multiformity: The Minutes of the Coetus of London, 1575, and the Consistory Minutes of the Italian Church of London*, (London: Huguenot Society of Great Britain and Ireland, 1997), 119–20. For the drift toward "aristocracy," consult Collinson, *Grindal*, 132–34 and, for Des Gallars' part against Morely, John Quick, *Synodicon in Gallia Reformata* (London, 1692), 56–57.

he returned with relish. He called Cartwright "a busy head stuffed full of singularities," a head, he said, that ought to be "bridled by authority."[56] But Grindal is not known for the bridling. That honor goes to John Whitgift, who chased Cartwright from Cambridge in 1571 and, twelve years later, succeeded Grindal as archbishop of Canterbury. Grindal is better remembered instead for having reluctantly presided over the suppression of prophesying and for having lost his influence at court and in the church as a result of his reluctance.

In 1576, soon after accepting appointment as archbishop of Canterbury, Grindal was instructed by the government to have his suffragans suppress the prophecies. First he polled them, looking for and obtaining endorsements that he could patch into an appeal to get the government to relent. He put off complying with the court's order and combed passages from the Bible and other early texts for proof that prophesying had been public in the earliest Christians' communities and that the apostle Paul commended lay participation. One *nota bene* in Grindal's collection of precedents seems to be exploring a compromise: Christians should come to the exercises to be edified, it counsels, but only learned laymen should venture to speak.[57]

The government, though, was less concerned with learning than with "over much vehemency," and Grindal's poll disclosed that the exercises brought out "great boldnesse in the meaner sort."[58] Officials at court assumed as much, specifically that subjects were "easy to be caryed [away] with novelties" during the exercises or the conversations immediately afterward. What they chanced to hear might convince them of their rights and abilities to judge religious positions, including the terms of the queen's recent arrangements for the church and prayerbook: rights they ought not to possess and abilities they did not. And the government knew to blame the "no small number" of firebrands "presuming to be teachers and preachers," working the crowds, spreading discontent. Grindal's concession, that only learned laymen be allowed to lecture during the exercises, might have closed on a remedy, but queen and council, probably presuming that education was no guarantee of acquiescence and suspecting the susceptibilities of commoners

---

56. *Remains,* 304–5, 336.
57. For Grindal's *Forma seu Modus Prophetandi,* LPL, MS. 2007, 129r, 132r–v, 134r. Also consult LPL, MS. 2014, 73r–74r; and Bodl., Selden Supra MS. 44, 64v–65r.
58. But note the suggestion that "vehemency" be pardoned if sermons were "delivered in the Latin tongue and not popularly taught," CUL, MS. mm 1.40, 373–74.

to "advanced" and subversive thinking about the laity, were taking no chances. "Considering the great abuses that have ben in sundry places of our realme by reason of assemblies callid exercises, we will and straightly charge yow that you do cause the same forthwith to cease and not be used."[59]

The government's preoccupations with "vehemency" naturally became those of its bishops "straightly charged" to enforce the cease-and-desist order. Some diocesans disliked the commission. Pastors of Peterborough thought their bishop among them. After all, he approved regulations for the exercises at Northampton, counseling the laity to attend, especially the commoners from "blynde corners," parishes seldom served by curates and hardly ever by preachers.[60] Parkhurst, bishop of Norwich, could not have been pleased with Elizabeth's directive. When Archbishop Parker previously tried to stop prophesying in Norwich because the diocese, he said, was infested with "puritaynes," Parkhurst resisted. Agreeing with his archbishop that the region was in a "miserable state," he attributed the problem, not to "puritaynes" but to patrons' propensity to nominate friends and family members to lucrative livings. The nominees, he argued, were almost always unsuitable for the reformed ministry. And the in-service training that Parker proposed to suppress was the only compensatory strategy on offer.[61] So when Parkhurst was told to stop the "vain prophesying," he stalled, sought advice from sympathetic courtiers, slyly misread his archbishop's intent, and declared his intention to discontinue only the "vain" exercises. Several months later, by spring 1574, however, Parker had clarified so that the most boneheaded bishop would know that all exercises were "vain," that none were "so good an help and mean to further true religion" as advocates argued.[62]

---

59. Large swatches of manuscript evidence for government instructions and stated concerns from LPL, MS. 2003, and BL, Lansdowne MS. 25, were printed by Stanford Lehmberg in his "Archbishop Grindal and the Prophesying," *Historical Magazine of the Protestant Episcopal Church* 34 (1965): 87–145. For "no small number" and "to cease and not be used," see Lehmberg, "Grindal," 142–43; LPL, MS. 2003, 40r, and BL, Lansdowne MS. 25, 92r–95r.

60. See BL, Additional MS. 27632, 47v, for Bishop Scambler's counsel and approval: "true laborers cannot but rejoyce when they see the work of their Lord . . . got forward as we did manifestly behold in these exercises." Also consult PRO, State Papers 12/78, 243r–244r; and BL, Lansdowne MS. 21, 4r.

61. BL, Lansdowne MS. 17, 129r, for Parker's position in 1573; Strype(1), 2.2:523–24, for Parkhurst's response.

62. See Ralph Houlbrooke, ed., *The Letterbook of John Parkhurst* (Norwich: Norfolk Record Society, 1975), 231–36, 241–47. Also note George Cornelius Gorham and C. S. Bird, eds., *Gleanings of a few scattered ears during the period of the Reformation in England* (London: Bell and Daldy, 1857), 484–92; and Collinson, *Elizabethan Puritan Movement*, 191–92.

Earlier, in a different context, Parkhurst confessed to being "a slow paced horse," and, into the 1570s, he obviously tried to slow Parker's pace. The archbishop, however, had the last word. The bishop of Norwich became hitched to Canterbury's plans to steer the church as the government desired, hitched as uncomfortably (yet securely) as several other suffragans. Cheney of Gloucester was reputed to have been more comfortable than most with his orders to suppress, yet he decided to spare one exercise in his diocese. Cooper of Lincoln promised that he would stop the prophesying whenever "base persons" were known to participate, but he preserved at least one exercise in his diocese and was rumored to be on the brink of restoring all the others he had "inhibited" just as Grindal got his instructions, roughly the same instructions that his predecessor Parker got from the government and readily, though not altogether effectively, circulated and enforced.[63]

What choice did Grindal have? Five years before succeeding Parker, he advised Girolamo Zanchi, a leading Heidelberg refomer, against appealing directly to Elizabeth on behalf of the English nonconformists. Grindal told him to approach the queen through her bishops.[64] In 1576 he followed his own counsel and cranked up a campaign to retain prophesying by canvassing his episcopal colleagues' opinions and, as we have seen, by soliciting their endorsements. Critics of the exercises as well as advocates replied. John Scory of Hereford, for one, said he suppressed prophesying several years before because he believed it gave enemies of the prevailing church order tremendous advantages against the church officials they pilloried. The dissidents pitched their remarks to market-day crowds. They were smarter than Cartwright, Scory said; they made presbyterianism appear compelling and the bishops who opposed it seem contemptible. Scriptural evidence for elders, though slight, could be made sufficiently strong to sway onlookers whose ignorance of the Bible made them easy marks for misleading interpretations and mistaken inferences. Scory went on to offer an alternative to suppression. He recommended restricting the public phase to a single sermon and requiring that Latin be spoken at all times, from the pulpits and in conferences.[65]

---

63. For Cooper, see LPL, MS. 2003, 29r; BL, Additional MS. 29546, 57r; for Cheney, BL, Additional MS. 29546, 56r; for Parkhurst, *ZL,* 1:98.

64. *Remains,* 342. Zanchi, however, bypassed the bishops and wrote to the queen, *ZL,* 2:339–53.

65. LPL, MS. 2003, 10v; and Lehmberg, "Grindal," 115–17. The "enemies of the prevailing order," in this instance, might have been critics who aimed to make Scory rather than

Ostensibly, that would have limited the usefulness of the exercises for the in-service training of undereducated pastors, but it would also have limited their use by those nonconformists who hoped to stir up public opinion against conformists. Grindal would presumably have welcomed the second result, unquestionably regretted the first, and so, on balance, must not have been keen on Scory's suggestion. On the whole, though, he was pleased with the survey results and gratified by the count in favor of retaining the exercises. Bishop Sandys of London saw to it that additional letters were composed for the dossier, long letters from lay supporters and from two archdeacons who had served as moderators of some prophecies. Endorsements, however, included one important stipulation: commoners were to come but not speak. Sandys' archdeacons, along with the bishops of Exeter, Coventry and Litchfield, and Gloucester, repeated that condition as if by prior arrangement. The consensus: in-service clerical training was too beneficial to risk for lay participation and later, as the queen continued to insist on suppression, for lay presence.[66]

Lay presence could lead to embarrassment. For example, Robert Dudley, Earl of Leicester, thought that prophecies were splendid occasions for "examinations." Pastors could prepare to impress their peers at the exercises "or become a reproof and a shame." Dudley was disinclined to humiliate the reformed ministry publicly. His plan was to have sermons preached and criticized at the clerical conferences that followed the prophecies' public phase.[67] But could the clerical confrontations be contained? Regulations were rather confusing. Preachers were encouraged to denounce "abuses" in colleagues' exegesis but warned to "meddle not with matters in controversie."[68] John Aylmer, appointed bishop of London soon after suppression, recalled that "meddling" was contagious. Younger clerics openly rebuked their seniors. The commoners then joined the chorus of complaint. Public censure was

---

episcopacy seem contemptible, for Scory's misconduct in office was soon afterward said to have been scandalous; BL, Egerton MS. 3048, 207r–8r.

66. LPL, MS. 2003, 5r, 8r, 13r, 16r; and Lehmberg, "Grindal," 97, 101, 108–9, 113. Neither Lehmberg's article nor the Lambeth Palace manuscript includes Cheney's letter, for which, see BL, Additional MS. 29546, 56v. A copy in BL, Additional MS. 21565, 26v, abbreviated yet misrepresented what Cheney conceded, reading "admit no layman" for the bishop's "admit no layman to speak."

67. Cambridge, Magdalen College, Pepys MS. 2503, 647.

68. Compare BL, Additional MS. 21565, 26v, with PRO, State Papers 12/78, 244v.

so much more disruptive than discreet peer review.[69] Arguably, laymen bene-fited from prophesying, able to hear some of their region's better preaching and sample various interpretations of the same generative biblical passages. But variety was a mixed blessing and became something of a curse when interpretations, spiced with criticisms of others' interpreting, embarrassed the ministry as well as those others. Even when clerical colleagues refrained from public exposure of "abuses," the laity was likely to compare, contrast, and choose favorites. That, too, contributed to what Aylmer perceived as a contagion of complaint. He took the disease so seriously that, as bishop, after suppression, he had a preacher imprisoned simply for "touchynge that which theye call exercise."[70]

Bishop Curteys of Chichester became something of an expert on dis-content and complaint. Unlike Scory, he preferred a menu of preachers at every exercise, so he would have been counted, for a time, among episcopal advocates of prophesying. Yet when, in part to appease Parker, he required less learned laymen to be silent, the exercises' more uncompromising sup-porters seem to have made common cause with his enemies from the cathe-dral close. Curteys was repeatedly and publicly condemned. Critics, he said, "afford me and mye officers manye ill words" and, worst of all, they put their protests before "the changeable people."[71]

If we knew how "manye ill words" were uttered at, around, or after the exercises, we would know more about the efforts to save and suppress them. We may be reasonably certain, however, that if the insults had been wildly provocative, Aylmer surely would not have pulled his punches and kept the news from us. And, had they been insignificant, Grindal would have for-mulated his concession differently when he rushed to restrict lay partici-pation, to see to it, *"ante omnia,"* that "no lay person be suffered to speak publicly."[72] Indeed, his dossier seems marked by desperation, which is diffi-cult to reconcile with the calm and the clerical character ascribed to early

69. BL, Additional MS. 29546, 57.

70. BL, Cotton MS. Titus B VII, 18v.

71. LPL, MS. 2003, 4; and Lehmberg, "Grindal," 110–11. For "ill words" and "change-able people," see Richard Curteys, *Two Sermons* (London, 1576), F7r–F8v. For Curteys' enemies and troubles, see Roger B. Manning, *Religion and Society in Elizabethan Sussex: A Study of the Enforcement of the Religious Settlement* (Leicester: Leicester University Press, 1969), 104–6; as well as Peter McCullough, *Sermons at Court: Politics and Religion in Eliza-bethan and Jacobean Preaching* (Cambridge: Cambridge University Press, 1998), 82–84.

72. *Remains*, 373–74.

Elizabethan prophesying. Moreover, had the exercises been straightforwardly didactic, monotonously clerical, and as tame as some now claim, why did they then seem so vexatious and prompt so much anxious thinking about the laity in the 1570s? Why was it lawful for subjects to gather for games that featured the legendary charms of Robin Hood's "Mayde Marion" and unlawful for them to assemble for prophesying?[73]

Paranoia perhaps. Suppression may not have been based on judicious assessments of real or potential harm. Possibly, as Wallace MacCaffrey suspects, rumors counted for more at court than reason. Elizabeth, on this reading, was first moved "by some bit of tittle tattle," then hustled "by private parties for factious ends" into the ranks of the exercises' critics. What happened at the exercises, the actual extent of lay involvement, therefore, was much less important than the intrigue around the queen.[74] Chronicler William Harrison looks to have preceded MacCaffrey down that same track. Harrison granted that reckless laymen "intrude[d] themselves with offense" at the prophecies, but what caused their suppression, he maintained, was satan's having infiltrated the government. At court, the devil tempted the queen's council to subvert reformed religion.[75] John Udall blamed courtiers and diocesan authorities as well. He composed quite a cabal for a barbed treatise on "the state" or status of the church. In a viciously, deliciously, funny scene, Udall has a crypto-Catholic court official coach a boardroom bishop to feign support for continuing clerical education while assailing those who had defended prophesying.[76]

Udall's bishop was probably a slap at John Whitgift. The court official was likely meant to mock Christopher Hatton who had taken Whitgift and John Aylmer under his wing by 1576.[77] Court opposition to prophesying, in literature and life, now appears to have been carefully choreographed, yet

---

73. BL, Additional MS. 27632, 49v, for "Mayde Marion." Collinson, *Grindal*, 233–41, makes the best case for calm.

74. See Wallace MacCaffrey, *Queen Elizabeth and the Making of Policy, 1572–1588* (Princeton, N.J.: Princeton University Press, 1981), 84–89.

75. *Harrison's Description*, 18–19.

76. John Udall, *The state of the church laide open* (London, 1588), H1r–H2r. Also see Lake, *Anglicans*, 80–84.

77. For Hatton, see O'Day, *Clergy*, 72–73; *Letters of Thomas Wood*, xxvii; and Simon Adams, "Eliza Enthroned? The Council and Its Politics," in *The Reign of Elizabeth I*, ed. Christopher Haigh (Athens: University of Georgia Press, 1985), 70–71.

whatever conspiracies there were in the queen's council would have been less consequential had there been no Southam and no Grindal. At Southam, near Warwick, "discentions for trifles" disturbed Dudley, the exercises' dependable support at court (although not a voice or vote for lay participation). What he thought of as reformers' immodesty and called "over busy dealing," Patrick Collinson now identifies as "the final crisis"—Grindal's responses assuring its finality. The danger at Southam might have passed, had Grindal not forced "the matter to a head," Collinson suggests, by questioning the government's authority to interfere. Grindal lectured the queen on the independence of her church, quoting Ambrose of Milan, a fourth-century bishop known not just for the odd circumstances of his election but also for having defied two emperors. Whatever Elizabethans thought about Ambrose's courage and whatever they may have made of prophecies and of the reformed church's prerogatives, anyone addicted to the queen's favor was dutifully and, if truly ambitious, dramatically outraged by Grindal's "wilfulnesse" and insolence.[78]

Grindal remembered things selectively. He insisted that he made inquiries "immediately" on hearing of the "discentions" at Southam. But the circumstances there were hard to sift, he said, and lay support for the prophesying was considerable. He wanted it known that his critics misjudged him. He was neither stubborn nor self-important but resolute, because, he explained, studying history convinced him "suche kinde of exercise [was] sett downe in the holie scriptures" and practiced in the earliest churches. The laity at the time had attended to good effect, and Grindal saw "no reason why people [of his time] shulde be excludit." Yes, he dared to call the government's intervention unwise as well as unwelcome. It would suppress preaching that attracted crowds to the exercises while requiring the reiteration of the church's standard-issue sermons (or homilies) which, he claimed, were far less popular and less edifying than what was suppressed. The court, in another's words, was reducing its "godly preachers" to "bare reading ministers."[79]

---

78. LPL, MS. 2003, 70v–71r; and Lehmberg, "Grindal," 139. Also, for Dudley's demurrer, see *Letters of Thomas Wood*, 15. For "final crisis," see Collinson, *Godly People*, 375, and "If Constantine, then also Theodosius: St. Ambrose and the Integrity of the Elizabethan *Ecclesia Anglicana*," *JEH* 30 (1979): 205–29 (reprinted in *Godly People*, 109–33).

79. BL, Lansdowne MS. 25, 163v, printed in *Remains*, 392–93. Grindal's protest ("not of my stubborness and wilfulnesse") was filed in Cecil's papers with a letter from Durham

Bishop Sandys of London agreed, to a point. He had helped Grindal compile the dossier defending the exercises, as noted, yet he also confided that it was difficult to supervise public sermons. Picking preachers for St. Paul's Cross, he relied on his episcopal colleagues' commendations, but some nominees turned out to be "fanaticall spirits" who incited the crowds and annoyed the court.[80] Grindal, however, spoke of the success of sermons at the Cross. He pledged that his suffragans would continue to vet public preachers, cork the radicals and malcontents, and control the crowds. His pontificate was wrecked, and the public phase of prophesying went under because Hatton, his allies, and the likes of Dudley as well were unpersuaded that Grindal or any diocesan official could deliver on that promise.[81]

Nicholas Bacon, Lord Keeper, expressed his skepticism in an address to parliament that put the government's spin on Grindal's scruples (his "disobediencie"). The realm's religion had to be "uniforme," Bacon said, going on to argue that prophesying, despite the bishops' best efforts, had undermined uniformity and would, if allowed to continue, leave religion "nulliforme." He touted what he and conformists considered antidotes to anarchy: homilies composed by sound, sensible reformers, read regularly during worship in the realm's churches. The scripts showed the provisions for lay education were in good repair, Bacon averred, presuming that officials of the established church were thinking of the laity's well-being when they published and prescribed them and when they suppressed or "removed certaine exercises and prophesinge used as well by the laie and unlearned people as by other." That Bacon believed the "removal" was necessary is clear; what he meant by "used by the laie and unlearned" is not, although he mentioned that advocates of the exercises supposed that "laye people should be parties," that the supposition was unwarranted, and that lay participation in prophesying was "nerely begune" or unprecedented. Apparently prophecies led to a leveling unlike anything the Lord Keeper had experienced in the parishes.[82]

---

declaring his "wilfulnesse and undeutifullnes towards his sovereign to be the just occasion of his troubles." See BL, Lansdowne MS. 25, 161v–62r, but also BL, Lansdowne MS. 25, 7r, 20r, for other parts of the archbishop's apology. I borrow the term "bare reading ministers" from Eusebius Paget, CUL, MS. mm 1.43, 446.

80. BL, Lansdowne MS. 17, 96r.

81. LPL, MS. 2003, 35v, 69v–70v.

82. BL, Harley MS. 36, 298r–99r.

Satan, Southam, Hatton, and Grindal are variously blamed for the suppression, and indeed the latter three are probable causes. Southam, by all reports, was "over busy." Hatton worked at court to discredit prophecies' partisans. And Grindal's "wilfulnesse" antagonized the queen. Satan, whom Harrison accused, appears a useless old swell in this connection, but the list of three that remain looks incomplete. The ordinary people who were "parties" to prophesying and, as Bacon noted, somehow "used" the exercises now ought to be numbered among the causes or conditions for suppression. Evidence ostensibly unrelated to the arguments of 1576 about the probity of the prophecies suggests we should be thinking of the laity when we add the history of prophesying and its suppression to the declamations and admonitions of the 1570s.

Commoners and prophecies, for instance, were very much on Richard Fletcher's mind when he wrote to answer critics of his father's ministry in 1575 in Cranbrook, Kent.

> It is a common thing now for every pragmaticall prentise to have in his head and in his mouth the government and reformation of the church, and he that in exercise that can speake thereof, that is the man. Every artificer must be [a] reformer and teacher, forgetting the state [he stands] in both to be taught and to be reformed. . . . We may say of our time as Seneca said . . . much of man's life passeth away either with doing ill or doing nothing, but the greatest part with doing other things such as do no whit appertain unto them or concerne them.[83]

"Every pragmaticall prentise [and] every artificer" forgot his station and pronounced on "the government and reformation of the church," Fletcher complained, intending only to defend his father but presenting excellent evidence that the prophecies had been as "over busy," in places, as their critics maintained.[84] Dudley Fenner, curate in Cranbrook less than a decade later,

---

83. DWL, Morrice MSS. B.2, 8, and C, 218.

84. Conceivably, John Stroud, a curate hired by Fletcher senior, was the pastor's most virulent critic and his son's chief target. Stroud's chief defender, a local schoolmaster named Good, likely preached at the exercises. He as much as said that he did during his deposition (DWL, Morrice MSS. B.2, 18r, and C, 228). The people of Cranbrook would not have been shocked. They were accustomed to hearing their schoolmasters preach. Inasmuch as many nonconformists deprived of their livings became teachers, however, curates would

recalled lay participation in local prophesying and mourned the loss of it. He also spotted a problem that had developed in the wake of suppression; since lively lay conversations had been discouraged, he reported, there was too little "exposition, interpretation, and application of the holy and wholsome word of God to the heart and conscience of the people."[85]

Fenner believed the exercises' enemies overstated the dangers and underestimated reformed parishioners' patience and good sense. Turning received wisdom on its tail, he argued that ordinary people bear with "contrarities and strifes" while their pastors careen and skid into all sorts of errors. A pastor, said Fenner, was more easily distracted than an entire parish; "One is sooner carried into ambition and covetousness than a whole church . . . into disorder." To be sure, such comparisons were after the fact, that is, Fenner was a late entry in the controversy over suppression, yet he claimed to know how diocesan and government officials during the 1580s could be reconciled to reviving the exercises. And he was prepared to assure them that if "others besides ministers are permitted to speake," they would not preach "out of the pulpit as with authoritie." Nor did he intend to cede "cariage of matters" to the commoners. He vowed prudent management of lay participation.[86]

Probably without realizing it, Fenner had recycled Laski's justifications for prophesying. He calculated that the advantages of a revival far outweighed the risks: laymen should have a forum to "shew their doubts," so pastors might not be surprised by that skepticism and, with others among the faithful, could address them before doubts became reservations, and reservations became resentments. But critics called Fenner a "makebate."

---

have been counseled to use discretion. Nonetheless, "in such scarcity of preachers" able and suitable laymen, "*laici idonei et habiles,*" were thought to be indispensable (LPL, MS. 2007, 131r; DWL, MSS. B.1, 276, and C, 338–39). They were trusted by the archbishop and by at least one of Sandys' archdeacons (LPL, MS. 2003, 13r), yet schoolmasters-turned-preachers—or deprived and turned back into preachers—could become dangerously disruptive. David Black in Cornwall was trouble for the bishop of Exeter, as was his pastor, Eusebius Paget (LPL, *Cartae miscellaneae* 12/15, 1v; Collinson, *Elizabethan Puritan Movement,* 276–77). John Leech, schoolmaster in Essex, betrayed the pastor he had befriended and preached in private homes during public worship; see McIntosh, *Community Transformed,* 207–11. Schoolmaster Good obviously plagued the two Fletchers.

85. DWL, Morrice MS. A.2, 131.

86. Dudley Fenner, *A defense of the godly ministers against the slaunders of Dr. Bridges* (London, 1587), 70–72; and Fenner, *Counter-poyson* (London, 1584), 30–31, 140–43.

They said he was pandering to commoners, making them think they were, or could become, competent "debators and judges." Fenner and his friends learned that the insult prefaced a summary statement to the effect that prophesying was suppressed to preserve the peace. They answered that Christ came not to bring peace but to spur debate and excite faith.[87] But their reply fell on deaf ears, much as had Grindal's recollection that "many" prophesied in the churches of the first century. Authorities also were deaf when an anonymous "gentleman in the countrey" proffered a specious bit of early church history, insisting that "all people of God" had once been "prophets." Grindal's "many" were too many; that gentleman's "all" was altogether unthinkable in 1585, with the queen on record against "popularitie." She, her privy council, and her bishops found nothing to prompt reconsideration of suppression, save Dudley Fenner and his small platoon of malcontents in the southeastern corner of the realm. And Fenner soon fled to the continent.[88]

Whitgift was just then stalking the reformed pastors who, he judged, were partial to Grindal's "programs." Fenner escaped, his hopes for a revival of prophesying disappointed because it "smelled of a popularity and bred disorder." But Whitgift, in this instance, was not sniffing; instead, the nose belongs to historian Marshall Knappen, whose work on Tudor puritan "programs" still repays study and, here, seems accurately to reflect the archbishop's sensibility.[89] To critics, Fenner among them, Whitgift seemed to be rehabilitating "old policie[s] of popish prelates" and suppressing the "discord" "necessarie" for the vitality of reformed Christianity. Whitgift, with Hatton's support, they charged, was imposing a papal "hush" on the English church. Yet when the archbishop joined Elizabeth's privy council and became censor-in-chief of the realm's political imagination, reformers of nearly every stripe were less and less likely to agree with Fenner and his friends, as

---

87. For their reply, see DWL, Morrice MSS. B.1, 411, and C, 377–78; and, for a comparable clerical petition that favored the exercises, BL, Lansdowne MS. 42, 208r. For early Stuart efforts to "construct room for disagreement and dispute," consult Lake, *Boxmaker's Revenge*, 233–42.

88. For Elizabeth's aversion to "popularitie," PRO, State Papers 12/176/68, 215r; for Grindal's "many," LPL, MS. 2014, 73, citing Matthew 7:22; and, for the anonymous gentleman's "all," *Register*, 175–76.

89. Marshall M. Knappen, *Tudor Puritanism: A Chapter in the History of Idealism* (Chicago: University of Chicago Press, 1939), 278; and, for Whitgift's sensitivity to Grindal's "program" and to populist sentiments, BL, Additional MS. 34729, 50v–51r.

we shall see in the next chapter. They were generally inclined, thinking of the laity, to agree with Whitgift and find discord noxious rather than "necessarie."[90]

Years earlier, in 1576, preacher Edward Dering, questioned by authorities about his attitudes and doctrine, wrote to Cecil and insisted his sermons "be judged by the hearers," not by his superiors. That insistence was what those who were suppressing exercises feared, especially if they read, that same year, that commoners customarily interrogated preachers "in their often meetings and conferences."[91] Suppression, however, was not the silver bullet conformists expected it to be. Preaching-obsessed puritans found ways to preach. Curious people found ways to "judge" and discuss what they heard. Notice what Catholic convict William Weston saw from his cell in Wisbech in 1586. Commoners gathered in a prison yard after public sermons had been delivered nearby; they talked about what they had heard and referred to their conversations as "exercises"; everyone seemed to be speaking, reading their Bibles and "comparing different passages to see if they had been brought forward truly and to the point."[92]

"A great multitude of puritan visitors"; that was Weston's count and characterization. He disapproved of them because they preferred preaching and prooftexting to his church's sacraments. Whitgift would have disapproved because they practiced what his government had long tried to prohibit. One libel had it that he liked laymen to be as "dumb asses [that] saye never a word."[93] It exaggerates, of course, yet one can imagine him yearning to have the loquacious Wisbech laity collared, muzzled, corraled, and lodged for the duration of his pontificate in the precincts of the prison they conveniently chose for their colloquy.

Wisbechs were relatively rare. The archbishop and his agents were generally successful keeping local officials alert for signs of "popularitie."

---

90. See William Overton, *Godlye and pithie exhortation* (London, 1582), B6v–C5r, discussing "necessarie" discord and the likelihood of an imposed silence the year before Whitgift became archbishop.

91. Barstow, *Safegarde*, 104r. For Dering's letter, see BL, Lansdowne MS. 17, 197r.

92. John Morris, ed., *The Troubles of Our Catholic Forefathers Related by Themselves*, vol. 2 (London: Burns and Oates, 1875), 240–41, for Weston. Collinson, "Puritanisms," 54, calls that Wisbech exercise "a holy fair."

93. *Strife*, 68–69.

Detection led to the depositions that now yield much of the little we know about lay initiative at the century's end.[94] In 1593, for instance, authorities caught up with Thomas Settle, who would then have passed as something of a born-again layman. He had renounced his ordination, "severed himself from the parish" he was serving in Suffolk, and come to London to listen to and worship with separatist Francis Johnson. Settle supplied little information about Johnson's ministry, but his deposition reveals what became of initiatives that ran into the 1570s and, as we saw, ran into formidable opposition. For Settle admitted that "he hath never served in any office in [Johnson's] congregation but he hath spoken in prophesie."[95]

94. See Collinson, *Elizabethan Puritan Movement*, 403–16, for the effectiveness of Whitgift's pursuits after 1589.

95. BL, Harleian MS. 7042, 59v.

FIVE

Patronage to the People?

Mistrust of the realm's commoners spread during the 1570s and into the 1580s, as did mistrust of the reformers who seemed to trust them. Conformist officials as good as admitted that the reformed laity was still "of verie small readinge and studie" two decades after Elizabeth's "alteracion"—the ordinary parishioners were still not prepared to choose their preachers. Undeniably, in the literature of late Tudor reform, the occasional "rudesbie" surfaced: savvy, theologically sound, and, as Perkins' Eusebius, sufficiently enlightened to assume leadership. Such fictional figures might have been deployed more often to buttress the arguments for lay authority and local control, were the very nonconformists who advanced those arguments not having second thoughts about the laity.

There were exceptions. Robert Browne of Cambridge, Norwich, then Holland, was troubled by striking structural similarities between the English reformed and old Catholic churches. He was especially disconcerted to find his fellow reformers deferring so often to diocesan authorities. To him, episcopal hierarchy had no place in a reformed church. Parishioners ought to have greater power; "anie" and "all" in each parish should select religious instructors and discipline delinquents. In Kent, Dudley Fenner distanced himself from Browne, who came to advocate separation and independence from Elizabeth's church. Yet Fenner came close to endorsing what Morely and Browne had said about the timeliness of further, democratizing reform. It made sense in late antiquity and through the Middle Ages, Fenner allowed, for church officials to concentrate authority among the few and reliable. That measure rightly restricted "partialities" and kept peace among Christians. But Elizabeth's "alteracion" removed all causes of the "continuall tumults" that plagued medieval Christianity. The church could again distribute power broadly, as did the earliest Christian congregations. That renaissance of lay power might invite controversies, yet resolving them publicly would be healthy for a reformed Christianity. The deliberations and resolutions would show the religion in a positive light. Plus, disagreements openly, amicably discussed seldom developed into festering resentments. To ensure discussion and resolution, Fenner proposed that congregations elect elders. He presumed, contrary to conformists, that the presbyters would calm rather than kindle controversy. Most reformers, though, thought of lay participation and patronage as powder kegs. The conformists were skeptical that ordinary people and their presbyters could prevent the queen's "alteracion" from slipping back toward Catholicism or skidding off course into "anabaptistrie." Only a rare voice was raised for the empowerment of "everie plaine man" in the parish. Into the 1580s, the plaine man's enlightenment and empowerment were simply too great a perfection for England.

Rudesbies

Archbishop Parker believed that Edwin Sandys was a stubborn man and kept him off the shortlist for promotion when the queen's council looked for a set of reliable new bishops in 1559. Sandys, though, soon managed to join fellow Marian exiles on Elizabeth's episcopal bench and quickly became one of the government's most valued diocesan officials. In consequence, twenty years later, with Parker in his grave and Grindal in disgrace, Sandys, then archbishop of York, was asked by Elizabeth and Cecil to answer a petition for church reform composed in the Commons. The stubborn streak Parker had noticed still showed. Sandys carped at the Commons for having failed to dismiss the "griefes" of "young ministers of these our times grow[n] madd." Their complaints blamed bishops for "abuses" Sandys thought administratively unavoidable. But the queen, council, and Commons wanted an investigation. Chancellor of the Exchequer Walter Mildmay conveyed their desire to the Lords in 1581, bearing with him "some things very requisite to be reformed," that satchel of "griefes" Sandys was summoned to answer.[1]

The sermons that opened the parliament of 1581 extolled Elizabeth's devotion to religious reform but also warned her against "innovation." They predicted that innovations led to "unquietness." By then Sandys and his episcopal colleagues were accustomed to disquiet, specifically, to the people's murmuring against "unlearned and unable ministers," excommunications "for every matter of small moment," pluralism, and absenteeism. Some of the more outspoken ministers expressed that discontent in their "griefes"; members of the Commons echoed them, and a few bishops in the Lords were sympathetic. Mildmay reported to the queen that several diocesan officials consented to appeal with laymen from the Lower House for the correction of "defects." But Sandys balked. He conceded that bishops and their deputies occasionally excommunicated offenders for small infractions, yet "the smaler the mater is," he went on, "the greater is the fault of . . . disobedience." Refusal to repent insignificant sins was a sin that warranted the severest censure. For insolence was "no matter of small moment," Sandys summed up.[2]

Pluralism, however, was the necessary inconvenience that enabled smaller parishes to survive. To compose an attractive salary, the revenues of and responsibilities for two parishes sometimes had to be combined. Sandys and his associates agreed at two points with the authors of the "griefes." Incumbents should reside in one of their two parishes, and the distances between the yoked churches ought never to exceed twenty miles. Sandys recoiled, however, at the suggestion that parishes with annual revenues of more than ten pounds remain independent. That provision, in effect, capped salaries, dissuading gifted men from the ministry. "If a man would deale covertly to pull awaye religion," Sandys inquired, "howe could he doe it better" than impose salary caps?[3]

---

1. Bodl., Tanner MS. 79, 152v, and *JPQE,* 302–3.

2. BL, Lansdowne MS. 30B, 206v, and *JPQE,* 283.

3. BL, Lansdowne MS. 30B, 208r. Also consult the anonymous *Answer to the two first principall treatises* (London, 1584), 343, on parish service and salary.

It seemed to Sandys that many young pastors and dissidents in the Commons were looking for excuses to "pull awaye" reformed religion as Elizabeth's settlement designed and defined it. Their petitions, he said, contained a revealing contradiction. At first they complained about "unlearned and unable" incumbents, but then they tried to pull the plug on pluralism, eliminating the one way diocesan officials might assure learned and able candidates would be drawn to smaller parishes. Sandys suspected that complainants knew what they were doing. Their criticisms of pluralism and the concern to "plant" a learned ministry in every parish were covers; they would be satisfied with nothing less than the implementation of Thomas Cartwright's plan for a completely decentralized church administration. Their "griefes," Sandys said, amounted to "an introduction" or conspiracy "to bringe patronage to the people."[4]

Sandys argued that consultations with commoners could have no beneficial effect. Candidates very seldom came from parishes to which they were assigned, so laymen there would be unfamiliar with nominees' virtues and vices. Hearsay rather than verifiable information would end up shaping parishioners' judgments. Sandys supposed that, even if there were adequate probationary periods, bishops were in an untenable position. If they decided to hear testimony at their cathedrals, they must somehow allow for the fact that only parishioners bent on repeating the worst about a probationer's character would undertake the journeys to testify. If bishops resolved to take testimony on site, they must expect the garrulous and querulous to take the occasion as an invitation to tell tall tales. Gossip would clog the system. Commoners' bias could block the best appointments. Ordering officials to consult with parishioners encouraged unhelpful delays.[5]

Sandys looks to have been mounting an Everest of obstacles to delay or deter further reform, and the queen was dissatisfied with his excuses and arguments. Mildmay heard her comment on her bishops' misrule, their "negligence" and "slackness."[6] Yet she was as far from "bring[ing] patronage to the people" as Sandys. Apparently, William Overton was the only bishop willing to contemplate accommodating the Commons petition for lay involvement in ministerial selection. His articles of 1584 permitted parish-

---

4. BL, Lansdowne MS. 30B, 203v–4r.
5. BL, Lansdowne MS. 30B, 203r.
6. *JPQE*, 303.

ioners in his diocese to evaluate a would-be incumbent after he served for a month, which would "acquaint parishioners with [his] person [and] gifts," in theory, giving the congregation a chance to detect and "prove against [him a] notorious default." Yet Overton failed to stipulate what would happen if a "default" should be proven. He failed as well to specify when, where, and how a fault or proof should be made known. Had he flinched at the prospect of public scandal and avoided setting procedures for airing any? Did he assume the threat of disclosure would be just enough to oblige unworthy candidates to resign? Or were Overton's articles, especially concerning popular participation and the month probation, empty gestures amounting to no more than a nod to local parishioners and, in parliament, to the partisans of broadly participatory parish regimes, all of whom the bishop ostensibly mistrusted?[7]

Such mistrust was long-standing and widespread. It made John Jewel cautious. As we learned, he defended the rights of ordinary people to read the Bible yet dreaded the results. Social theorist Thomas Smith similarly supported having commoners read scripture, all the while worrying they might yield "too quick assent either to their own invention or to other men's."[8] Into the 1580s, the "other men" were Jesuits and "Romish traytours" who, "under the habite of hurtlesse sheepe sought in the church of God to playe the part of ravening woolves."[9] Overton thought that commoners in Coventry and Lichfield were likely prey, too fond of "vain popish trish trash" to put up resistance. Many churches there were unprotected; relatively few reliable pastors were in place. Overton described his diocese in 1582 as "the very sinke of the whole realme." "Little reform," he concluded, was "to be looked for."[10]

The few partisans of participatory parish regimes who survived into the 1580s were thinking differently of the laity. On occasion, they acknowledged commoners' ignorance, obstinacy, and indolence. But they supposed pastors selected by the people would have a greater say in parishioners' rehabilitation. Hence, a truly, pervasively reformed church would rapidly emerge in the realm. Not so, said Matthew Sutcliffe, dean of Exeter Cathedral, who

---

7. See Overton's "Articles," *EEA*, 168.

8. Smith, *Discourse*, 63, 127, 134.

9. Anthony Munday, *A briefe and true reporte of the execution of certaine traytours at Tiborne* (London, 1582), A2r.

10. BL, Lansdowne MS. 36, 46r–49r; and *EEA*, 163.

denied there was or could ever be a connection between lay empowerment and pastoral effectiveness. "Rudesbies," he claimed, would remain rubes, ignorant and insolent, whether they elected or simply accepted incumbents: sooner teach an ass to harp or a sow to dance than preach a prole to piety. Sutcliffe aimed to deflate the puritans' confidence that reformers could count on commoners before—but certainly after—their preferences were put in pulpits. He capitalized on skepticisms similar to those that Overton, Jewel, and Smith expressed and on the suspicions that Elizabeth, Cecil, Sandys, and Whitgift harbored. None had much faith in the rudesbies, and all declined "to bringe patronage to the people."[11]

Whitgift was determined, possibly because he believed that the laity favored candidates for the ministry who "cleane alter the order of the service and the administration of the sacraments and other things by law appointed." Nonconformist ministers were a clever lot, he suggested. They "so framed theire parishioners" that few if any complaints were lodged against their innovations. And when a nonconformist was suspended from the ministry, laymen in his parish, "so framed," preferred a replacement exactly like him.[12] Whitgift explained why the nonconformists had their way. Rudesbies and renegade pastors, he noticed, were cut from the same cloth. The latter, "for the most part yonge in years and of verie small readinge and studie," moved among the commoners, for the most part, companionably, effectively spreading a resentment of more senior prelates.[13] Moreover, from what happened when nonconformists were dislodged and "driven to their shifts," one should infer that informality and companionability with ordinary people came naturally to them. For example, John Stroud lost his living in Cranbrook and turned to a trade he practiced part-time while pastoring. Critics scoffed, yet his friends insisted that "printing is no baser than tentmaking or fishing." Stroud, they said, chose the apostles' way of conforming to the world of work while refusing to conform to the ways of the world, refusing, they meant, to observe rules of the realm's partially reformed church. Richard Gawton took up carpentry when he was deprived of his pulpit in Norwich. The trade had been good enough for Jesus, he said, when told it was contemptible. The dean of the cathedral chapter doubted that Gawton and the gospel of Mark (6:3) that he cited could be trusted, claim-

---

11. See Sutcliffe's *Treatise of ecclesiastical discipline* (London, 1590), 20–21.
12. LPL, MS. 2002, 75v.
13. BL, Lansdowne MS. 42, 185r.

ing it was typical of nonconformist pastors of small reading and less study to rely on the reports of rudesbies in Nazareth and draw a self-serving conclusion from the words of proles prone to error![14]

The dean's response, real or richly imagined by Gawton, seems extreme. Mistrusting the evangelists was risky business. Mistrusting sixteenth-century rudesbies, however, was second nature to the likes of Sandys and Whitgift. Nonetheless, "rash and rude" commoners had gained a certain celebrity by the 1580s. The friends of Stroud and Gawton were not the first Elizabethans to refer proudly and defensively to the apostles' simplicity and rusticity. John Foxe, Anthony Gilby, George Gifford, William Perkins, and Robert Crowley transformed rudesbies into lay theologians. Especially in Foxe's pages, they became the most formidable adversaries a Catholic, catholicizing, or conformist cleric might expect to encounter. Rudesbies were not just perfect foils for pretentious, "popish" clerics in the literature of late Tudor religious controversy; they also became splendid prompts or models for the reformed laity, who were "not [yet] much commended for any forwardnes in the cause of religion."[15]

The fictional rudesbies were remarkably self-assured and unreservedly anticlerical. They were cousins of "Playne Piers," whom Crowley's mid-century editions of *Piers Plowman* introduced to generations of Elizabethans. Foxe's *Acts and Monuments,* from the first edition of 1563, offered them an assortment of rudesby muckrakers. Foxe flat out revered his cooks, cowherds, and other commoners whose confrontations with officials he had scripted to emphasize the resourcefulness and cunning of ordinary laymen. By the 1580s, copies of Foxe's *Acts* were placed alongside the English Bible in every cathedral church in the Canterbury province.[16]

George Gifford's *Country Divinity,* first published in 1581, circulated well but not as widely as Foxe's *Acts.* Yet his Zelot, much as Perkins' Eusebius,

---

14. "The troubles of Richard Gawton," *Register*, 398–99. For Stroud, see DWL, Morrice MSS. B.2. 21r, C. 324.

15. The report on indifference and "forwardnes" appears in a description of the laity in Lancashire which dates to the 1580s, PRO 12/235/4. Anthony Gilby explicitly rated his rustics above "popish priests" in his *Pleasaunt dialogue conteining a large discourse betweene a souldier of Barwick and an English chaplain* (London, 1566), 15r.

16. See Ritchie Kendall, *The Drama of Dissent: The Radical Poetics of Nonconformity, 1380–1590* (Chapel Hill: University of North Carolina Press, 1986), 125–28; John King, "Robert Crowley's Editions of *Piers Plowman*: A Tudor Apocalypse," *Modern Philology* 73 (1976): 342–48; and David Loades, *Revolution in Religion: The English Reformation, 1530–1570* (Cardiff: University of Wales Press, 1992), 110.

whom we met in our first chapter, is an excellent specimen of the reformed rudesby theologian. Atheos, Zelot's sometimes churlish interlocutor, maintained that God was unlikely to punish Christians who did their best to please him. Their best, by Atheos' calculations, amounted only to an effort to obey the ten commandments and a sincere remorse for sin. And that expectation and calculation were probably representative of the views of late Tudor laymen who were attending their churches in ever-increasing numbers. To them Gifford's Zelot replied that attendance, good behavior, and remorse purchased no reward from God as long as a reward was expected and as long as the dutiful and remorseful failed to be faithful as well, that is, failed to "feel the power of Christ's death."[17]

Atheos resisted his intended mentor's meddling. He resented puritans of his acquaintance, "busie in checking every man," and stood ready to credit preachers who turned a good phrase, seemed informative and informed, and were relatively undemanding. Atheos claimed several times that he was too dim to do more. True to his name, however, Zelot was relentless; he explained that "it is not learning alone which must judge of sound preaching." God's spirit would "inwardly" teach commoners to tell the difference between a muddle and a masterpiece. Rudesbies formerly beguiled by biblical citations or by beautiful words would be able to appreciate substance over sound, to sift what they heard and the preachers from whom they heard it.[18]

Zelot and his hope were parts of an Elizabethan literary strategy that cast the commoner as "a centre of right-thinking theological gravity," a strategy that gave way at the century's end to the suspicion that rudesbies were called rude for a good reason. Atheos would then be taken as the typical layman; Zelot and Eusebius as overidealized, rather preposterous effigies of the common man.[19] But the opinions and the very persistence of rudesby mentors in late Tudor literature seem to me all the more striking when we factor in a growing suspicion of lay initiative and assertiveness. Reformers

---

17. Gifford, *A briefe discourse of certain points of religion which is among the common sort of Christians, which may be termed the countrie divinitie* (London, 1598), 48–49, 132. For church attendance, see MacCulloch, *Later Reformation*, 140–41.

18. Gifford, *Countrie Divinitie*, 11–17, 26–28, 80–90.

19. See Martin Ingram, "From Reformation to Toleration: Popular Religious Cultures in England, 1540–1690," *Popular Culture*, 109; Craig, "Reformation Politics," 14–18; Kumin, *Shaping*, 243; and Marsh, *Popular Religion*, 212–13.

of various stripes, into the 1580s, still figured that something better than Atheos' Pelagianism might come from below. But the best evidence for their dreams or schemes is resistance to broadly participatory parish regimes. The schemers left less behind than the likes of Sandys, Sutcliffe, and Whitgift. And the articulate and forward, fictional lay protagonists of Gilby, Gifford, Perkins, and Foxe hardly document a movement to empower the masses. Yet the resistance was real, as is the small stock of memorable and resourceful commoners in the literature of Elizabethan reform. And two outspoken partisans of lay participation suggest, if not a concerted or conspicuous campaign or movement, the survival of some palpably positive thinking about the laity.

Browne and Fenner

Robert Browne studied for the ministry at Cambridge in the early 1570s. Conceivably, he witnessed the debates there on lay patronage and prophesying, the same discussions we overheard in the previous chapter. He remembered that he was "soare grieved" by the slow pace of church reform at the time. He also recalled turning to the Bible, where he learned how the first Christians organized their communities. He subsequently drew up proposals that left much to be determined locally and laically, by "the voice of the whole people guided bie the elders and the forwardest." Pure democracy seemed unworkable to Browne. The "whole people" could not be trusted to complete the reform of reformed Christianity or even get reform off to a good start: "the kingdom of God was not to be begun by whole parishes but rather off the worthiest, were thei never so fewe." Browne went from door to door, on the lookout for some smoldering discontent with current church discipline. He would know the "worthiest" by their level of dissatisfaction. Cambridge householders, however, disappointed him; he came to see the city as something of a stopover. He believed "the Lord had appointed him there to be occupied onelie to trie and prepare him to a further and more effectual message." Parishioners at St. Bene't "gathered him a stipend" to settle his ministry, yet he was persuaded his future lay elsewhere. In Cambridge only the few "forwardest" thought as he did. He refused to blame the rest but railed instead against "the wickedness of bishops [and] against their whole power and authoritie." They permitted poorly trained and indolent men to serve the churches in their dioceses. As a consequence, "blind busserdes" and "idol shepherds" discredited the ministry. Even when candidates were carefully examined and exceptionally gifted, however, diocesan administrators were wrong to have imposed them; schooled in scripture, the realm's bishops ought to have known that neither Christ nor the apostles dared to "thrust ministers upon any congregation."[20]

Browne's brother bought him a license to preach, but he would not accept it because, he asserted, the archbishop had no authority to sell it. Browne seemed bent on controversy. In 1579 he renewed his friendship with Robert Harrison, who was visiting Cambridge from Norwich. He serenaded his old college comrade and prospective ally with his criticisms of church officials. He declared "he was nowe so far from seeking license, ordaining, authorising at [a bishop's] handes," adding that he "abhorred such trash and pollutions as the markes . . . of Antichrist."[21] Harrison took some convincing but soon came around to Browne's position and passion, putting him up when he arrived in Norwich and accompanying him through East Anglia. To local magistrates, Browne and Harrison posed a threat. They warned the pair "to be carefull of [their] proceeding," confiding to the privy council in 1581, though, that the two dissidents were unlikely to comply.[22]

The magistrates guessed correctly, and when further measures were taken to suppress the pair's "proceeding," Browne told other friends from prison to prepare to flee the realm. Scotland accommodated a presbyterian polity, yet Browne and Harrison figured that the far side of the Tweed "framed itself . . . to please England toe much" and would be unsafe. Instead, the two looked to the continent and made plans for exile, "ffor their [followers'] meetinges together, and ffor their exercises therein,"

> for exhortation and edifiing, ether by all men which had the guift or by those whiche had a special charge before others. And for the lawefulnes of putting forth questions to learne the trueth, as iff anie thing seemed doubtful and hard, [it would be appropriate] to require some to shewe it more plainlie or for anie to shewe it him selfe and to cause the rest to understand it. . . . Againe, it was agreed that anie might protest, appeale, complaine, exhort, dispute, reprove as he had occasion, but in due order.[23]

---

20. *Browne*, 397–404, 477–78.
21. *Browne*, 406–7.
22. BL, Lansdowne MS. 33, 167r.
23. *Browne*, 422–23.

"Exhortation and edifiing . . . by all men which had the guift"; "putting forth questions"; pressing for plain talk and a general understanding among "companions," clergy, and laity: what church officials worried prophesying might become in the 1570s, Robert Browne imagined his congregation becoming in the 1580s. He made arrangements for the mutual exhortation, examination, and edification of reformed Christians, "seeking holines and happiness by Christ in his church."[24]

According to Browne, reformed Christians may find "holines and happiness" only in a congregation where "anie might protest, appeale, complaine, exhort, dispute, reprove." Historians could be right to say that "Browne's chief contribution to separatist ecclesiology was to place his church-ideal in the context of a covenant relationship."[25] Arguably, the covenant replaced the clergy, in some measure. "We make not the minister . . . to be the essence, substance, or life of the outward church," Browne explained, "but the keeping of the covenant by the outwarde discipline and government thereof."[26] He accused moderate ministers of dishonesty. "Somewhat conformable," they devised "tolerations, mitigations, and other trim distinctions" to keep bishops at bay and to appease ordinary people who might otherwise have pressed for a more thorough reformation of church polity and discipline.[27]

It is impossible to determine whether Browne (1) planned to distribute power in the congregation to "anie" and "all" because he hated hierarchy and was disappointed with conformist colleagues or (2) resented bishops and moderate clerics because he was so committed to leveling and lay empowerment. The first looks likelier, for he repeatedly criticized episcopal tyranny and clerical temporizing. Furthermore, he never comprehensively commented on the relationships between "the whole" congregation and its "forwardest" members. But Browne continued to advocate broad participation

---

24. *Browne*, 257.

25. Timothy George, *John Robinson and the English Separatist Tradition* (Macon, Ga.: Mercer University Press, 1982), 41–42; and, for Browne's "unusual, mutualist, conditional" covenant concept, see Barrington White, *The English Separatist Tradition from the Marian Martyrs to the Pilgrim Fathers* (Oxford: Oxford University Press, 1971), 53–59. But consult Stephen Brachlow *Communion of Saints: Radical Puritan and Separatist Ecclesiology, 1570–1625* (Oxford: Oxford University Press, 1988), 174–76, for a dissent.

26. *Browne*, 447.

27. *Browne*, 334–35, 340–41.

during his exile. He advised Christians who had withdrawn from "conformable" neighbors to assure themselves the opportunity to choose from their number "those which had a special charge before others."[28]

Harmony between "the whole" and the "forwardest," between those who chose and those chosen to fulfill "a special charge," was an objective no separatist congregation managed to meet for any length of time. For Whitgift and his colleagues, harmony in the parish depended on conformity in the pulpit. On orders from the archbishop, diocesan administrators in southeastern England commanded that all pastors subscribe to three articles declaring the propriety of previous legislation for conformity, the orthodoxy of the prayerbook, and the ecclesiastical authority of the queen. Failure to subscribe led to suspension. Whitgift's commissioners forced known dissidents to answer interrogatories under oath and to swear their obedience. Some summoned ministers protested the procedures. Their friends at court objected that interrogations without specific accusations were unlawful. Whitgift replied by pointing out that "a greate number of disordered causes" never came to light "by complaint and open accusation," principally because nonconformist pastors conned their parishioners and clerical colleagues. The churches were in "a crasie state," Whitgift's secretary later reported; they required "gentle purges." Thus bishops were justified acting on hunches and rumors: starting with some sense of a clerical colleague's disaffection was "a thinge often tymes most necessarye in the government of the church."[29] Ordinarily, one might prefer to begin investigating after specific complaints or charges were registered. But "a vehement suspicion sufficeth to make such enquirie," Richard Cosin let on, and "sufficeth" as well, to oblige self-incrimination under oath—the objective of this extraordinary proceeding, to ferret out the likes of Dudley Fenner.[30]

Fenner refused to subscribe to the three articles and was suspended for his refusal. During the previous decade he echoed Cartwright's statements and complaints, following him to Antwerp. But he then returned and settled

---

28. *Browne*, 408. He also urged his parishioners to participate in discipline, specifically in "church rebuke," as he called it in 1582 (269), but he himself was rebuked and "utterly forsaken" by his church in exile soon afterward (428), returning to England less contemptuous of the authorities and living conformably well into the seventeenth century.

29. See LPL, MS. 2002, 72r–78v; and for "crasie state," George Paule, *The life of the most reverend and religious prelate, John Whitgift* (London, 1612), 61–62.

30. Richard Cosin, *An apologie of and for sundrie proceedings by jurisdiction ecclesiastical* (London, 1591), 83–84, 158–59.

in Kent, as a curate in Cranbrook, where we found him in the last chapter. Whitgift was just then stoking his campaign for conformity, and it looked to Fenner as if the archbishop were firing up "a civill war of the churche." It seemed, that is, as if the archbishop had prepared to lead the church back to Roman Catholicism and, along the way, to misrepresent the principled puritan dissent as sedition and insurrection.[31]

Puritan protests, Fenner argued, amounted to nothing more menacing than "sorrowful complaining." He said that he and his colleagues never meant to "impugn" or "diminish" Her Majesty's majesty. They desired "no alteration of the estate, either in church or commonwealth, but the perfection of both." Far from being compulsively contrary, as the conformists claimed, they were loyal subjects, Fenner continued, neither seditious nor malicious. He and his associates would change no part of the faith they shared with Whitgift and other English Calvinists, "but out of it," they would "deduct the right ecclesiastical government of the church."[32]

"Deductions"? John Bridges, answering for the conformists, thought Fenner's "right ecclesiastical government" unrelated to any commonly accepted faith. It was a private and "miraculous revelation" deduced from nothing but rather devised *de novo,* Bridges observed, challenging Fenner's distinction between "alteration" and "perfection." Nonconformists, for their part, trusted that their plans for parish polity would hold up their end of the bargain (or covenant or contract) that God once made with the faithful. God's promises were conditional on Christians making strenuous efforts to complete the reform of doctrine and discipline by establishing "the right ecclesiastical government of the church," the perfect polity which they must "deduct" from their reformed faith. Fenner understood that "deductions" should be tested against the regime reported in, and prescribed by, the Bible. He added that (unnamed) historians of Christian antiquity agreed with the partisans of broad parish participation that the churches depicted in the Acts of the Apostles functioned in many respects as democracies. Patronage then belonged to the people; Christian commoners chose their leaders and had

---

31. Dudley Fenner, *Defence of the godly ministers against the slaunder of Dr. Bridges* (London, 1587), C2v–C3r. Cartwright charged that Whitgift, his commissioners, and his apologists "fathered" political subversion on Fenner and on him as well; *Briefe apology of Thomas Cartwright* (London, 1596), C1v.

32. Fenner, *Defence,* B1v, D1v–D2r, 121–22.

a say in where they led. Hierarchy subsequently developed as a proportionate response to "continuall tumults, partialities, and disorders." Fenner's interpretations of the Bible, the covenant, and the history of hierarchy dovetailed with his defense of puritans' dissent in a concluding question: inasmuch as religious reform had removed all the causes of "continuall tumults," why not return to reformed parishioners the parts their ancestors and apostles reserved for the faithful in the selection of their pastors?[33]

Conformists countered that there was nothing to give back. That "the primitive church used always to elect her pastors by the suffrages of the people" was unprovable, Thomas Bilson said, arguing that the New Testament proved just the opposite, namely, that itinerant apostles and prophets appointed local churches' leaders. Perhaps for short spells, during persecutions, "when prophets failed," parishioners temporarily took charge, Bilson conceded, but by the fourth century Christian magistrates made decisions "without depending on the voyces of the people." The notion that mobs knew more than magistrates about the ministry would have been as unwelcome then, he went on, as it was in the sixteenth century. Bilson finished with the familiar conformist refrain: Elizabethan church officials in concert with the queen ought to manage church affairs without attending to "the rashness and rudenesse of the many that are often ledd rather by affection than discretion." Here was thinking of the laity that was overtly contemptuous of commoners, Bilson would have had to admit, though he believed it irrefutably biblical to boot.[34]

Fenner's *Counter-poyson*, written soon after he was suspended from the ministry, was as defensive as his earlier *Defence of the godlie ministers* against Bridges and the likes of Bilson. Fenner took issue in both treatises with the assumption that the early Christian commoners could not be, and had not been, trusted with power on a regular basis. Quite the contrary, Fenner said, local officials knew that they had nothing to fear from the "rashness and rudenesse" of their people. Leaders had learned how to keep "altercations" orderly. Christianity survived its infancy and its first controversies, which had been caused more by curiosity than by "rudenesse," and its survival should be attributed to the wise decision to air rather than suppress disagreements.[35]

---

33. Fenner, *Defence*, 61–68. Also see similar statements from his *Counter-poyson*, printed in *Register*, 432–33.

34. Thomas Bilson, *The perpetual government of Christ's church* (London, 1593), 88–89, 353–60.

35. Fenner, *Counter-poyson* (London, 1584), 32–35, 144; and Fenner, *Defence*, 130.

The solution then and in the sixteenth century, Fenner said, was to tolerate certain levels of dissent. Should the government encourage discussions of religious disagreements, churches would become something of an early warning system. Prelates might sift sentiments before they turned subversive. Fenner did not forget that nonconformists and conformists sifted differently and found danger at varying levels of discord, so he specified that reformed presbyters handle the sieves and that their goal was to report resurgent Catholicism, to "finde out Jesuits" and not to harass radicals.[36]

For Fenner, spirited discussion was spiritually bracing and could be politically hygienic. The puritans' fondness for lively talk, he argued, did not make them "persuaders of rebellion." He assured that "rebellion [is] avoyded" and "poperie is rooted out" when curiosity, inquiry, and heated discussion were allowed, even encouraged. He probably would have endorsed historian John Guy's view that "disputations and controversy were [the] lifeblood of reformed religion."[37] But inviting dispute while avoiding disaffection could be tricky. Fenner assigned that task to presbyters, dismissing the notion of critics of presbyterian polity that "eldershippe" was "a meere conceit of our age."[38] Fenner and his friends never tired of finding biblical precedent for presbyters, though they also argued that the requirements of reformed polity made them especially indispensable. Presbyters had been present at the start, and they should also be parts of "the right ecclesiastical government" in the sixteenth century, when they would serve as a check on the rudesbies' rashness, which made conformists shudder, and as impresarios of the congregational consensus, which made puritan advocates of participatory parish regimes swoon. They were to "compose the controversies about the faith," to resolve intramural quarrels, and to elect and depose ministers in a public assembly and with the authority of the entire church.[39]

How representative of and responsive to their parishioners might those lay elders have been? Fenner required them to "yield to the challenge of some not so well instructed." He recalled the apostle Peter had "to beare with

---

36. Fenner, *Counter-poyson,* 153, and *A defence of the reasons of the Counter-poyson* (London, 1587), C4r.

37. CCCC, MS. 121, 142; Fenner, *Defence,* 125; and John Guy, "The Elizabethan Establishment and the Ecclesiastical Polity," in *The Reign Of Elizabeth I: Court and Culture in the Last Decade,* ed. John Guy (Cambridge: Cambridge University Press, 1995), 126.

38. Bilson, *Perpetual government,* 172–73, 195.

39. BL, Harleian MS. 6879, 127v; and Fenner, *Sacra theologia sive veritas quae est secundum pietatem* (London, 1586), 121r.

[persons] contending against him and peacablie to give them not onelie the hearing, but the satisfaction." Conformists had noted that rudesbies in Jerusalem ultimately "yielded" to Peter, and Fenner granted them the point, though he fixed on Peter's having "give[n] them the satisfaction" of an answer.[40] The implication seems to have been that elders or presbyters were representative when they were responsive and were responsible when they were courteous. Arguably, Fenner was disinclined to go much further. One imagines him only grudgingly giving ground to the "not so well instructed." He was, after all, on record as a proponent of the learned ministry and, presumably, he recognized that learning afforded pastors and presbyters some privileges. Nonetheless, in his *Sacred Theology*, one passage appears to undercut his emphasis on learning. At the time it would no doubt have raised some brows. For Fenner ruled outright that patronage in the parish belonged to the people, that choices were to be made *ex judicio totius ecclesiae, vel majoris partis.*[41]

Yet he could have been clearer. *Vel majoris partis* is ambiguous. Did "greater part" denote a majority vote or refer to parish elites? Fenner was straightforward in combatting the idea that parishioners must be excluded, yet when he explained (or did not) how or to what extent they might be included, he left issues unresolved. And if we start elsewhere, with the comment on direct elections he dropped into an unrelated argument for the authority of Hebrew scripture, his position on direct parish democracy gets no clearer. Fenner was compiling "wryters, holy and prophane, who have continually alleadged the sentences and commaundments of the Olde Testament" when he named Cyprian who took up the Pentateuch "to prooveth the election of the people." Quite likely, for this example and others, Fenner consulted François de Saillans, whose collection of biblical and patristic passages concluded that the "election" of pastors "ought not to be made without the plaine and expresse consent of the people." When English conformists criticized the collection, Fenner rushed to its defense, so we might argue that he supported what de Saillans wrote about the "mechanics" of popular participation. But, alas, de Saillans was no more precise than Fenner. We can only say with certainty that the two attempted to persuade read-

---

40. Fenner, *Defence*, 70–71, citing Acts 11.

41. Fenner, *Sacra theologia*, 105v–6r. Also see John Morgan, *Godly Learning: Puritan Attitudes Towards Reason, Learning, and Education, 1560–1640* (Cambridge: Cambridge University Press, 1986), 232–33.

ers that, if ever discouraging words were heard from the Fathers and the councils of Christian antiquity, they must weigh the negative against a more imposing, authentic patristic witness for lay authority and local control. Partisans of broadly participatory parish regimes might not have learned from Fenner or de Saillans all that they needed to make those regimes work, yet they would have been told that "plaine and expresse consent" was as patristic as the few prohibitions of same that conformists might cite. And the readers of Fenner and de Saillans would also have heard that those prohibitions did not always mean what they said. For instance, "as concerning that which the decree of the Council of Laodicea ordaineth, that the election and choice of pastors should not be made by the people, that must be understood of the people alone, to the end that election should not be made confusedly and without good order."[42]

From the negation of the council's negation ("should not be made by the people"), we may safely infer some commitment to the positive ("should be made by the people"), although Fenner's *vel majoris partis* ("or the greater part thereof") is vexing. Might it be that he proposed a "due consent," a "plaine and expresse consent," that was, as Stephen Brachlow now asserts, "not much more than a rubber stamp"? Perhaps when Fenner and his friends, along with other nonconformists, wrote "consent" they referred rather to a recondite consensus of sorts, to what Brachlow now calls a "guaranteed public affirmation of judgments enacted by ruling elders in the name of the congregation."[43]

A *Briefe and plaine declaration concerning the desires of all the faithful* suggests otherwise. Circulating by 1584, it lays out the nonconformist arguments for a broadly *and* comprehensively participatory parish regime. Historians think that either Walter Travers or John Field composed it, but a good case could be made for William Fulke, now that we have his equally forceful statements in the Cambridge debates the previous decade. The *Declaration* is as "briefe and plaine" as Fulke had been and as its title promises.

---

42. De Saillans published his *Treatise* as Bertrande de Loque. The British Library copy (shelfmark 3936 aa40) has an "Admonition to the Reader" by Richard Vaughn, with conformists' criticisms to which Fenner responded. For that response, see DWL, Morrice MSS. B.1.511–22, C.555–67. For Laodicea and "plaine and expresse consent," see de Saillans, *Treatise of the church*, trans. Thomas Wilcox (London, 1581), 39–40; for "wryters, holy and prophane," Fenner, *Counter-poyson*, 94–95.

43. Brachlow, *Communion of Saints*, 122–23, 190–91.

It stipulates that nothing ought to be done without the congregation's consent and commends nothing to which Fenner might have objected. Moreover, without reducing "consent" to a "rubber stamp," the *Declaration* cautions, as Fenner did, that power not be "so diffused over the whole church" that the parishioners "hear," "try," and "determine" everything. Elders, "the segnorye," assisted "because the judgment of the multitude is confuse[d]." According to the same document, however, elders or presbyters should "be moderated that their judgement may be rightly accounted the judgement of the holy churche." Such was the will of those "faithfull ministers" for whom the *Declaration* claimed to be speaking. But was the plan to submit elders to the authority of the whole church, the "whole multitude," or, as the text also has it, to that of "the holy church"? The former seems likelier because "the desires of all the faithful" were that the seniory or consistory be doubly accountable to all parishioners. First, the lay presbyters on the panel were to be elected by the entire congregation. Then,

> the second point for moderation of the elders' authority in such sort that their sentence may be the sentence of the churche is this: that when the consistory hath traveled in examining of causes pertaining to ecclesiastical discipline and agreed what judgement [it] ought to passe upon matters, [members] propound it to the whole multitude that it may be confirmed by their consent.[44]

"Their consent" cannot categorically be distinguished from Brachlow's "rubber stamp." For, as often as nonconformists dared to "return" power to parishioners and tried to assure presbyters' decisions reflected, and were "rightly accounted[,] the judgement of the church," they hedged a congregation's right to consent and limited it to "cases of greater weight."[45] Or they assumed that regular elections of elders assured accountability. Undeniably, however, they were thinking ambitiously about the laity because conformists were fearful. They accused Fenner, Fulke, and their associates of holding pastors hostage to the commoners' whims. Fenner was heard to propose that "the people ought in everie church . . . to choose their owne ministers," and when those ministers do not do well "to put [them] out and chose other."[46]

---

44. *Briefe and plaine declaration* (London, 1584), 81–84.

45. For example, see Bodl., Ashmole MS. 383, 70r, 81v. The anonymous author of this treatise on "the sacred doctrine of divinity" professes to be continuing Fenner's work.

46. BL, Lansdowne MS. 30B, 211r.

He denied it, stressing that he would never have given the laity such "sway." He took care to put distance between himself and Robert Browne: "wee doe more then mislyke [his] doinges and writinges."[47] And a portion of that "wee," still pressing for congregational autonomy and presbyterian polity into the 1580s, now looks to have turned a bit timid as the decade wore on and especially as Browne seemed to swerve to "the left," that is, toward what conformists and nonconformists alike considered unwholesome separatist experiments. But Fenner continued to assume that controlled consent was possible within every congregation, consent fashioned and "guided," as he said, by panels of presbyters who could brake parishes short of faction and anarchy. Their job would be to think not only about the laity but, on occasion, to think for the laity. Whitgift would not take that prospect very seriously, or, to be precise, he took it as a serious miscalculation. He believed history had proven the mob a monster. "Marvelous contentions" had disrupted church elections in Alexandria and Antioch, he remembered, and there had been "a marvellous stir and sedition" in fourth-century Rome.[48] Even if history suggested that lay consent could be managed and order maintained, Whitgift would never have trusted nonconformists' willingness to manage their constituents and to uphold the prevailing order. Those very nonconformists, after all, were forever challenging episcopal prerogatives, the requirements associated with the prayerbook, and their own suspensions from the ministry. Arguably, those three challenges were the sum and substance of their discontent. Fenner said as much. Nonetheless, rumors reached Whitgift and others that dissidents were ready for war and readying fellow radicals—according to Bancroft, as many as one hundred thousand—to change the terms of the religious settlement.[49] Conformists sensed some "unlawfull execution" of the puritans' "distempered designementes" was imminent. Radical reformers might talk of truce and say they only wanted a further opportunity to discuss their discipline, but it was all "to cover their lewd purposes until by the multitude of lewd complices they be able by force to putt the same in practice . . . to the utter overthrowe" of episcopacy.[50]

---

47. Fenner, *Counter-poyson*, 149.
48. *Whitgift*, 1:446–47.
49. Bancroft, *Dangerous positions*, 138–39.
50. Oxford, Queen's College MS. 280, 172v. A decade earlier, John Field mentioned "the multitude" might sieze ground that the church authorities refused to cede. Nonconformists rarely, if at all, repeated the threat, although their critics picked it up to discredit

And conformists wrote as if the destruction of episcopacy would be only the beginning. They predicted that radicals were unlikely to stop at the cathedrals; they would level hedges and manors and all markers of, or monuments to, affluence, influence, order, and rank. An apologist for episcopacy, pondering in print "whether it be fitt . . . to pull downe cathedrall churches," seems now to have reflected the temper of those times when he grimly counseled that capitulating to religious "innovation" would leave "a very barbarouse and fowle example" for all ages, and would leave every testament to Tudor achievement in ruin.[51]

Christopher Hill thinks alarmism of this kind contrived. He says that talk of monstrously disposed multitudes set priests and propertied parishioners against commoners. Conformists built their coalition, he claims, by forecasting appalling social and economic costs, should the realm's congregations decide to elect and eject clerical leaders. It seemed a cost that the kingdom could ill afford into the 1580s, when the crown and commoners were "in a greate distresse of money by warre." War, rumors of war, high taxation, escalating inflation, severe food shortages—what historian William Hunt now calls "popular immiseration"—was a recipe for unrest. Conformists' chefs, one could argue, stirred the pot to the puritans' great disadvantage, but most puritans themselves wanted nothing done "confusedly" and "without good order" during those troubled times. Increasingly they favored restraint.[52]

Too Great a Perfection

Troubled times. Wallace MacCaffrey writes of an "atmosphere of dread." Worries about the worst that could happen were often trumped by events.

---

them; Collinson, *Religion of Protestants*, 189–90. And, nearly a century later, they were still at it; see Peter Heylyn, *Aerius Redivivus* (Oxford, 1670), book 7, 298–300.

51. LPL, MS. 2016, 28r.

52. Consult William Hunt, *The Puritan Moment: The Coming of Religion in an English County* (Cambridge: Cambridge University Press, 1983), 41–63; and Christopher Hill, "The Many-Headed Monster in Late Tudor and Early Stuart Political Thinking," in *From Renaissance to Counter-Reformation*, ed. Charles Carter (New York: Random House, 1965), 296–324. For unrest and the "epidemic" of violence in the 1580s and 1590s, see Roger Manning, *Village Revolts: Social Protest and Popular Disturbances in England, 1509–1640* (Oxford: Oxford University Press, 1988), 187–210; the essays by R. B. Outhwaite and Peter

Protestants' military and political setbacks on the continent during the late 1570s left the regime without allies abroad. How other outcomes across the Channel may have affected reform in England is pure speculation. But we have no difficulty imagining why conformists grew cautious into the 1580s, because Patrick Collinson has so aptly summarized their predicament. They were caught, he tells us, between "militant puritanism" and "an equally vigorous Catholic revival," "two deeply antithetical and intensely politicized religious fanaticisms [which] confronted a hardline archbishop of Canterbury, John Whitgift, backed by a queen impersonating a rock, *semper eadem.*" Any agitation for broadly participatory parish regimes would have been associated with a deliberate destabilization. Puritans who aspired to careers within the national church were adjusting and beginning "to present themselves as but the evangelically zealous and activist, genuinely protestant, and therefore genuinely politically loyal, face of the English church." They knew changes had no chance of implementation, unless they promised some further concentration of power and authority, not its dissemination among commoners, for order increasingly was identified with oligarchy.[53]

So the chroniclers of withdrawal consulted in our first chapter were onto something when they collected England's elites at one pole and its commoners at the other, the pole to which the conformists, notably Bancroft, banished puritan partisans of "due consent." Bancroft's methods remind Collinson of Senator Joseph McCarthy's. Both the bishop and the notorious senator exploited their respective "atmosphere[s] of dread"; indeed, they helped create them. They were masters of polarization, and, as Anthony Milton understands, polarization was "the function of polemical debate rather than its trigger."[54] The shame is that the conformists' incendiary and insistently dualistic rhetoric, dividing their world between the irrepressibly profane and the acquiescently pious, encourages historians thinking of the

---

Clark in *The European Crisis of the 1590s,* ed. Clark (London: Allen and Unwin, 1985); and Mark Burnett, "Apprentice Literature and the Crisis of the 1590s," *Yearbook of English Studies* 21 (1991): 27–38.

53. MacCaffrey, *Elizabeth,* 8, 51, for "dread"; Tittler, *Reformation,* 188, 208–9, 242–43, for "incursion of oligarchic rule"; Collinson, "Ecclesiastic Vitriol: Religious Satire in the 1590s and the Invention of Puritanism," *Reign of Elizabeth,* 150, for Whitgift's dilemma; and Lake, *Boxmaker's Revenge,* 12–13, for moderate puritans' choices.

54. Anthony Milton, *Catholic and Reformed: Roman and Protestant Churches in English Protestant Thought, 1600–1640* (Cambridge: Cambridge University Press, 1995), 5, 16; Collinson, *Elizabethan Puritan Movement,* 397.

laity to lose sight of England's "extensive middle territory in which people blended their orthodoxy with their assumptions about authority, piety, conviviality, and play."[55]

Into the 1580s, that "middle territory" was not so much lost from view as viewed with growing suspicion. Commoners there were thought susceptible to what diocesan officials feared as radical puritans' initiatives, disgraced by preachers' obvious preening and pandering, to topple the established church. Officials were suspicious of unregulated preaching even after their government suppressed the public phase of prophesying. Reformed Christians were often traveling distances from their parishes to listen to the sermons of pastors from other churches and occasionally to those of unlicensed preachers. That going abroad or "gadding" resembled a pageant or pilgrimage— and represented a serious threat, said some, to the parish system. To the conformists, "gadding" was a bad but breakable habit, a nuisance that needed watching until commoners could be kept and corrected in their own parishes. The puritan premise, however, was that no Christian was "imbued with God's spirite, but such as run to hear preaching."[56]

Dudley Fenner looked forward to the time when "no man need goe above five myle to hear a sermon."[57] Frequently gadding to fartheraway sermons, though, likely struck him as a reasonable interim measure. It was a form of lay patronage, an "election," in which commoners voted with their feet. What understandably concerned conformists was that the vote was invariably against conformity, hierarchy, prayerbook liturgy, scripted homilies, and—what they took to be—order. Were Whitgift familiar with gadding's offspring, he might have warned of trouble in every tent revival. But in 1583 he was more alarmist; puritans parading to hear preachers or conferring with them in the privacy of their homes, he said, were "manifest sign[s] of schisme" and "causes of contention in the church."[58]

---

55. Paul Griffiths, *Youth and Authority: Formative Experiences in England, 1560–1640* (Oxford: Clarendon, 1996), 233.

56. Gifford, *Countrie Divinitie*, 44.

57. Fenner, *Counter-poyson*, 68.

58. Collinson, *Religion of Protestants*, 248, quoting Whitgift. Also, Collinson, "Popular Culture," 46–50. Lake, *Boxmaker's Revenge*, 179–88; Lake and Questier, *Lewd Hat*, 583–610, record similar complaints about "strands of religious radicalism" running through the London puritan "underground" during the next century. But Patrick Collinson, "Sects and the Evolution of Puritanism" in *Puritanism: Transatlantic Perspectives on a Seventeenth-*

Secrecy breeds suspicion in an "atmosphere of dread." The queen's council heard that Catholics covertly met "for massing" somewhere in Oxfordshire every day. Attorney John Norden feared more was afoot; he warned that small squads of recusants in the realm regularly huddled and conspired to bring back "the cloudy darkenes of Romishe religion."[59] Nonconformists shared Norden's concern, but their secrecy was as suspect to the conformists as was that of the Catholics. Authorities in Sussex, for instance, were distressed by nonconformists' meetings at midnight in Mildenhall, where dissident Thomas Settle stalked.[60]

Whitgift fretted. He imagined that puritan partisans of participatory regimes had gotten their ideas about polity from anabaptists on the continent. He predicted that imported notions of "democracy" would make a Münster of any English town puritans populated, because their "democracies" would obliterate critical differences of property, erudition, age, and gender, differences on which order, oligarchy, and hierarchy depended.[61] That was a common refrain. There had long been anxiety that the radicals returning from exile might be tempted to give "equall ryght" to all and to "slide into anabaptistry." University, diocesan, and government authorities were put on alert. Even ardent reformer Laurence Humphrey at Oxford was impatient with sentiments that "smelleth of anabaptisme."[62] Yet Whitgift and his associates succumbed to the fear retailed in the more recent literature purporting to disclose the "barbarous, brutish" anabaptists' plans for "anarchy," for a leveling so comprehensive that it could destroy marriages, families, municipal governments, and local churches. If radical, late Tudor levelers should have their way, it was said, "none maie obei other." In 1583 the conformists accused Fenner of being an English anabaptist.[63]

Century Anglo-American Faith, ed. Francis J. Bremer (Boston: Massachusetts Historical Society, 1993), 147–66, argues that informal gatherings were safety valves releasing much of the pressure for local autonomy and lay authority.

59. John Norden, *Mirror for the multitude* (London, 1586), 18–19, 43–45, 63–64, 107. For Oxfordshire, *APC* 13:233–34.

60. LPL, *Carta miscellanea* 12/19, 2v.

61. *Whitgift*, 1:128–29, 353; 2:516.

62. Laurence Humphrey, *The nobles or of nobilitye* (London, 1563), B7v; CCCC, MS. 106, 539.

63. For reports of "anarchie," see Niels Hemmingsen's *Commentarius in epistolam Pauli Ephesois* (London, 1576), 137, 148, translated by Abraham Fleming as *The epistle of the blessed Apostle Saint Paul to the Ephesians* (London, 1581), 197, 215.

Fenner replied indignantly. The accusation was preposterous, he said, distancing himself from the anabaptists, as he had from Robert Browne. Anabaptists were mistaken to have proposed "meere popular elections not governed with the fore-direction of the elders," Fenner observed, adding that others in favor of participation were more astute. They favored regimes in which "due consent of the people" would not preclude "the foreleading of the presbytery."[64]

An anonymous *Dialogue concerning the strife in our church* replied quite differently in 1584 to the accusation that pastors suspended the year before, Fenner and his friends, had "the very properties of anabaptists." *Strife*'s Philochrematos sided with Whitgift and berated Orthodoxus, who represented the suspended, for trying to make "everie man a controller." According to his accuser, Orthodoxus passed off anticlerical drivel as doctrine. He lured laymen from their parish churches to hear sermons far afield and preached unlawfully. He supported the commoners (whom he would make "controllers") though they were "addicted to heare some and not othersome" and likely to be stirred by any sermon's "hatred and malice" that played to their "vaine humor." Not so, said Orthodoxus; commoners craved instruction not insurrection. They were neither "factious" nor "fantasticall," as Philochrematos charged; the preachers they preferred sounded spiteful to conformists, only because "it seemeth the greatest hatred in the world unto carnall men when any mislike their waies." The conformist critics had mistaken urgency for malice, Orthodoxus argued; commoners and preachers alike wanted to save their church, to embarrass its contemptible "corrupt ministrie" so officials would be compelled to reform it before Jesuits and other Roman Catholic critics capitalized on lay disaffection.[65]

Strife's highly placed conformists were predictably off the mark and rancorous, besides. They were the church's "great men" who preyed on "the small," feeding them nonsense, keeping them ignorant.

> When yee tell men God is mercifull, all men sinne, what shoulde yee make your self more holy than other, yee overthrow all the doctrine of regeneration and all the precepts which the apostles give for walking worthie of the gospel. You make the good and bad in one condition. . . .

---

64. Fenner, *Counter-poyson*, 24–25.

65. *Dialogue concerning the strife in our church* (London, 1584), 6v–7r, 50–54, 102, 109, 128–29.

But wherefore doe great men now a dayes take it so grievously [that] anye difference of men should be made? Surely I will tell yee the cause. They would not have their treason against the church of Christ espied when they thrust upon [it] wicked and unlearned masters. . . . Nay, yee like best, as yee confesse, of those that be ignoraunt. And why? Because they are quiet. Indeed, you are least troubled of those which be most ignoraunt for they can not espie your dealing. Such as have knowledge in God's word can saye, what a wolf this is: he hath three benefices and . . . doth visite them once a yeare to see they doe him no wrong in his tithes.[66]

Strife's solution was to increase the number and influence of those "such as have knowledge in God's word." The objective was not to replace the clerical staff but take control from bishops who "thrust upon" their churches indifferent pluralists who then hired irresponsible curates. It is now nearly impossible to tell whether Orthodoxus was trying to win over clerical colleagues or threaten them as he built to his final argument that "yee cannot faile in your duetie, but everie plaine man [is] able to controll yee by the Word of God."[67]

Strife's message, that a strong ministry depended on an enlightened, empowered, energetic laity, probably got a warm reception among the self-styled "simple men of the country," persons "of the inferior sort," who filed surveys with the Commons two years later to detail the deplorable condition of their ministry. The church was understaffed and the staff was terribly underqualified, they concluded, and Job Throckmorton justified parliamentary intervention in terms reminiscent of *Strife*'s. When "wise men of the court should be so backward" or "too sleepy," he explained, "simple men" must see to the reform of their churches.[68] Their most concrete proposals, offered in 1586 with their *Lamentable complaint of the commonaltie*, were unlike *Strife*'s transfer of control. Instead, *Complaint* asked that the government cover costs of "plant[ing a] holie ministrie in every place."

---

66. *Strife*, 98–102.

67. *Strife*, 69. To Orthodoxus, the Bible shows "plaine" men—for example, the "inferiour persons" whom God appointed prophets to the Hebrews—often reprimanding and "controlling" priests and princes to good effect; *Strife*, 82–83.

68. For Throckmorton's speech, see John E. Neale, *Elizabeth I and Her Parliaments*, 2 vols. (London: Cape, 1953–57), 2:150, but also Collinson, *Elizabethan Puritan Movement*, 306–8.

Complainants acknowledged such a strategy would require endowing semi-naries and augmenting parish chests. Was it not worth the effort, they might have asked, to have supply catch up with the demand for preaching? They knew patrons had the power to frustrate campaigns for improvement, so complainants proposed something slightly more ambitious and more am-biguous that did approach *Strife*'s commendation of lay "control." Arguing that "the leprosie of spoyling of the church hath pearced [patrons'] bones and marrowe so deepe that it cannot be washed away by any good law," the "simple men" said that "the only way and remedie is to restore presentations to the church." This "only remedie," lay participation and local choice, was critical to the success of *Complaint*'s financial provisions for seminaries and salaries. And, complainants said, "the only way and remedie" was perfectly safe; faction and anarchy were out of the question because "many skilfull and vigilant eyes" in each parish would keep order.[69]

The queen stopped deliberations before anyone in the Commons thought to inquire how many of those "skilfull and vigilant eyes" were to have belonged to the commoners, to rudesbies? Petitioners assumed parish-ioners were watchful, honest, irenic, and eager for instruction. Experience taught the queen, her councillors, and her bishops that the laity was list-less, incurious, very often wilfully ignorant. Councillor Christopher Hatton launched what one historian calls "a massive counterattack" on the puritans' proposals.[70] By 1587, parliament's discussions of petitions and parish surveys were adjourned indefinitely. Participatory parish regimes suggested by *Strife* and the *Lamentable complaint* were set aside. Advocates of laicization and local control fell silent for the remainder of Elizabeth's reign. The resistance to having "our sheep teach their shepherd[s]" proved too much for them.[71]

Yet resistance was building within their own ranks as well as in parlia-ment. The puritan partisans of lay and local control wondered whether the ambitions they had (and had voiced) *for* the laity were, in fact, the ambitions *of* the laity. They questioned whether commoners could be trusted. Rome,

69. *The lamentable complaint of the commonaltie*, in *Register*, 206–10, 218–23, 242–43.

70. Neale, *Parliaments* 2:158–63.

71. Norman Jones, *The English Reformation: Religion and Cultural Adaptation* (Ox-ford: Blackwell, 2002), 144–45, citing Francis Alford, who endorsed the government's "dis-taste for the democratic enthusiasms of presbyterian preachers." Alford knew what few historians now doubt: into the 1580s, "the royal will was trumps" (Lake and Questier, *Lewd Hat*, 488).

after all, had drawn "the best wittes out of England . . . to traine them" and to return them to the realm "for perverting of [the] simple and ignoraunt."[72] Ambitious thinking about the laity in England understandably spawned concern about lay susceptibilities and, specifically, about the still Catholic sentiments of Protestant commoners. Empowering them could well and widely have seemed to court catastrophe, to be a colossal mistake. Even the partisans of broader participation must have been haunted by the prospect that parish elections could return the wrong sort of pastors to their pulpits. In 1584, without rehearsing the proposals for or the arguments against local control or lay authority, James Hales offered an observation that appeared astute to an ever-increasing number of those discussing power and patronage in their parishes. Hales, that is, mentioned the inevitability that commoners were moved more by "shewe" than by substance. They too were easily swayed, he said, by "smooth and fayer tongue[s]."[73]

Confidence in "plain" and "simple" parishioners was not, at day's end and century's end, unshakable. After all, they remained plain and simple. Puritan chronicler William Harrison regretted that neither the laity nor the time was right for "so great [a] perfection" as a local, lay, broadly participatory parish regime.[74]

You may recall that, at the start of this chapter, Walter Mildmay had warmed to the prospect of "bring[ing] patronage to the people." In 1587, however, he predicted to the Commons that the "election by many" in each parish was unlikely to result in the election of incumbents any worthier than those selected and presented according to prevailing practices. Was Mildmay driven "into a conservative frame of mind by the extravagances" of the puritans who advocated lay participation, as John Neale guesses, or by the realization that he and they had been thinking of the laity too optimistically?[75]

---

72. Thomas Bilson, *The true difference between Christian subjection and unchristian rebellion* (Oxford, 1585), A2v–A3r.
73. PRO, State Papers 12/69/31.
74. *Harrison's Description of England*, 110.
75. Compare Neale, *Parliaments*, 2:161.

Afterword

What happened afterward, after discussions of lay participation in parish administration were discontinued in the Commons? By then Fenner and Thomas Lever were dead. Cartwright, Fulke, and Dering were quiet and possibly contrite. "Consumer resistance" to puritan evangelism may have given advocates of localization and laicization second thoughts about consumers' competence. Conformist critics nonetheless were unrelenting. A summer of seditious streetside preaching in 1591 gave them the chance to exaggerate "the dangers of populist puritanism."[1]

William Hacket previously announced he was the messiah come to condemn church officials and complete the realm's reformation. He and two accomplices took that message to London and were arrested. Hacket was executed, yet his critics would not let him die. They chronicled his "conspiracy" to prove that "evangelical Calvinism" was politically subversive. Three sly Richards—Cosin, Bancroft, and Hooker—insisted that parish referenda would lead to riots, "tumults, tragedies, and schisms." Perhaps they only wanted to put the queen and council on alert, but, of course, they put nonconformity at a disadvantage for decades. "Frantick Hacket," the false prophet who quoted scripture so seditiously, was a perfect argument for the urgency of religious conformity and episcopal oversight. The church "which hathe once made the said canon or regester of the scriptures" must

---

1. Alexandra Walsham, "Frantick Hacket: Prophecy, Sorcery, Insanity, and the Elizabethan Puritan Movement," *HJ* 41 (1998): 64–66, for the Hacket prosecution and "the dangers of populist puritanism."

"preserveth the same" against incendiary exegesis. A century after the affair, historian Thomas Fuller confirmed that "this business of Hacket happened very unseasonably" for all dissidents and that the few remaining puritan partisans of broad lay participation "could not wash his odium so fast from themselves but their adversaries were as ready to rub it on again."[2]

From the 1580s, and especially after Hacket's "tumult," puritans looked inward for signs of authentic reform. They looked to personal piety and not to polity. William Perkins' Eusebius was visited by God "inwardly," at home, in conscience, and without benefit of clergy. John Winthrop urged reformed Christians to "close with Christ," become their own confessors, and experience the "discomforts of anguish" and an assurance of election "inwardly" and directly from God. Often, unregenerate Christians might need a good shove to make their runs from indifference to remorse and redemption. A bad decision and a guilty conscience got Eusebius started. Winthrop would walk for miles, gadding to sermons that would provoke his "godly sorrow" for having sinned. It seems to have mattered little to Winthrop whether preachers were locally elected. He was concerned with content rather than parish consensus. The devotional literature he consulted, which included Perkins' stories, concentrated on religious sentiment and not on social policy.[3]

Perkins and Winthrop did not complain that congregational deliberations took place less frequently. Perhaps they did not even notice when more exclusive forms of parish government were developed, some now say, to protect the Elizabethan elites from the whims of "inferior" parishioners.[4] After a fashion, though, those "inferior," "plain," "simple" people welcomed oligarchic parish regimes. Few commoners had managerial responsibilities, yet there is no record that any contested the concentration of parish authority in select vestries. Possibly the silence was "financial." Costs of leadership were increasing. An economic downturn in the 1590s was terribly devastating for tenants of middling sorts in the countryside and for under-

---

2. Thomas Fuller, *The Church History of Britain*, vol. 5, ed. J. S. Brewer (Oxford: Oxford University Press, 1845), 62; Bancroft, *Dangerous positions*, 168–83; *Laws*, 8.7.6; and Richard Cosin, *Conspiracie for pretended reformation* (London, 1592), 73–81.

3. For Perkins and Winthrop, in this connection, see Peter Kaufman, *Prayer, Despair, and Drama: Elizabethan Introspection* (Urbana: University of Illinois Press, 1996). Also consult Fulke, *Text*, 132v–33r, and, for subsequent puritan self-study, Tom Webster, "Writing to Redundancy: Approaches to Spiritual Journals and Early Modern Spirituality," *HJ* 39 (1996): 35–52.

4. Kumin, *Shaping*, 248–55; Duffy, *Morebath*, 30–32.

capitalized craftsmen in the cities. The rich were resourceful and got richer. Wardens drawn from their number, the "chiefe men" of their parishes, rose to the challenge. They were told to deal with the destitution of the poor, no longer by parishioners but by the queen's council and its commissions. Into and through the next century, churchwardens and vestrymen chose their successors, audited accounts, corrected "defects and defaults"— without broad parish participation.[5]

Curiously, as leadership in the local churches became more oligarchic, what literary historians now call "the popular voice" passed into the literature of the late English Renaissance, some of which reveled in leveling. But that popular voice often was expressed only to be suppressed in fictions that underscored the importance of rank, dignity, and order.[6] True, we are innings away from any decisively compelling interpretations of those fictional encounters between social "superiors" and "inferiors," but it may help the interpreters to know that by the time William Shakespeare drew his King Henry V into amicable conversation with prole soldiers and scripted Coriolanus' outright contempt for the plebes, conformist critics had successfully claimed democracy was a monstrosity. The local parish and body politic must do without their many heads, each pursuing its "commodity" instead of the commonweal.[7]

The conformist critics who feared faction, sneered at the commoners' "commodity," and deprecated their competence owned the immediate afterward of our story. They imagined that "plaine" and "simple" people would "fall to [their] old fashions," which meant the revival of "most cruel poperie."[8] Conformists stressed the barbarity and ruthlessness of the rudesbies. Hence by 1610, it was obvious to Lord Ellesmere that the proles were implacable; concessions only incited them to agitate for greater power than had been conceded, *plebis importunitas cedendo accenditur*. Ellesmere's Latin was Livy's; his anxiety, older still and, unlike this "Afterword," *sine fine*.[9]

---

5. CUL, MS. Oo.6.93, 29–34.

6. Helgerson, *Nationhood*, 205–7.

7. Bodl., Selden Supra MS. 44, 18r. To sample interpretive alternatives, consult Stanley Cavell, "'Who does the Wolf Love?' Reading 'Coriolanus,'" *Representations* 3 (1983): 1–20; and Annabel Patterson, *Reading Hollinshed's Chronicles* (Chicago: University of Chicago Press, 1994), 187–214.

8. Charldon, *Sermon*, D8r (1595).

9. Elizabeth Read Foster, ed., *Proceedings in Parliament, 1610*, vol. 1 (New Haven, Conn.: Yale University Press, 1966), 276–77.

Index

Acts of the Apostles, 42, 107–10, 116,
    151, 154
Admonition controversy, 17, 107–9,
    114, 119
adultery, 87–89
Alcock, John, 54–55
Aldersay, Thomas, 86
Alford, Francis, 164n.71
Allerton, Ralph, 54–56
Allin, Edmund, 32, 55–56
Ambrose of Milan, 111–12, 132
anabaptists, 124, 161–62
anticlericalism, 34–36, 55–56, 145–47
Ardern, Thomas, 81
Augustine of Hippo, 94–95
Aylmer, John, 61, 73, 129–31

Bacon, Nicholas, 72, 133–34
Bancroft, Richard, 22–23, 35–36, 89,
    117, 157–59, 167
Banks, Pierce, 83
Barstow, John, 115–16, 137
Beza, Theodore, 90–91
Bible, English translations of, 31,
    38–40, 64, 93–95, 145

Bilson, Thomas, 152, 165
Black, David, 135n.84
Bles, Joan, 84
Boleyn, Anne, 37, 51
Bonner, Edmund, 47, 53–57
Booth, Anna, 87
Bownde, Nicholas, 25–28
Bridges, John, 25, 151–52
Briefe and plaine declaration concerning
    the desires of all the faithful,
    155–56
Browne, Robert, 139–40,
    147–49, 157
Bruen, John, 78
Bucer, Martin, 42–43, 46
Bullinger, Henry, 105, 124
Bury St. Edmund's, 106–7
Byrne, Roger, 88

Calfhill, James, 69
Calvin, John, 18, 41–42, 58, 72, 76
Cambridge, University of, 9, 69,
    106–13, 148
Campbell, Mildred, 21n.27
Carlson, Eric, 81

Cartwright, Thomas, 107–9, 114, 117–18, 126, 142, 150–51, 167
Cecil, William, 72, 75–76, 109, 114, 137, 144
Chaderton, Laurence, 107
Chambers, Richard, 60
Champneys, John, 32–33
Charldon, John, 61n.85, 169n.8
Cheney, Richard, 128–29
Christchurch, Oxford, 69
Chrysostom, John, 94, 108
churchwardens, 63–64, 120–21; duties, 80–86; election of, 85–86; enforcement of discipline, 86–89, 100; social status, 63–64, 80–81. *See also* parish administration
Clark, Edith, 88
Clement VII (pope), 37
Coke, Tristram, 87
Collinson, Patrick, 16–18, 72–73, 97, 119–20, 122n.46, 159
Cooper, Thomas, 128
Cosin, Richard, 106, 150, 167
Cox, Richard, 91, 123
Craig, John, 81
Cranbrook, Kent, 134–35, 144
Cranmer, Thomas, 4, 31, 36, 42–50, 86
Cressy, David, 27n.44
Cromwell, Thomas, 36
Crowley, Robert, 145
Curteys, Richard, 61, 130
Cyprian of Carthage, 95, 112–13, 154

Dent, Arthur, 19
Dering, Edward, 18, 118–19, 137, 167
Dialogue concerning the strife in our church, 162–64
Doderidge, John, 106n.3
donative curacies, 106–7
Dowley, John, 58–59
Drury, John, 34
Duffy, Eamon, 49n.51, 67n.10, 81

Easton, Jane, 87
ecclesiastical commissions, 65, 68, 72, 114
Edward VI (king), 4, 32, 42–52, 64, 76, 106, 123
Elizabeth I (queen), 15, 51–52, 63–76, 98, 131, 141; first parliament of, 66–67, 71–72; mistrust of "the multitude," 8, 64–65, 73–76, 122, 136n.88, 139, 144, 161; as religious reformer, 5, 65–67, 99–101; suppression of prophesying, 126–34
Elyot, Thomas, 23–24
Emden, 58–59
enclosures, 20–21, 48–49
Eucharist, 47, 55

Fairlambe, Peter, 124n.51
Farel, William, 43
Feckenham, John, 75
Fenner, Dudley, 5, 19–20, 134–35, 140, 150–57, 160–62, 167
Field, John, 17, 59, 100, 103, 114–15, 118–19, 155–57
Fleetwood, Edward, 70–71
Fletcher, Richard, 134
Foxe, John, 13, 24–25, 34–35, 53–57, 145–47
Frankfurt, 58–61, 124
Fulke, William, 6–9, 17, 19, 92, 103, 107–15, 118–19, 155–56, 167
Fuller, Thomas, 168

Gallars, Nicholas Des, 125
Gardiner, Stephen, 47–50, 54, 56
Gawton, Richard, 144–45
Genevan consistory, 42, 58
Gifford, George, 12–13, 23–25, 145–47
Gilby, Anthony, 61, 145
Gilpin, Bernard, 14
Godwyn, Thomas, 107–8

Gorboduc, 74
Greenblatt, Stephen, 39–40
Greenham, Richard, 13, 18–19
Grindal, Edmund, 61–62, 67, 72, 75–76, 97, 104–5, 125–36, 140
Guy, John, 153

Hacket, William, 167–68
Haigh, Christopher, 75
Hales, James, 165
Hall, Arthur, 119
Hall, Basil, 45–46
Harding, Thomas, 93–96
Harrison, Robert, 148
Harrison, William, 20–21, 28, 131, 134, 165
Hatton, Christopher, 131, 134, 136, 164
Hawkin, Robert, 105
Hawks, Peter, 79
Hemmingsen, Neils, 161n.63
Henry V (king), 169
Henry VIII (king), 4, 31, 36–37, 40
Heveningham, Arthur, 80
Hill, Christopher, 22–23, 158
Holie discipline of the church, 114, 117
Holland, Robert, 87
Hooker, Richard, 41–42, 89, 167
Hooper, John, 46
Horne, Robert, 60–61, 69, 72, 76, 97
Howard, Henry, 109, 113, 118
Hudson, Anne, 35
Humphrey, Laurence, 161
Hunt, William, 158

idolatry, 76
income, parish, 82–83

Jerome, 94–95
Jerusalem, council in, 110, 154
Jesuits, 52, 69, 143, 153, 162
Jewel, John, 5, 15, 61, 64, 66–67, 72–73, 91–101, 143–44

Johnson, Francis, 138
Jones, Norman, 68, 72, 164n.71
Julius III (pope), 51
justices of the peace, and local magistracy, 49, 69–72

Knappen, Marshall, 136
Knox, John, 61, 124–25
Kumin, Beat, 77

Lake, Peter, 3n.3, 18, 29n.50, 107n.6
Lamentable complaint of the commonaltie, 24, 163–64
Laodicea, Council of, 155
Laski, Jan, 43–50, 123–24, 135
Latimer, Hugh, 4, 14
lay lectors, 63, 78–80
Lee, William, 37
Leech, John, 135n.84
Leicester, Robert Dudley, Earl of, 96, 129, 132
Leo I (pope), 109
Lever, Thomas, 2, 73, 78–79, 98, 103, 113–14, 118–19, 167
Levine, David, 16, 20
literacy, 32, 92–95, 139, 144–45
Livy, 169
Loades, David, 70, 85
lollardy, 31–36, 40
Luther, Martin, 36–37, 40–41, 57, 95

MacCaffrey, Wallace, 131, 158–59
MacCulloch, Dairmaid, 43
Machyn, Henry, 66
Marsh, Christopher, 40, 120
Mary I (queen), 4, 32, 50–54, 61
McIntosh, Marjorie, 16, 28
Micronius, Martin, 124n.50
Mildmay, Walter, 141–42, 165
Milton, Anthony, 159
Monmouth, Humphrey, 36–37
More, Thomas, 39

Moreels, Henrick, 125
Morely, Jean, 90–91, 99–101, 108, 125
Morwin, Isabel, 35
Munday, Anthony, 143n.9
Münster, 161

Neale, John, 71, 165
Netter, Thomas, 33
New College, Oxford, 69
Newgate Prison, 84
Nixon, Roger, 87
Norden, John E., 161
Northumberland, John Dudley, Duke of, 49–51
Norton, Thomas, 74
Nowell, Alexander, 73

Obedience of a Christian man, 37
Olde, John, 50
Onslowe, Richard, 74, 119
Overton, William, 137n.90, 142–44
Owen, Gareth, 77–78
Oxford, University of, 36, 69, 93, 161

Paget, Eusebius, 83, 133n.79, 135n.84
Paget, William, 48
parish administration, 23–25, 38–40;
    congregational participation in,
    2–6, 103–4, 108–16, 149–57;
    Edwardian reform of, 42–43,
    49–50; lay leadership, 63–64,
    81–82, 153–54; in refugee
    congregations, 43–46, 59–62, 96,
    124–25. *See also* churchwardens;
    presbyterian polity
Parker, Matthew, 66–67, 75, 78–79, 97,
    127–30, 140
Parkhurst, John, 61, 69, 72, 127–28
Parkyn, Robert, 49
Paul VI (pope), 52
Paulet, William, 44

Peacock, Reginald, 33
penance, 33
Perkins, William, 3, 8–14, 22–24, 139,
    145–47, 168
Perne, Andrew, 111–13, 117
Peterhouse, Cambridge, 111
Pettegree, Andrew, 45, 52–53
Philip II (king), 51
Phillip, John, 18n.21
Piers Plowman, 145
pilgrimages, 33, 68
Pilkington, James, 61, 65–67, 75,
    96–100
Plumbers' Hall, London, 104–5
pluralism, 78–79, 141–42, 163
Pole, Reginald, 32, 51–53, 56, 61
Ponet, John, 59
poor box (parish), 82, 88
Practice of prelates, 38
presbyterian polity, 6, 16–17, 89,
    108–9, 116–18, 121, 142, 153–57
prophesying, 104, 121–37, 160
purgatory, 48
puritanism: definitions, 3, 14–20; and
    parish regimes, 3, 23–25, 120–21,
    142–47, 161–65; and parliament,
    71, 142, 164–65; and the pulpit, 9,
    76–77, 86, 90, 144, 160; and social
    discipline, 17n.15, 21–29

Rather, George, 88
Redman, William, 109–12, 117
Ridgeway, Joanna, 87
Ridley, Nicholas, 44
Roye, William, 37

Safegarde of society, 115–16, 137n.91
Saillans, François de, 154–55
saints, 84
Sandell, Richard, 76
Sander, Nicholas, 69–71

Sandys, Edwin, 61, 66–67, 121, 129, 133, 140, 145
Sawyer, Richard, 35
Scambler, Edmund (bishop), 127n.6
Scarisbrick, J. J., 77
Scory, John, 50, 128–30
Scot, Cuthbert, 93
select vestries and parish elites, 15–16, 77, 86, 154
Settle, Thomas, 138, 161
Shakespeare, William, 169
Shaw, Richard, 65–66
Sherlock, John, 82
Shuger, Debora, 25n.40
Siddall, Roger, 88
Smith, Thomas, 20–21, 143–44
Somerset, Edward Seymour, Duke of, 48–49
Southam, 132–34
Spufford, Margaret, 13, 17n.15
Standen, Nicholas, 100
Stone, Lawrence, 88–89
St. Paul's Cathedral, London, 65–66, 73
Stroud, John, 134n.84, 144–45
Sutcliffe, Matthew, 89, 117, 143–44, 147
Sweeting, William, 34

Tewkesbury, 106
Theodoret, 94
Thomas, Thomas, 85
Thomson, John, 81–82
Throckmorton, Job, 163
Tittler, Robert, 29n.50
Travers, Walter, 155
Trent, Council of, 47, 96

Trinity College, Cambridge, 107, 109
Troubles begonne at Franckford, 59–61
Tunstall, Cuthbert, 36
Tyndale, William, 4, 31, 36–40

Udall, John, 131
Usher, Brett, 57

Velsius, Justus, 125
Vermigli, Peter Martyr, 42–43, 46, 73
vestments controversy, 97–101
Vulford, Richard, 34

Walsham, Alexandra, 3n.3, 65
Warner, Alice, 57
Watson, John, 79
Westminster disputation (1559), 66
Weston, William, 137
White, John, 67n.11
White, William, 105
Whitgift, John, 90, 107–11, 117, 131, 136–37, 144–47, 150–51, 157–62
Whiting, Robert, 49n.51, 67n.10
Wigan, 70–71
Wilcox, Thomas, 17–19, 100, 114–15, 118
Winthrop, John, 168
Wisbech, 137
Wittenberg, 37
Wood, Thomas, 59, 123
Woodman, Richard, 54–56
Wrightson, Keith, 16–17, 20, 29n.49
Wyclif, John, 33–34

Zanchi, Girolamo (Zanchius), 128
Zaret, David, 22–23